TRIAL BY ILLUSION

JUDY DAVOUST

BALBOA.PRESS
A DIVISION OF HAY HOUSE

Balboa Press books may be ordered through booksellers or by contacting:

Balboa Press
A Division of Hay House
1663 Liberty Drive
Bloomington, IN 47403
www.balboapress.com
844-682-1282

Because of the dynamic nature of the Internet, any web addresses or links contained in this book may have changed since publication and may no longer be valid. The views expressed in this work are solely those of the author and do not necessarily reflect the views of the publisher, and the publisher hereby disclaims any responsibility for them.

The author of this book does not dispense medical advice or prescribe the use of any technique as a form of treatment for physical, emotional, or medical problems without the advice of a physician, either directly or indirectly. The intent of the author is only to offer information of a general nature to help you in your quest for emotional and spiritual well-being. In the event you use any of the information in this book for yourself, which is your constitutional right, the author and the publisher assume no responsibility for your actions.

Any people depicted in stock imagery provided by Getty Images are models, and such images are being used for illustrative purposes only. Certain stock imagery © Getty Images.

Print information available on the last page.

ISBN: 978-1-9822-7319-4 (sc)
ISBN: 978-1-9822-7321-7 (hc)
ISBN: 978-1-9822-7320-0 (e)

Library of Congress Control Number: 2021917171

Balboa Press rev. date: 09/01/2021

To my beloved husband
and our daughters

Dear Reader,

This is an intriguing life story with some extraordinary times. These are my memoirs. I have chosen to change some names and details of a couple of events to protect those I love and to honor their privacy.

Further, I have changed my name to Annalee Grace, my mother's first choice. It was, however, rejected by my father in favor of my name, Judy. As an honor to my mother, I chose to use it in this work. I chose as well to honor the privacy of my children. When I asked them what name each would choose in my narrative, my older daughter asked me to choose. I, immediately, chose Eleanor, the one I preferred, but was rejected, coincidently, by her father in favor of the lovely name she now carries. The younger daughter chose the name, Emma.

As you will understand in the course of the book, all of what I have just told you does not matter. You will see that it is all illusion.

Judy

Nothing ever goes away
until it has taught us
what we need to know.

Pema Chodron

I found him in the corner, strapped in a wheelchair with his chin resting on his chest. He was dying. But as much as he needed to leave his body and step to the Other Side, the will of a warrior and champion was still promoting resistance, true to his characteristic stubborn nature. Clearly over-medicated for the convenience of the under-staffed nursing home, he sat motionless with a bit of drool at the corner of his slightly-agape mouth. After refusing to see me for the last seven years, he now could offer no protest, no judgment and no further rejection. His power had vanished into the empty spaces inhabited by the cruelty of Alzheimer's. I felt no relief in finally seeing him once again, nor did I relish that I did not need to be on high alert for the surprise power struggle that was his signature communication ploy. I discerned no hope of connection. As I steadied myself, processing all that this encounter now signaled, I walked slowly to his side, put my hand on his shoulder and kissed the top of his drooping head.

It must have startled him because he raised his head with enormous effort and stared forward. Quickly positioning myself so he could see me, I smiled as I said "Hello, Dad."

"Oh, daughter, I'm sorry. I'm sorry. I'm sorry," he said, hurriedly, with no breath between sentences, followed by a flood of emergent tears.

Before I could reply or ask a question, the lucid person of a few seconds before had vanished, replaced by a empty-person with a vacant stare. I said to him, but mainly to myself, "Dad, do you know who I am?" hoping to reclaim the moment before that brought some hope of elementary conversation. Nothing. He was gone, his cognitions vaporized into the ethers.

What was he sorry for? Was it not responding to my many years of letters, not being kind to my brother, not being a family man, not knowing how to parent, not being there when we needed him most, not being supportive when we hurt or failed, not praising our accomplishments, not prioritizing us over trivial interruptions and so many other offenses? Still, sitting opposite this man-shell, I saw the Divine in him more in that nursing home wheelchair than I ever had before. I wept, knowing that for all his shortcomings and grievous faults, I loved him.

While making the four hour round trip drive to the nursing home every two weeks, I mentally reviewed our history together. I often cried, laughed, spewed expletives into the empty passenger seat or blessed the opportunity. Dad was not an easy man. Our history was as colored, varied, explosive and volatile as his temperament. I so wanted to please him, receive acknowledgement of my accomplishments, avoid his harsh criticisms or even discern a hidden hint of love. All the wishing and waiting was for naught. I was now sitting once again with a body uninhabited by a personality, unable to admonish or express any coherent message.

The third visit was to be an experiment. My meditation teacher had suggested that we anoint him and use massage oil to rub on his body. My hope was that I could relax him and, perhaps, give him some sensation of caring, love and blessing. As we entered his sparse room, now absent a newly-departed roommate, he was moaning, thrashing and warning fellow soldiers about incoming artillery. His body was balled up tight as he periodically screamed orders to his unit. He was fully engaged in the battle of Bloody Nose Ridge in the Pacific, fighting Japanese from every direction in indescribable conditions, with death happening continually and bodies heaped upon each other. His distress was difficult to witness, and I considered that the over-medication protocol might have been preferable to the awareness of horrific memories and unending angst. The Battle of Peleliu in 1944, the highest death toll of any amphibious assault in military history where 28,000 soldiers landed on the atoll, and 9800 were wounded or killed, was his ever-present focus for the last few days, as reported by the orderly. As we began to arrange his body so that we could massage his legs first, we caught sight of the unattended bed sores. Further inspection exposed the absence of his wedding band and the new Nikes I had put in the closet on a previous visit. Making a note not to complain, but to report the theft and state that I would be dropping by unannounced henceforth, I got the attention of management. They would not like me, but they would take better care, making the trade-off profitable.

After almost an hour of massaging and humming lightly, the thin legs of my father began to unwind, allowing us to stretch them out and fully massage his withering muscles--the very same muscles that ran track races in Madison Square Garden, won tournaments for Purdue University and had qualified for the cancelled Olympics in Cross Country. This decaying man had a history of significant achievements for an Indiana farm boy with little exposure to life outside his hometown of two hundred or so folks--until he received the valedictorian scholarship to Purdue. As he registered for classes on the first day of college life, the counselor asked what he was majoring in. Not knowing what to answer, he turned to the young man adjacent to him, asked what his major was and then repeated it to the registrar. He was going to study civil engineering. It was a serendipitous moment because Dad excelled in math and science.

While walking to his boarding house after class one day, he passed the track and field arena and saw the athletes practicing. He quickly inquired how a young man could join the team, and the coach said: "Well, son, let me see you run. I'll time you." The story goes that Dad took off his shoes, crouched and ran like hell when the coach signaled. Learning that he had the second fastest time in qualifying runs, he became a bona fide member of the Purdue track team. Athletes were automatically given scholarships, so his room and board were then covered. He often joked that he ran for his dinner! The truth was that he had run several miles to school and back for most of his youth, and he had run cross country for the feeling of freedom it gave him. However, now he had teammates at school with a similar passion.

As we began to massage his feet, my friend asked how he had injured his big toenails which were rounded humps of nail tissue. I recited the saga I had heard many times in which Dad had run a cross country race in the hills of Ohio where the steepness of the downgrade was such that his big toes bled due to being jammed forward into his hard leather track shoe. He lost both toenails that day...and finished the race.

Always liking the idea of the military, he joined the ROTC, which was accompanied with a stipend and a guarantee of second lieutenant bars at graduation. Pictures of him in the late 1930's showed a lanky, handsome man with a hint of swagger and confidence. Apparently, the boldness of the pending graduate had persuaded an equally lanky freshman co-ed named Evelyn to marry him. In September of 1939, they wed. My mother once told me she was upset that a friend had interrupted their wedding reception to report that England had declared war on Germany. Dad had turned to her and whispered that they should fully enjoy themselves for the next two years because he would soon be drafted. Soon after, indeed, he was drafted into service for World War II. His life and personality were to be changed forever. And the consequence of a protracted and hellacious Pacific war was now playing out in far-off memories embedded in a demented mind.

While listening to his screeches and high-pitched orders to imaginary soldiers, I, for the first time, suspected that he had chronic post-traumatic stress disorder--something unknown or undefined after wars before the 1970s--a disorder that my dad would certainly have disavowed. He did not allow himself any obvious psychological shortcomings.

His life-experience arsenal was filled with fear, anger and mistrust, often broadcast by the loudest voice and the most auspicious threats. His reputation pre-warned any adversary that this opponent was skilled, brilliant and committed to the immediate task. He seldom lost, leaving many emotionally wounded souls in his wake. I, however, never witnessed that he felt any measure of pride of achievement after his many verbal altercations. He dusted off and walked onward.

His limbs relaxed, and we stroked his arms and chest, keeping rhythm with his exhalations. I began to softly pray out loud that our caring touch would bring comfort to this warrior's transition that was nearing closer each day. Knowing that the body was only temporary, that his essence was eternal, I prayed for an easy release from this world back to the all-encompassing love of an awareness source that we call God. Dad was fighting every war ever fought, commanding all military units ever formed, ensuring freedom for the wives and babies left at home and giving his full measure of courage, patriotism and intellectual guidance. He, most of all, was an officer with battlefield promotions to Captain and Major doing all he could to protect his men and earn their trust in him. It was a mission he completed with success, resulting in medals, commendations and a lifetime of destructive, nightmarish recollections.

For all his success on the battlefield, he was miserably incompetent at expressing honest emotion, trusting his own self-worth and using his superior intellect to expand his world view beyond the engineering degree that defined and legitimized him. He was a tortured soul having great difficulty with his impending exit. Religion, country, family and military experience simply had not prepared him for this moment, regardless of the absence of cognitive ability. He had not lived his life in such a manner that he could turn his perceived wounds into wisdom, his grief into new joy down the road or his experience into insight, thereby making his life much easier. Dad, somehow, always seemed to make life harder for himself and everyone close to him. He was the proverbial "cut-off-your-nose-to-spite-your-face" guy that could never quite realize his self-fulfilling prophecy dilemma that defined him to be the victim and not the victor. He was the irascible, sacrificial child of the Great Depression who was hungry for a long time, ate mostly potatoes with his four brothers for over two years, was used as share-cropper labor in the fields with his dad, and self-schooled until he could finally return to classes and graduate as valedictorian of a class of eight in rural Indiana. As an adult, he had employed his dad and three of his brothers as laborers and foremen in his construction company, still feeling responsible as the oldest to help them earn a living and feed their families. Eventually, they all quit, finding him difficult to work for and causing intermittent family feuds known county-wide and heard by complaining residents nearby wherever the altercations took place. He, lifelong, saw his siblings as ungrateful and unappreciative of his philanthropic intentions.

My teacher and I asked the orderly for help to turn him over carefully, attend to his bedsores and position him so we could massage the broad shoulders and muscular back of the soldier. He was now compliant. Our bequest of love and blessing seemed to be well accepted and nourishing to the previously uneasy warrior, now a willing recipient of our intentions. We were supplicants for peace, rest, acceptance and surrender. Instead of being the offering of peace, I was becoming peace. I felt his awareness of letting go, of allowing, of forfeiture and of ultimate surrender to the moment. The only time that exists, the only gate to higher consciousness and the goal of all humans is the return to Love. This experience with my dying father was teaching me what I most needed to know and understand.

I, accidentally, touched a bedsore and was immediately refocused to the purpose at hand. Two hours of touching had had a soothing effect upon all three of us. Dad was sleeping peacefully, and my teacher and I gathered our things, blessed the body in the bed and left. Not a word was spoken on the two hour trip home, but when she left the car my teacher thanked me for the opportunity to be a part of such a blessing. I understood that words were inherently inadequate when trying to describe a spiritual experience as a gift.

When I put the garage door down, I sat in my car with my forehead on the top of the steering wheel and sighed. I had now fully accepted that Dad was gone; we were just waiting for the eventual pneumonia to quiet the lungs and let the heart come to a full stop. His body no longer served a purpose. I needed to do so many things on the list to prepare for our daughter, Eleanor's, wedding, but I knew, without a moment's doubt, that I needed to sit and process what I was feeling. I could no longer be a random observer. I felt the stamp of my father upon my being, the unwitting incorporation of his goodness and the repulsion of his distasteful behaviors and opinions. He was a major player in my life of fifty-plus years, and I could not deny that his imminent departure had meaning and consequences for my own psyche and my own search for peace.

I sat for some time, struck by the remembrance of our first meeting in the nursing home where he uttered the breathy sentence repeated three times: "I'm sorry." Knowing that it was meant for me, and me only, because he rarely, if ever, used my given name, rather referred to me life-long as "daughter," I could not escape that the apology was directed at me, and for me to consider and accept. It still had almost no credulity since I could never recall having heard an apology from him...Never! His tears were throttled by emotion for those few seconds. That was the third time I had ever seen him cry, and, as with the first, it looked to devastate his whole being. He knew he was leaving me...leaving with so much undone. And those first tears, shed decades before were when the most important person in his life was leaving him...with a whole life together undone.

There had been years when I did not want to consider forgiving him. Feeling angry, rejected, abandoned and forsaken were easier emotions with which to maneuver through our mine field of conversations. Unabashed honesty, transparency and love were dangerous and provided no exit plan or safe harbor. Now, forgiveness was easily felt, as though it had no need of rehearsal or curtain call. Forgiveness was, as it always should be, natural and comforting.

I was going to sit, sip on my glass of wine and revisit the tsunami of memories. Not feeling a need for chronological order or hierarchy of significance, I would just let years and events float in as they chose to make themselves known.

My chest filled with pain that signified the remnants of hurt and sadness that had yearned for a daddy's elixir, or at least a few words of sympathy or empathy. For years I had felt that intermittent pain and had relegated it to another day, knowing that the end game was a silly dream never to be fulfilled. I had spent the past forty years learning of a different and more productive way to navigate life in a manner that might bring relief, hope, contentment and a spiritual awakening. I also had more university degrees than needed in an attempt to hope that education and research would fill in the gaps with more understanding and breadth of acceptance. The degrees had served to interest me in a spectrum of studies, provided me with a satisfying profession and an ability to dissect and analyze my history with articulate proclamations, but none of it had soothed the family history dynamics with a result of minimal comfort. I, simply, could not find a way to erase the dysfunction that had orphaned me, left me adrift to find some welcoming shore. Yet, sitting in my living room with a glass of wine decorated with droplets of moisture, I smiled. I had the secret of being able to withstand any obstacle, love any rascal, seek awareness at every conscious moment and enjoy the illusions. I had Sissy Jean. The recollection of my introduction to her was gilded with so much joy and thankfulness that I allowed myself to drift into the memory of our first meeting some forty-five years prior.

In the province of the mind, what one believes to be true either is true or becomes true.

John Lilly

2

I walked focused with a sense of urgency, dragging the tattered, grey sheet, replete with paint stains, that I had rescued from the trash several years ago. Headed to my private sanctuary, I felt the usual, anticipatory thrill as I approached the forest that soon would be transformed into my private quarters.

As was my childlike custom, I would gather the sheet around me like a cape that imbued me with powers beyond the reality of a ten year old girl sneaking out of the modest house to play imaginative games in the forest: a woods of about a hundred trees or so a quarter mile from home.

With a minimal amount of preparation, the sheet became a tent, a palace or a nap site. In this shrouded space, so magically hidden in the canopied elegance of elderly oaks, I nestled into the coveted, quiet retreat all my own...a hideaway filled with wonders, imaginations, love of a creative, fertile mindfulness, but most of all, a sense of eagerness tethered to something much bigger than myself. The small, protected space offered the promise of unbridled thought that wondered in all directions, free of any restrictive rules. Fantasy became the sweetness that satiated my appetite for frequent adventure into this secret realm. I found the excursions delightful and repeatedly inviting.

From my earliest remembrance, I was full of questions. Questions, in themselves, evolved into a game. I loved games, competition, winning and feeling proud. My dad, a self-appointed mentor, never stopped pressing me with questions. My head often ached after a dinner table quiz session which was usually punctuated by confrontation, minimal phrases of praise and an admonition that I needed to study more. He seemed to delight in pop quizzes of math computations, matching historical figures with the century of their accomplishments or current events of which I had zero interest. Logic was always paramount. Honestly, logic was the only exercise that actually engaged my interest. Math was easy; history was boring and current events always came accompanied with emotion and his raised voice. Logic was interesting, formulized and, ultimately, tinged with the subjective. I excelled at logic. Dad would relent by becoming quiet. That, for me, was success. I could finish dinner.

But I had a secret place to escape! I could relax. I could ask questions out loud, hearing the soft echo in the trees and wind that carried my voice to a hollow where all sound evaporated into nothingness. I felt safe. I felt a freedom that I had never experienced in another place. I tried repeatedly to transfer this sensation of unadulterated freedom to the quiet of my bed at night, to the prayers in the Sunday school class, to the mandated quiet time at my three-room school house or even to the back seat of the Ford where silence was the absolute rule. This was seldom successful. In these attempts at replication of the "freedom of the forest," I squeezed my eyes shut, hoping to find a transport to my wooded sanctuary. It evaded me. So I yearned for the times I could escape my mother's list of duties and return to the only place I knew would bring joy...and the hope of an encounter with the unknown thought or fantasy that young girls so crave as delightful entertainment. Indeed, these fantasies were the desserts of my imagination.

It was one of these fun and self-indulging, magical forays into the sheeted sanctuary of the woods that I first heard it. Turning my head toward the call of my name, I feared I had finally been found out. As I sat perfectly still on the moist leaves of the forest floor, I drew my knees up tight against my chest and continued to carefully look around. A survey of the trees that I could see over both shoulders as my head slowly did a grid-directed analysis of everything in sight found no interloper. I was careful to look for rustling of leaves or evidence of someone hiding behind one of the substantial oaks. An equally precise survey of all that could be seen in front of me produced nothing but frustration, mixed with a small amount of fear. Then, I heard the soft, lilting call of my name again. And fear began to turn to very guarded anger. There was definitely someone in my personal forest, invading what was my secret place which had become sacred. And I didn't like the game that seemed to be in favor of an antagonist-in-hiding.

For the third time : *"Annalee Grace."*

Well, it had to be someone I knew that had followed me here. Only my family and friends knew my full name. And, so, after keeping the secret of this place for the past few years, I would now have to share. My chest began to ache a little, and my head lowered.

"Come on out. It's okay. I know you're here somewhere," I said with resignation.

Nothing. No response. Total silence. Even the sounds of the woods had stopped. I listened for the incessant chirping of the swallows and sparrows that always provided a cacophony of dissonant calls. The breeze had slowed, and stillness was everywhere. I got to my feet, walked around, kicked leaves in frustration, grabbed my sheet and began to run home. I could feel the tears welling at the edges of my eyes. Knowing that crying was not allowed, I wiped my face on the dirty sheet, put it in its hiding place in the hollow of a dying maple tree near the house and entered the kitchen. As I apologized for being late to do my chores, Mother smiled and handed me a small sprinkling bottle to dampen all the cotton clothes and roll each piece into a tight bundle, then stack them in the refrigerator. I was now old enough to do the ironing, except for Dad's work shirts and pants. Usually a chatterbox, I silently finished my chores, lost in my own sorrow and bewilderment at the memory of the unknown forest invader.

I stayed away from the woods for a few days. I kept a vigilant ear and eye for any clue that might identify the visitor that had invaded my special den. My mind raced with plans of retribution upon the one who had dared to disrupt my wooded haven. I had a plan. I determined to take a mirror the next time so I might see more easily behind me. And I would not construct the tent-like room where I napped, day-dreamed or rambled out loud. There was a very minor clearing near the edge of the woods where my viewing would be enhanced. I would be gracious upon meeting the intruder...or pretend to be gracious and inviting. Being mad or territorial would seem to serve no purpose.

After Dad picked us up from Mass on Sunday, he and Mother always retreated to their bedroom for a nap. They routinely locked the door, so I had some playtime to do as I pleased. I left the sheet in its hiding place. I could not risk it being stolen or mishandled by the stranger. Carefully approaching the woods from a different angle than was my custom, I walked to the small clearing on the far side. The afternoon sun was uncomfortably warm in the more exposed area of the woods. I much preferred the coolness of the canopy, an arbor of perfect temperature. So after a few fidgety minutes of sweating in the summer heat, I moved inward to my haven where comfort was guaranteed, and I felt a sense of ownership. A sudden sense of confidence accompanied my decision. My Aunt Leona used to say, "If Annalee lacked anything, it sure wasn't a lack of confidence!" The memory of those words bolstered my resolve to claim my usual encampment site...and wait.

After some time, I succumbed to the invitation of easy slumber as I lay curled beneath the grandfather oak that was my favorite. Only the spitting of a light shower awakened me. As I pulled the lightweight summer blouse up around my neck and back of my head, I quickly did a visual 360 degree survey of my environment. There was no evidence that anyone had been there. I could see no tracks or disturbance of any kind.

Admitting to myself that I enjoyed a well-developed imagination, I began to open the door to the belief that my recent encounter with someone calling my name three times was simply a trick that a vivid imagination could play upon its hostess. That <u>must</u> be it! No one had bothered me today, and I certainly saw no evidence of any visitor to the woods.

As I began my walk toward home, I thought for a second that I heard the faint call of my name once again. I walked faster as the brewing, summer thunderstorm drowned out any possibility of further imagined annoyances.

Soon, summer began to fill with recreational activities. Vacation Bible School, waterskiing, fishing, daily swimming, running through the sprinkler hose and 4-H projects were the most memorable. That was my first year to enter a project at the County Fair. It would be a beige linen place mat, perfectly sewn, pressed and carried between two pieces of tissue paper to guarantee its arrival in immaculate condition for the eyes of the judges. Plus the tapioca pudding for the food preparation entry. Geez!!! Tapioca, void of lumps, is hard to make! My family was blessed with a lot of experimental attempts to create a perfectly smooth pudding. Success and the blue ribbons were pinned to my projects when Daddy finally agreed to walk the dusty midway of the County Fair to the 4-H exhibit building.

I thrilled with the experience of competition. I always won the math and spelling bees at school which were fun for a while, but the teacher had relegated me to the tutor corner to help others while the contests were now held without me. Although I understood, I missed the rush of the "win." Most of all, I was horribly bored. I sat in a classroom with two, sometimes three, grades being taught by one teacher. It was easy to learn what all three grades were doing, so I just assigned myself the task of doing all the lessons for subjects of all three grades. My reward was to skip a grade. And now I had found a new activity that not only allowed for the competition game, but also, over the years, would teach me life skills such as homemaking skills and discipline. Every summer for the next seven years would be fully filled with 4-H projects. Food preparation advanced to full meals, soufflés, French pastries; clothing construction that started with the linen place mat gradually culminated in construction of a ball gown and a man's tailored overcoat. I felt accomplished…at least in the mind of a young girl in a small Indiana town where my picture appeared on the front page of the weekly newspaper when I won championship ribbons at the Indiana State Fair.

As my tenth summer was ending with just weeks left before school started, I ached to return to the woods. I had so much to think about. And, indeed, so much was pure pride that I could express in private. Mother admonished me to be humble. Daddy said I had a lot to learn, but that it was good that I was learning woman's work. In my mind I had many responses that I swallowed for fear of being admonished or punished. Yearning to say my thoughts out loud in defense of myself, I took comfort in knowing the trees would listen, offer no judgment and respond only with the sounds of nature. Here, safe and hidden, I found permission to be honest, self-advocating, experimental and real. The feeling of being whatever I wanted to be was quite intoxicating. I was King Arthur for a while. Lancelot did not appeal to me. At other times I enjoyed stepping into the role of Ivanhoe (the latest book I had finished), or my favorite, Queen Elizabeth II, waiting for her coronation. In my drama, I felt the burdened weight of her new responsibility.

Then it happened. I was deep into a feeling of gratitude for my secret place when the softness of her voice lightly penetrated the breeze that had begun to cool my shoulders. I dug my toes into the now-crunchy leaves and stiffened slightly. I knew it was a female pronouncing my full name. She made it sound regal, with a compassionate inlay. This time I felt no fear, no anxiety. Curiosity defined the moment, followed by an immediate determination to find this person and interrogate her. I liked games, but this one was all too frustrating. Yet, I somehow trusted the nature of the stranger. I felt something I could not describe. My apprehension dissolved. An eagerness welled up in my torso in the form of a heartbeat that gradually announced itself in my ears. With the heart of an Olympian, I quietly focused and sat cross-legged with my eyes closed. Minutes passed. I drifted into an altered state of being…kind of outside of myself. I could see me, sitting, quiet and perfectly attentive.

"Annalee"

"Yes. I hear you. Please come closer so I can see you."

"I am here, my child. I am very near."

I eagerly opened my eyes with great expectation! No one was there.

Lowering my head in dismay, I closed my eyes once more. I felt somewhat suddenly exhausted.

"Gracie, I would like to talk with you,"

"Don't call me that. You have no right. Only my brother can call me that name. We agreed. I call him Fippy, and he calls me Gracie."

I had a bunch of "handles," as Dad called them. Mom called me Annalee. I knew she loved that name. Dad called me "daughter" as if it were a title of some sort. All my friends called me A.G. This phantom stranger that I could not see knew my favorite, but restricted, nickname. All of a sudden, I felt a bit dizzy like when I rode the Tilt-A-Wheel at the County Fair.

I lay back, hoping to lose the lightheadedness and regain my sense of well being. My throat was dry, my lips somewhat parched and my legs were almost numb. I rested, composed myself and sat upright once more.

After a time, the voice said: *"I would like to talk with you."*

"That's fine with me. But I would like to meet you. Would you please come out of hiding so I can see you?"

"Child, I am here. If you can hear my voice, you know I am near. Close your eyes, go into your heart space, and I will meet you there."

This was so strange. I could not see anyone in my vicinity. However, I could hear her clearly. I could "feel" her presence. I accepted the invitation to do what she suggested. I squeezed my eyes shut and went into that space where I knew my heart to be. I was transported. To where, however, was beyond my understanding. I relaxed. I succumbed. I waited with immense anticipation.

"*First, you need to know I will never do you harm. My purpose is to let you know that you are loved, and that I am always with you. You are never alone.*"

"Okay. Thank you. I get that you will not hurt me. And I already know that my family loves me. But you are wrong. I come to the woods where I can be alone. It is my favorite place in all the world. This is the first time I have ever heard a voice in the woods. The woods protect me."

"*I tell you that you are never alone because I am always with you. It is my purpose to be with you, to love you and to comfort you.*"

"Really, everything you say doesn't make much sense to me. It is impossible for someone to be with me all the time. I don't even think I would like that very much. Actually, it's sort of rude to assume that I even want to be your friend. And, by the way, could we just quit the game, and you can come sit here for a while. We can begin by you telling me your name."

The voice softly pronounced a name that sounded like an impossible combination of s's and e's. When I asked for a repeat, she kindly offered that I could use a name that sounded close to what I thought I had heard. After saying some options in my head, I blurted out "Sissy Jean!" I could almost hear her smiling. She assured me that the name was, indeed, a good one. That was our first agreement. And I felt like we were on more even ground now. Annalee and Sissy Jean.

"Okay! Come show yourself, Sissy Jean. Let me see what you look like. And how old are you? And what you like to do for fun? And where you go to school?"

"*Annalee, this may surprise you, but I am fortunate not to have a physical body. I am a non-physical being. You cannot see me. You are able to hear me and feel my presence, but that is all.*"

"Geez! Are you a ghost? I thought ghosts were imaginary…and just used to scare little kids on Halloween. But you don't feel or sound scary."

"*No. I wouldn't say I am a ghost. I, actually, am the perfect part of you. I am the perfect Annalee. I am that part of you that carries the Truth.*"

"Boy, you sure do talk a lot of what my Daddy calls gibberish. Normal people don't talk like you do. Most people won't be as patient with you as I am. And Mother says that everyone should tell the truth, even if it gets them in trouble sometimes."

After waiting thirty seconds or so, I had a question.

"I don't always tell the truth. Sometimes I fib. I like that word better than lie. Mother says there are white lies. I think what she means are the fibs someone tells so she doesn't hurt another person's feelings. But you said you are a part of me that carries the Truth. I don't get it."

"We beings who are not in physical form know everything about the universe. We know the true nature of every soul. Do you understand what a soul is?"

"Yeah. It's that part of you that goes to heaven after you die. And, then, I guess it just stays there. The priest at church says 'bless your soul' a lot."

"My job for the rest of your life is to teach you about your soul, to teach you about the Truth and to bring you peace."

"Well...why didn't you say you are a teacher in the first place? I thought we were going to be friends. Besides, Mrs. Van Dyne is my teacher, and I like her a lot. She's really nice, and she makes stuff interesting. I am not changing schools. So nice to NOT meet you, Sissy Jean. And I would appreciate it very much if you would stay out of my woods."

"I will do as you say as much as I can. I will always be with you, but I will not speak until you ask. I am with you for eternity. We are not separate. We are one."

"I don't know where you teach, but I pity the poor kids that have to understand you. I am late, and it's chilly. I'm headed home. Bye."

I ran, knowing I was late to set the table. I had trouble catching my breath, my thoughts all jumbled in my head like a jig saw puzzle when it was poured out of its box, and all those pieces looked like they would never fit together. Daddy would laugh at me when I spent my allowance on another puzzle that would take weeks to finish. He would tease me when I showed him the finished product and mockingly ask me what had I learned. Sissy Jean was a puzzle, and I didn't have the faintest idea of how to make sense of it all, much less put the pieces of our conversation together. I shook my head and opened the back screen door to the kitchen.

The Miracle is this:
The more we share
The more we have.

Leonard Nimoy

Being raised in a Midwestern state was a blessing. There were actually three months to each season. Winter was marked by the onslaught of snow that turned grey after its initial coverlet of pristine white. Buds, birds and tractors announced spring in dramatic fashion. Rains, lightning bugs and longer days defined the muggy, humid summers, and, best of all, the colors of fall vanished into the small stacks of burning leaves and acorns raked by kids in the neighborhood. Even better was being a kid in a small, northern Indiana farm town with a summer tourist lake. The town was small enough to know almost everyone if you grew up there, and it was big enough to have enough players from the local high school to compete in the widely recognized obsession of basketball mania. School was regularly dismissed during tournament season, and pep rallies were monster events, inciting the spectators to a seasonal frenzy. I often lost my voice, a consequence of my youthful enthusiasm!

On a very muggy night, rare for late in the summer, I tossed and turned in the bed in my second floor bedroom. The lone window, small and open, brought no gift of breeze. As I lay wishing for some comfort and the onslaught of welcome sleep, my mind returned to my conversation with the soft-spoken Sissy Jean.

I found myself fascinated. Replaying the conversation ver- batim, I catalogued the questions that popped into my head. So much of what she said made little sense to me, but I felt a feeling of intrigue… and a bit of curiosity mixed with a willingness to spar with her. She had left me with the impression that she was patient and not easily ruffled. I resolved to talk to her again.

It was quite difficult to focus on my chores and get my school supplies in order because my mind was constantly at the woods. After hours of hurried and erratic, mindless work at home, I quickly gathered my noontime sandwich and ran for the trees. Winded and hungry, I plopped down beneath the grandfather oak, sighed, and inhaled the daily noon diet of bologna and Miracle Whip sandwich.

Soon enough, I felt the peace that was the allure to this ever so special nest of mine. I sat for a while. My anticipation was a mixture of excitement and a lingering, tentative belief that she was real and would answer my call. Finally, I said her name out loud. Amazingly, the conversation started.

"*Yes, Child, I am here as I promised.*"

"Oh, boy! I am so glad you answered me. I was afraid you might have gone away after I left so abruptly yesterday. I apologize. Mother says there's never a reason to be rude."

"*I know your heart Annalee. You were not rude. You were simply a child with lots of questions on your mind. Just so we're clear, I want you to remember what I told you. I am always with you, and I will never, ever leave you. I live inside of you, just like the Holy Spirit lives in your heart.*"

"Well! I wasn't expecting that! Inside of me? How can you do that?"

"*I am an awareness that stands down your spine. I am Light brought from the Other Side. I want you to imagine a beautiful rod of pure white light going all the way from the tip of your head to your heels. I live, so to speak, in that rod of Light. No harm or oddity will ever result from my being part of you. You will just be more loving and aware because you know me and know I am part of you.*"

"The other side of what? I don't see any Light."

"*Light is the energy of the One. You and I are part of the One. The Other Side is where Light, Energy and Awareness of the One abide.*"

"Sissy girl…you need to slow down and explain. You told me you are a teacher. If I don't understand something, my teacher at school tells me to raise my hand. She says she can't read my mind, so I need to let her know. So, I am raising my hand! Explain things so I can understand, pleeeease."

"*My Child, thank you. You are right. You are my student, so I will do it differently. I first want to tell you that you are in a classroom every day you are alive on your planet. Earth is a schoolroom where souls come to learn. Every person has a lifetime journey in which to explore, learn, evolve and come to physical death. You, sweet one, are on a path of discovery as is everyone else. You will explore, feel joy and success, pain and isolation, suffering and ecstasy, anger and excitement. All of these emotions are part of your human journey. But none of these are your purpose. Your purpose is very much bigger, authentic and transforming.*"

"Holy Cow, that's a lot to take in. I think I understand that everybody has all sorts of different emotions and experiences, but what do you mean when you say that all the living stuff I do and feel is not my purpose? I try hard to be a good girl. I'm really good at my studies. I say my prayers, and I try to help others if I can. I actually think a lot about these things."

"*Child, I know you do. One of the reasons that you can hear me and converse with me is that your heart and mind are open, inquisitive and eager to live more fully than many of your school friends. All your friends have the same possibility to experience what you and I are experiencing. Every person on your planet has a unique journey to live and learn and the ability to connect with the non-physical.*"

"I think I understand...a little. It's kind of like when I talk to God I get a sense that He's there. Sometimes it even feels like I sort of 'feel' an answer...but not really hear Him. Father Cochran says that's the Holy Spirit I feel. I am not sure I get that at all! But Father says I will understand in time."

"*Annalee, that feeling you get has a name. It is called Knowingness. That simply means that you feel that you know something. You don't exactly know why or how you know it. It seems like a mystery to you. And because it is a mystery to your human mind you may start to doubt yourself and your feelings. You may even dismiss them...or forget them. But Knowingness is real. It is your connection to the Other Side, to the One.*"

"Miss Sissy, can I lose this connection to the One?"

"*Dear One, you can never, ever lose your connection to the One. You are part of It, and It is part of you. However, it is possible to FORGET the connection, or not believe in the connection. It does not matter what you believe or don't believe; the connection ALWAYS exists. However, most humans have separated from their knowingness. We will talk about that when you are older.*"

"I think that's a good idea. You say a lot that makes my brain ache. I have a lot to do. In addition to homework, friends and family, my questions about things you say make me feel really tired. But I'm excited to learn more, and I think it may be a while before I get the gist of everything. So please be patient with me, Okay?"

"What if I'm naughty or stupid or really bad to my parents or my brother? I really get mad at them sometimes. I told my mother last week that I was going to run away from home because Daddy had spanked Phil and me. She said she would miss me and smiled. I know I should not have said that to her. I felt really sad for a while. But

Mother isn't like Daddy. She doesn't get upset very often. Daddy gets mad a lot. He hollers and yells and uses cuss words. Mother doesn't say anything when he acts like that. Phil and I often get scared, and we go outside or to the basement. We only go to the basement in the winter because it's too cold to go outside. But the basement isn't our favorite place because that's where we have to go if we are going to get spanked."

"Sissy, I know when I deserve a spanking. But the one Daddy gave me last week was so unfair! Phil and our boy cousins were being rowdy and didn't mind like they were told. So Daddy said we both would get a spanking when we got home from Grandma's because Phil didn't behave. Since I was the oldest cousin it was MY responsibility to 'corral them.' That was impossible with those boys. They never listen!! Do you think that's fair? Do you?" finally taking a deep breath.

"*I know that it certainly didn't feel fair to you. But, be assured, in everything that happens to you in your life, from now until you leave your physical body, there will be a blessing. You will be taught something valuable from each experience.*"

"So, wait a minute here! You call getting spanked for no good reason a 'blessing?' I still don't quite understand where you come from, but here in Indiana we certainly don't call a spanking a blessing. Gee whiz!"

"*Annalee, please believe me when I tell you that there is a purpose to everything you experience. Nothing, absolutely nothing, will ever happen in your life that does not have a lesson contained within it. That is what you signed up for when you chose to come to this planet with these parents in these circumstances. And I promise you that you are fully capable of embracing all these lessons.*"

"Whoa! I get to choose the lessons! How do I know which ones to choose? At school I get to do something special if I get all my lessons done early."

"*You will choose your lessons according to what you need to learn. It may be a lesson in compassion, patience, acceptance, forgiveness or many other things. You will choose many, probably most of them without knowing you are choosing. That, too, has a name. It is called 'unconscious choosing'.*"

"Let me get this straight. I have to go to this life school you talk about, and I have to learn things that I don't even know I want to learn?"

"*Yes. That is part of your purpose for being a physical being. You chose to be here and walk this path for a while, embracing all the lessons that will come with it.*"

"I don't know anything about choosing to be here. My mother says I am here because she and Daddy loved each other and made a baby...and that was me. Seems to me that my folks did all the choosing. And I certainly don't remember having any say in any decision. I just got born!"

"*Well, let's just agree for now that you are here, you are very aware, and that you are here for a reason, just like everyone else. You will not always recognize a lesson when you are going through the experience, but the consequence will be enlightening to you at some useful time. You may see the meaning of it while it is happening, or it may be years before you allow yourself to see the blessing that came from living through it. You must know that no matter what the lesson, you are always safe. Emotions may cloud that truth, but you are safe.*"

"This is a lot to understand. Did you forget that I am just ten years old? You talk in grown-up language that I sort of understand, but it also sounds a little scary. You're saying that I am going to live a life with stuff happening to me that I won't really have much of a choice about, but that I secretly choose, but don't know it! And that I probably won't feel safe, but you say that I will be fine. Is that about the gist of it?"

"*I would say that you are a very good listener. You have heard me accurately and have reacted appropriately. Do you remember that I said you have a purpose for living your life here? That purpose is only one thing: to learn to love!*"

"Well, that's gonna be easy. I already love my parents and brother and grandparents and some cousins, plus a lot of other names. I even love my doll collection, but I don't really play with them anymore. I put all but one of them in an old footlocker that my daddy gave me. So, maybe, I already know the lesson."

"*Annalee, you have a heart so full of love like most children who have a home, parents and other comforts. And it is good that you respond to love with love. You also give love freely without being asked. However, I am talking about a love that is so special, so beautiful, so exquisite, so amazing that when you feel this love your entire being feels at peace. It is quite like the love that the One feels for every piece of matter, every morsel of the Universe, every human alive.*"

"That's a lot of love. The One is amazing! So, how do I learn to love so that I have peace? And, by the way, what does peace feel like? At Christmas I always see Peace, Joy, Love. You say I will learn about Love; I think Joy means being happy. But, I guess I don't get what Peace is, and it sounds like I better or I won't learn the lesson."

"Peace is the result of pure Love. Peace naturally comes when we know the Truth, when Ego disappears and we know that we all are one and part of the One."

"Ya know, Sissy, we're gonna take this one step at a time. A lot of what you're saying is beyond me. I think you know what you're talking about, but it's a whole lot more than I can swallow all at once. You're gonna have to repeat a lot of it along the way for me to remember and get what's important. I'm pretty smart, but not THAT smart. Is there more?"

"There IS more. You must lead a life of service. As you mature, the call of service will naturally come to you. You already know how to help others. You help the little ones get on the school bus, and you let them play marbles with you at recess even though they are not skilled. You help your next door neighbor, Mrs. Jennings, with her evening dishes because you know she has debilitating arthritis. And you leave the nickel she pays you in her pink piggy jar that she keeps by the kitchen door. You are patient in your tutoring of those who are bewildered by math. I have witnessed your joy in helping others."

"Well, yeah, I like helping. Why not? The 'service' assignment won't be hard. Piece of cake. What else?"

"There will be many things that we will talk about. I want you to always feel free to consult me. I will do my best to help you with your journey. I think your understanding of daily life will be helped by a lesson called Meditation. You already have grasped some of its elements. When you sit under Grandfather Tree and close your eyes and empty your mind for seconds at a time, you are closely aligning yourself with a meditative state."

"Now you really lost me! If my daddy were here, he'd be saying "Holy Jesus, Mary and Joseph!" Some of this stuff will just have to wait until I'm older. You pretty well wore me out today. Please, don't get me wrong. I like talking with you. You talk in a funny way sometimes, but it mostly makes sense. So I will come back and talk again, if I may. Thanks. I have never had a friend like you. Nice."

"Child, please know I am always available and with you. I am always a part of you. We can talk at anytime wherever you are. You need not think to limit your access to me to the woods only."

"That makes me happy. You say I will know you forever. That's a long time. You are older than me. I can tell. What happens when you die? How will I know?"

"Dear Annalee, you will have much to encounter and deal with in your life. There will be hardship, loss of loved ones, betrayal and great happiness. But I will never die. I promised I will always be with you."

"Sissy, we have a lot to talk about because I know everyone eventually dies. So the next time we talk, maybe you can explain yourself. Right now, I am late again. You have a way of making me happy and getting me in trouble at the same time. See you later."

Adolescence is like only having enough
light to see the step directly in front of you.

S. A. Allen

4

I had turned eleven years old and was gradually being given more skilled chores, mostly ironing and some cooking. Mother was a patient and complimentary teacher, but she didn't tolerate procrastination or excuses. As a result, it became more and more difficult to journey to the woods...or for that matter, even find much time for myself.

I tutored at school, bypassed recess much of the time to quiz students who asked for help, did my chores when I got home and washed dishes after dinner. Family time around the radio was filled with episodes of with Hopalong Cassidy, Roy Rogers, The Shadow and Amos and Andy. Luckily, I had no homework because I always finished it at school.

I desperately ached to talk to Sissy. I remembered that she had told me that I could talk with her anytime and anywhere. However, that was just impossible at school or on school bus rides because of the incessant noise of laughter, giggles, squeals and boys' fights. Regrettably, my only quiet time at home was in my bed at night. Unfortunately, I was so tired I often fell asleep immediately. The next morning I jumped on the bus a little after seven for the hour ride to the country school house. I began to realize that there was no sacred, dedicated time for Sissy Jean and me, and my stomach was beginning to hurt every day. I had to do something.

Finally, I gathered the courage to talk to my mother. Surely, I could make her understand how important it was to have private time with Sissy. One Saturday I asked if I could talk with her in private. She agreed and made time for me after lunch. We sat in the big two-person wood swing on the front porch while Dad was on the lake, and Phil was at a friend's. Perfect.

"Mommy, I need your help. I have someone special in my life, and I really like talking with this person. I learn a lot from her, and she makes me think about things. You would like her. She is soft-spoken, kind and helpful. I talk with her on my trips to the woods, but I am so busy now that there really is no time to visit with her.

So could I please not do so much ironing or cleaning so I could go to the woods? I could stay up later to get all the chores done."

"Annalee, it is so nice that you have a new friend. And you seem to really like her. I would like very much to meet her. Please invite her to dinner, maybe tomorrow after Mass. Does she live close-by? And what is her name?"

"Her name is Sissy Jean. She says she is a non-physical being. So I have never really seen her. But our conversations are interesting. She makes me think. She tells me stuff I have never heard before. And she says she is always with me. I feel very comfortable when we talk. But I can't invite her to dinner. That just wouldn't work."

"Annalee Grace, you have always had such an expansive imagination! I have no doubt you communicate with your new imaginary friend and, probably, have very interesting conversations. That is all extremely entertaining. But...you are eleven years old now, and it is time for you to give up imaginary friends and spend more time with your schoolmates. We can have Karen or Wanda or Marilyn over for Sunday dinners. Maybe one could come home with you every now and then for a sleep over. I can call their mothers and arrange it."

"No, Mother! You don't understand. I want to talk with Sissy Jean. I can talk to the girls at school. Please, please let me have some time to be with her. I promise to help you more. Please, mommy?"

"Annalee! Stop. I am not permitting you to go to the woods anymore. You are too old for this! You are a young woman now, and you need to start taking more responsibility and stop thinking about such foolish things. Secondly, I am going to ask a favor of you, and I want you to agree. You must not tell others about your imaginary friend. Do you promise?"

"Yes," I answered with my watery eyes lowered.

"And the other thing is that you need to stop calling me Mommy. You know you are not a little girl anymore."

I got up slowly from the swing, walked down the front steps and went to the orchard in the backyard. Leaning against a peach tree, I cried, making no noise whatsoever.

For the next several months I could feel myself withdrawing inward. I played along with conversations, was polite, but engaged minimally. Even my teacher, Mrs. Van Dyne, talked to my mother about my change in personality. And it was then that Mother shared the biggest, most embarrassing secret in my whole life. She told my teacher that I had "gone through puberty," and that I was sometimes sullen. Mother was sure that it was hormonal and would pass as I grew.

I not only had "gone through puberty," but I had done it a year earlier at TEN. TEN!!! Why did that have to happen to me? No one else in my grade (or even the next two grades) had to endure the embarrassment. I secretly made sure that the sanitary napkin was hidden in my school pack and made sure no one ever saw it. I made excuses for when incapacitating cramps interfered with softball practice or swimming in the summer when I had a period. Sanitary napkins and swimsuits did not go together! "Making sure" was my constant, exhausting duty. I was a freak.

Being a freak was one thing, but being a "woman" was way more burdensome. Mother had gently, but firmly, informed me at the onset of my initial menstrual cycle that I was now a woman. My body would begin to develop more rapidly, and I could have a baby like any normal female. Feeling like a freak was one thing; BEING a freak was overwhelming. It was too much to comprehend or appropriately handle. I withdrew more. I wanted nothing to do with my mother who had betrayed me or my dad who always demanded more and more from me. Surely, adulthood, whenever that occurred, would be preferable to this hell. Numbing myself to my situation was a brilliant solution. I began to feel very little. Doubt about everything in life consumed me. Parents didn't understand. Teachers were robots. Friends were fickle. Sissy Jean was a figment of my imagination. Boys were stupid. Girls were silly, and I, in particular, was lost, bewildered, hurt and so alone.

I decided that adolescence was the long-awaited, numerically double-digit time that, ultimately, became the most embarrassing period of life, and one could only hope to sneak through without being noticed or devastated.

Trying desperately to remain numb to this unavoidable and excruciating passage in life (which was not working particularly well), I decided to search for another more viable option. Truth be told, numbness was boring and frustrating. So my new plan was embracing hurt and self-pity. I would channel my energies to activities which would allow an acceptable form of rebellion. I certainly didn't care to set myself up for more negative attention or parental criticism. Within days, I was confident that I had the perfect, clever solution. I thought of it as an end run around depression and adult judgment. Even the thought of the upcoming execution of the plan energized me!

Knowing that my body was not athletic, either in form or desire, I chose activities that encouraged the drama of all kinds of expression: Speech Club, Drama Club, school plays, Debate Club, and quasi-political involvement in Student Council and school governmental issues. These organizations all had the requisite approval of school officials and side-lined parents. And, to my surprise, I enjoyed and promoted with all spectacle of teen-age enthusiasm, the chosen activities. I was quite sure that my new-found interests successfully detracted me from the darkness and consuming doomsday drama in which I had so pitifully entrenched myself. Retrospectively, it was a good and productive choice, albeit a result of somewhat vengeful and retributive anger.

Now that I was in high school, although a bit earlier than most since I had skipped a grade, I was finding myself mildly repulsed by the silliness of girls and the abject stupidity of boys. Even my brother, to whom I had, historically, been closer to than anyone was being a dope. The girls in my freshman class were totally focused on hair, make-up, clothes and boys. The boys focused, mainly, on sports, stupid comments, teasing and spitballs. I had to admit I might have been a bit precocious and judgmental, but this stuff was SO juvenile that I saw it as embarrassing. I stayed busy and focused with the clubs and the many invitations for speeches at Kiwanis and Lions Club events. The debate team traveled on the weekends for regional competitions, becoming an unexpected bonus to distance myself from my invasive and interrogative parents. I began to think I was a pretty smart cookie to have plotted a course that successfully saved me and, at the same time, entailed events that brought much needed pleasure and praise.

Friday night home football games and basketball games were always followed by a sock-hop in the gym. Literally, after the game most all the kids in high school placed their shoes neatly in the outer entrance to the gym and paid a quarter a couple to dance on the polished wood floor of the gym that smelled of locker room sweat and cigarette smoke with just a lingering scent of buttered popcorn from the concession stand, now closed.

Elvis Presley, Chubby Checker, Buddy Holly, Fats Domino and Little Richard provided the music via the school DJ from his arsenal of 45's. David Cessna and I danced in the dimly lit gym, enjoying the closeness of bodies and the experimental kisses when the lights would occasionally go totally dark. I was pretty certain the DJ not only controlled the music and the light, but also promoted the nascent romances evolving on the dance floor. I liked David. He was respectful, romantic, shy, a great kisser and an average dancer. All in all, he was a nice boy that cared about talking to me, dancing with me and looking me in the eyes. Most of the jerk guys in high school talked only to my chest.

I hated my chest. I felt some gratitude that I had a Marilyn Monroe curvaceous body, but I more than hated the Jane Russell boobs. Having developed early, I sported fully blossomed breasts by the age of 13. I had experienced twenty year old men asking me for dates. They were not pedophiles or dirty old men...they were just guys who thought I was twenty. And I was not prepared for how to respond to their advances. I was a neophyte, a child in a fully developed body with unwanted opportunities for dating and awkward invitations. As I progressed through high school, I slowly exited the relationship with sweet David, and purposely gravitated toward a young man who would be the valedictorian and who had all the manners of a Southern gentleman. He was more intellectually interested in me that physically attracted to me and posed no threat whatsoever. I was safe from the gawkers, the idiots, the aggressive bullies and the hormonal hand grabbers. Still, realizing that I craved safety, I thought of Sissy Jean.

I had spent minimal time with Sissy for two reasons: I had very little reflective or meditative time, and I, simply put, was full of myself. Basking in the praise that a small Indiana community so willing offers their hometown actors and athletes, I did not sip at the cup of praise and pride...I, full-heartedly, gulped the recognition unapologetically. Sissy talked about such serious and worldly things at a time that I was so willing to bathe in the immature and fleeting spotlight of small town and temporary glory. She did not slip away; rather, I trotted along my self-serving course with no attention or gratitude for her friendship or mentorship. I had left her; she had not left me.

As I was busy with my burgeoning and multiple school activities, my dad was rapidly becoming financially much more successful. He was exponentially creating an affluence that was so unknown before--and somewhat uncomfortable for me. It felt foreign to dress in store-bought clothes and to go out to dinner at the country club. We rode in his Cadillac and began to talk with the "rich" people in town. Dad had become a reasonably big fish in a smallish pond. He began to drink too much on the weekends. Mother seemed to like the idea of "Manhattans," which I knew to be some kind of exotic alcoholic drink served with orange slices. Dad would come home and drink something called 7 and 7. All of this was accompanied by his loud regaling of the days' events of success or failure. Worst of all, I began to hear rumors of Dad's car in front of Sharon Krueger's house in the afternoons. Mrs. Krueger's daughter, Karen, was a school friend of mine who always got the lead in the school plays. I liked her, but I hated, hated, hated her mom. She must have been a real Jezebel that enticed my dad to stop at her house where the whole neighborhood could see his truck in the driveway. When Karen and I would meet at play practice or in the school hallways, we both exchanged that knowing look of daughters who absolutely wished to avoid what we feared...what we knew. I felt her pain. Her expression told me she felt mine. We were decidedly more mature than our respective parents.

One day after school when I was talking on the phone to a friend, Dad walked into the living room and demanded I relinquish the phone so he could do business. Before I could politely hang up, he yelled: "Don't you have more important things to do than yak-yak with your girlfriends?" To which I snippily replied: "Don't you have more important things to do than visit YOUR girlfriend in the afternoons?"

I promise I don't know where the courage or audacity came from to utter that response. I expected to go flying across the room as a result of the back of his hand, although he had never slapped me across the face. In fact, I distinctly remember my last spanking was in my tenth year. He stared at me. I was certain he had stopped breathing. He abruptly left the room. I hung up the phone, knowing my friend had heard every word. I ran out the door, grabbed the sheet from its hiding place and headed for the forbidden woods. When I said her name, she replied immediately.

"Sissy, I hate my life. My folks aren't the same people they used to be. My brother is beyond immature. My friends are silly. There is no place for me in this world. I don't know what to do."

As I sat with my head in my hands, hidden and depressed, I heard her soft voice once again.

"*My child, I am sorry that you are experiencing this sadness. I know that it seems so real to you. But I tell you this truth. This world you are experiencing is not real. It is an illusion. It is your story that you have created to learn what you came into form to learn. None of what is happening serves any purpose other than to be a lesson that you invited yourself to learn. It cannot hurt or harm you, only enlighten you. Do not be saddened.*"

"Sissy! Stop with all your craziness about my life not being real. I came to you for comfort because you said you were always with me and that you love me. Spouting fairy tales and nonsense is NOT helping. There is NO way that I would go around choosing to be hurt or to have parents who are out to lunch or ever ask for pain. I thought you would help. Right now I could use some really good advice. You got any?"

"*I do. Find a way to go inward. Search for a time and place where you can get to know your true self. Find a sacred place inside where you can feel peace, contentment and joy. In that place the answer will come. It is much more important for you to find it than for me to teach it to you at this time.*"

Having yearned for an immediate elixir from my mentor, I felt disappointed, frustrated and resentful. I needed someone I could turn to. This was too big for me. I couldn't be disrespectful to my dad. At the same time, having little respect for him, I loved and needed him. He was successful at producing great fear in me. Insanely, I would do almost anything to earn his praise. My mom seemed oblivious or, at least, acted that way. I really wanted to run away from this family that embarrassed me. And in spite of what Sissy had just said about going inward and finding my true self, I would have gladly been transported anywhere else except where I was. All I thought about was that in two more years I would be in college far away from this small town and my family. I knew I would leave and never, ever come back to face the stares and silent ridicule that I was so convinced were occurring daily.

"*It does not take courage to know yourself. Love is the only requirement. In all your quiet moments remember love, always love. Your life, the one you now seem to hate, is really just a dream you have made up. It is not real, but your mind keeps telling you a lie and convincing you that the events are real. Not so. When you are ready, we will talk about this at length."*

I had no doubt she meant well, but I believed she had no way of knowing how difficult this was for me. Feeling more alone than ever and not understood or comforted by the one person I saw as my last hope, I said my goodbye and walked home.

In the days and weeks that followed, Dad began to spend his new-found wealth as if there were an unending supply of dollars. Business must have been really great because we moved into the nicest new house in town. He bought a Piper Cub airplane and a sailboat. Always sort of scary and bellowing orders, Dad, now inquired about our school activities. He even attended the two school plays and one of my speech contests. He showed up at the 4-H county fair with Mother to see my championship ribbons and tell his buddies at the coffee shop how talented his daughter was. Not a word was said about the purple ribbons won by my sweet brother. Phil was simply not around much of the time. As a result, he avoided questions, trouble and punishment...and the noticeable absence of praise.

Tiptoeing through the daily routines at home, I slowly began to feel like I could breathe normally and go about my chores without looking over my shoulder and feeling shame. It took enormous effort to invest in the new house, mainly because it was contemporary, designed with a sterile simplicity and absent of warmth and old treasures. And, most of all, my sacred woods were nowhere near. I drove the Ford that Dad had for errands out to my beloved woods one time, but I could find no space in which to park that would have not been trespassing on another property. I left, knowing I was leaving my childhood behind. It was gone. The memory would be the only proof that I had loved that place better than any other plot of earth on the planet. I, once again, cried silently as I returned to the new house, careful to make sure that my red eyes were hidden from scrutiny or comment. Only the weak cried. The no-crying rule existed as long as I could remember. I recall vomiting in my mouth one time when my broken ankle was more painful than I thought I could endure without screaming. The admonishment that "big girls don't cry" echoed in my ears for years each time there was a good reason to scream or cry with one of the inevitable breaks, scrapes or agonies of childhood.

The spring morning was glorious with a slight breeze, pleasant sunshine and a perfect temperature that seemed to demand some adventurous outdoor activity. When Dad walked into the kitchen on his return from the daily "buddy-meeting" at the coffee shop, he asked if I wanted to go flying. It was a school day without significance or exams or any necessary attendance. And wow...my dad had asked me to go with him, knowing full well that it was a school day. I felt emboldened to skip school and do something I never thought I would do. I was going to fly in an airplane. Dad was still a student pilot, and I was unaware that it was illegal for him to carry passengers. It wouldn't have made any difference. I was invited, and, by golly, I was going.

The fabric-covered, bright yellow tail-dragger had tandem seats so Dad sat in the front, and I belted myself into the back. I could not see a thing ahead of me except the back of his head. As we taxied, without radios, and with minimal navigational avionics, my heart began to race. I was going to escape gravity! As he reached the end of the grass runway, we turned around to face where we had just come from and the throttle-push forced the plane to gather speed as we bumped along the grassy path and became airborne. The field was now below us as Dad made the plane climb. Everything below became smaller and geometrical. Perfectly seeded fields became little squares. Roads crisscrossed, and houses began to look like dots randomly placed on a massive green palette.

Midway through the flight that took us over familiar places around the community and near-by farmland, Dad asked if I would like to fly the airplane. At that moment I truly never felt more trusted, more honored and more capable as I took the stick in front of me in the dual control aircraft and began to feel my way to guiding the plane into straight and level flight. As I was gaining confidence and trying desperately to control the thrill of being momentarily in control of the flight, Dad began to instruct me in the slow process of turning, climbing, descending and leveling our aircraft. I was far beyond exhilaration. I was touching the heavens. I vowed that sometime in my life I would get my pilot's license and own an airplane because it would be impossible to forget the most exciting thing I had done in my fifteen years of living. Dad and I had reconnected through both loving an adventure that seemed to leave a mortal world behind.

Summer meant constant work on numerous 4-H projects which

included complicated sewing construction of a ball gown with 30 satin-covered buttons down the back, a difficult soufflé of many trials forced upon the family as dessert, the re-upholstering of an antique Victorian chair and a craft project of an original modern art design of Cleopatra embroidered upon an exquisite, narrow, long piece of linen that, ultimately, won first prize at the Indiana State Fair. This was my swan song after years of effort that, gratefully, culminated in teaching me every homemaking skill needed to survive and thrive.

All the summer weekends were spent at the St. Joseph, Michigan Yacht Club and Marina where Dad had a slip for the sailboat. On Friday afternoons, after spending all morning packing groceries, beachwear and the potato salad in the ice-filled cooler, we would head for the other side of the northern Indiana border to the boat. Those weekly trips were exciting, exhausting and memorable as Dad swore his way through South Bend traffic with a loud collection of cuss words, many times of original thought. I knew all the usual ones, having heard them for years, but the newly-initiated ones were often laughable. Phil and I would spit on our thumbs and slam our palms in recognition of a newborn, profane utterance. Mother turned and asked what on earth we were doing. We assured her it was a new game that we invented. She wasn't stupid by any means, and we were pretty sure that by mid-summer she had figured it out. The slight upward turn of her mouth when new expletives were exclaimed gave her away. She never said a word of admonishment to us.

To be fair, I couldn't wait for the weekends that summer. Phil and I were always allowed to take one friend (who were always forewarned of the possible expletives) so that our parents had free time. This allowed Phil and me to have a good time with our best friends.

Betty and I scoured the beaches, collected stones like they were shells from an ocean instead of Lake Michigan, flirted with the only teen-age boy in the marina, gossiped like Olympians and traded the most precious of secrets. Betty's dad and mom were both alcoholics, but fun people. I was the only person who knew how bad her home life really was. She had asked me one time what I did when my daddy beat my mom. I said that never happened, and she told me I was a very lucky kid. It's no wonder she loved to go to the boat with us, but she wasn't permitted often enough. I suspect her parents were cautiously trying to guard their secrets, so they limited their exposure via an influential family in town.

On the many weekends that Betty was not allowed to go with us, I spent the time on the boat, waiting to leave the slip in the marina and venture into the pure, blue waters of Lake Michigan. As our vessel would exit the long, concrete jetties of the harbor, I would hurry to position myself securely upon the bowsprit, which now I considered a place of reverence.

I had finally found it again! The bowsprit was the new sacred place where I could privately talk with Sissy. After leaving her the last time, I began to miss her daily. In searching for that peaceful, beautiful and lovely place from which to connect with her, I had almost given up. But the first time I ventured forth to straddle the magnificent bowsprit, I knew the invitation was beckoning to visit with my non-physical, sweet friend. We were easily reconnected, accompanied by a loving and needed embrace that feeling and openness allowed.

I loved riding the protrusion of the sailboat, imagining that I was discovering a new world and that I mattered as an inhabitant of this planet. With enough thought and discernment, I could find newness and fragrance in this seemingly hostile world. It was of these things that I wished to speak about with Sissy Jean.

Being on a sailboat meant that the wind was always in my face. And being on Lake Michigan meant that the waters were calm, and the bowsprit never dipped to the water as might happen in rough weather. Dad was a fair weather sailor, so the rides were pleasant and long which gave me plenty of time to think, ask questions of Sissy and listen to the wisdom conveyed in her answers. I protected my time with her and never mentioned her (non) existence to another human being after my mother had forbidden it. As I grew older, I began to understand that telling about our friendship could definitely cause trouble for me. Outright alarm and reaction from the caring individuals in charge of my well-being would not bode well for me. I never questioned our connection. Although I admit to not always understanding or appreciating some of the lessons she shared.

Firmly wrapped around the bowsprit, I thought for hours on end about what I wanted to do with my life. Certain that I would enter college in another year, I just assumed I would study science and math, using it as a stepping stone to some field of study that would catch my interest. My parents had always encouraged college studies. They never said: "when you go to college," but said "when you go to Purdue." Both were alumni of that great Indiana institution. In all those years of knowing that I was headed for college one day, I never considered anywhere but Purdue. There was no other acceptable institution of higher learning! I had already been informed by a recruiter that I would be receiving a scholarship for four years if I kept my grades at the acceptable level. Knowing about the free ride at Purdue, my dad would have forbidden any other consideration anyway.

Occasionally, I would inquire of Sissy about things she had said. She often repeated that the world was not anything but imagined perception. The illusion is something we humans create in order to learn a lesson. Our Spirit Mind knows that we need the experience. She reiterated that there are two minds in every human. The Ego Mind creates illusions of control, material wealth, judgments, self-conscious bodies and a myriad of useless and exhausting emotions and ideas. When she paused during her description of human (ego) mind, I said that all she spoke of seemed quite normal to me. Everyone I knew was, to some degree, invested in the Ego Mind feelings and activities of which she spoke. How could what she was saying be true for the world I knew?

"*Child, I assure you that you purposely chose to come to this planet, purposely chose your family, and now, purposely choose to investigate your reason for being and invest in the quest for Truth. You will live a long life in pursuit of the answers that elude you now. It is the most important thing in your life that your dedication and focus be on finding your Truth which will align with The Truth, The Oneness. This quest will be rigorous, but it will result in eternal joy and abiding love. And I am always with you.*"

"Sissy, you said there were two minds. What is the other one?"

"*The other mind is the Spiritual mind. It knows the Truth, looks always to the Light and knows that the only true emotion is Love. The only true purpose is giving and receiving love. You will come to know this mantra: "Nothing but love shall come to me, and nothing but love shall go forth from me." It will not be possible to live on your planet with pure love, unaffected by the intrusions of daily life, but it will be possible for you to know your true self and the Truth of The One. And it will be possible to change your behavior to align with the intention of love.*"

"Well, thank God, you have let me know that the perfection of love of which you speak is unattainable on Earth. But, nevertheless, my purpose is to focus on that goal!"

"It is good to see you express gratitude to The One who dearly loves you, asking only love in return."

"Sissy, is it possible you are mocking me? Is it really possible that you have a sense of humor?"

"Of course. Love is often conveyed via a bit of humor."

Sissy and I bantered for hours on the bowsprit pulpit. I grew in my abiding love for her. She, obviously, needed no growth or praise or direction. She simply and completely loved. I enjoyed her immensely. And a part of me knew how big she was…how big what she talked about was…how big life was.

There is no death, only a
change of worlds.

Chief Seattle

Labor Day weekend was the end of our summer delight. Betty and I made the rounds of all our favorite places along the beach, said good-bye to summer friends and danced to a rock and roll band at the Yacht Club. We felt so grown-up and wise as evidenced in the erudite topics we often discussed late into the night as we sat on the hillside that sloped down to the marina. Moonlight danced quietly on the water, looking very much like a Hollywood film scene.

We both were excited about entering our senior year, and we knew that after this last year in our small high school we would start a new life away from the semi-safety of the only place we had even known as home. Neither of us expressed any fear or trepidation-- only resolve. I told her that my Uncle Ford had recently told me that I would never again feel as important as I would as a senior in high school. But then he added that I would have to start at the bottom again. He had regaled in laughter and pinched my cheek. Sharing this tidbit of family wisdom with Betty made us both laugh out loud, echoing our sounds of fun over the water and into sleeping staterooms on boats anchored close by. The security guard politely suggested we retire for the evening. The next morning we packed and were entertained by my father's expletive-filled ride home.

Seniors always wore their newly-painted "cords" to the first day of school. September was still too warm for corduroy pants or skirts, but the honor of the senior cord outweighed the discomfort of heavy clothing. Almost every senior had painted his/her cords with symbols of their school activities, sports' letters, favorite sayings and the graduation year in bold letters. It was a somewhat discriminatory tradition because the poor could not afford the cords and paint. The underachievers and introverts had no activities to record upon their cords, and many had minimal artistic ability, so some cords became the butt of jokes. Lingering immaturity did not perceive the need to help or protest the unfairness or inequality. We were too excited to consider what love and compassion should have offered.

Sissy and I talked often. I had so many questions that would invade my thoughts during study hall or breaks in debate tournaments. It became difficult to take debate topics seriously after spending time with Sissy. The arguments seemed so mundane and useless compared to the mandates of finding one's true self while discovering love in everything and everyone and embracing the concept that all events in life have purpose and are a blessing.

December was dismal. White snow piled up along the plowed highways and became dirtier and darker daily. Sidewalks often had snow piled at the edges that exceeded the height of children walking with their parents. The bright spot, of course, was the coming of Christmas. Small towns excel in pageantry, Nativity displays, church chorale concerts, snowmen of extraordinary artistry, decorations and homemade sweets of innumerable varieties. I found it entertaining to work as a temporary clerk at the town haberdashery, secretly knowing almost every dad's Christmas present. I saved money for presents Phil and I would buy for Mother and Daddy. It felt like an act of respect to earn the money rather than Mother give us some to go shopping. Phil was made to work for Dad on construction jobs or in the equipment yard, but without pay. It was an unspoken rule that anytime we were given or earned money we split it. We had each other's back, and I don't think the folks ever knew about our agreement.

Early in December, Mother and I went to Washington, D. C. on a week's trip as the result of a speech contest prize I had won several months earlier. It was interesting that the young man who was the second place winner was asked to give his speech in the Capitol. I was permitted to go on the trip with a chaperone, but not to speak. At the national contest there were no female contestants. Mother and I both took note of this anomaly. She told me that I could help change that prejudice in my lifetime. Although my mother was quiet, submissive and somewhat cunning, she quietly wove a permission of rebellion into her daughter. I think she thought I had more courage, more hutzpah and more delight in edging toward the boundaries of acceptable behavior. I had often felt her secret relish of delight when she listened to speeches I gave that touched upon controversial subjects. Her clever manner of giving encouragement to my bridled, yet rebellious, nature was always complimentary and never admonishing about my subject matter.

As we traipsed through the White House, the National Mint, the Capitol and all accompanying monuments on the Mall, the Naval Academy and the Houses of Congress, I began to notice that Mother opted out of some of the tours. She begged off, saying that she hadn't slept well and was tired. At one point, I said, resentfully, that she was not appreciating my efforts and successes. She demurred, but without gusto.

Christmas was the usual present-opening on Christmas morning around the tree that Phil and I had decorated. We mischievously veered off the traditional pattern and had added fun little decorations with our own secret meanings. None were naughty, only personal. I opened gifts that would be needed in college, and Phil got the usual sports equipment. Dad tried on his new shirt from the haberdashery, and Mother seemed really pleased with the silk blouse from Blumenthal's, the local ladies' clothing store.

I spent most of Christmas vacation helping Mother with all the post-Christmas duties: disassembling the tree, storing house decorations and yard lights and figurines and freezing the excess goodies given as gifts from our many generous and kind friends.

In late February, I heard sniffling in the bathroom that was between the master bedroom and my room. As I knocked on the door, I feared waiting for an answer so I just walked in. Mother was in the tub, weeping with a washcloth over her face trying to muffle the sobs. I went over and knelt down. I stayed quiet but close. As she lowered the washcloth, I looked into a face that was ashen with enormous dark circles under the blue-grey eye color we shared.

"Mother, something is wrong. You never cry. Please tell me so I can help. What can I do?"

"Help me out of the tub, darling. I don't feel very stable. And then please hand me the bath towel," she said softly.

After helping her dry, I walked her to her bed and helped put her feet up. As I did so, I noticed her extended abdomen, particularly noticeable on her very slight frame.

"Mother, are you ill? Maybe I should call Dr. Herendeen. He makes house calls, and I know he would come to check on you."

"Annalee, I don't think we should do that. It's Sunday, and that poor man hardly ever gets a day off. Besides, your daddy just flew to Ohio for the week to see about one of his construction jobs that started last week. I don't want to worry him. Let's wait until tomorrow, and then I will go see the doctor."

I knew, instinctively, that waiting at the doctor's office was not a good idea. Dr. Herendeen didn't take appointments. As one of the two doctors in town, he, like Dr. Rowe, just had patients walk into his waiting room, sign in and wait their turn. Often, he would be called away for an emergency or to deliver a baby, so it could be an all day wait if a baby took its time or the emergency was significant. I could recall times in which we were sent home and asked to return the next day, while keeping our place in the queue. So I decided to take matters into my own hands. I could withstand whatever admonishment might come, but my stomach hurt just viewing my mother's frail body as I covered her with her favorite hand-knit cashmere blanket. She was asleep within minutes.

Mrs. Herendeen was exceptionally polite when I identified myself and apologized numerous times for interfering with their Sunday afternoon. When Dr. Herendeen answered the phone in his characteristic slow, baritone voice, I paused a little too long. He asked rather firmly why I was calling.

"Annie, is something wrong? Are you okay?"

"Doctor, something is wrong with my mother. My dad is away on business, and I am scared because she looks really sick. I didn't know who else to call beside you. I'm sorry. I know it's Sunday."

"You did the right thing," he said. "Tell me why you think your mom is sick."

I reported the bathroom scene, her weakness in walking and the bulging abdomen. The doctor said to take her temperature, and he would be there in the hour. Breathing a sigh of relief that help was on its way, I disobeyed the doctor, and did not wake my mother to take her temperature. I just sat and waited fearfully.

I prayed. I talked with Sissy Jean. I rocked. I listened for his car to come up the hill and pull in the long driveway. Hurrying out to meet him, he gave me a quick sideways hug and asked if I were a senior this year. As we entered the house, I directed him to the master bedroom at the far end of the first floor. He looked at her, looked at me, and asked me to wait in the kitchen.

The longer he was gone, the more frightened I became. Some minutes later, he asked to use the phone. He was instructing the person on the other end to prepare a room for her and dictated a lot of foreign-sounding instructions. Then he turned to me and said that he was checking my mother into the hospital. He helped me get her into our Ford and told me to go to the back entrance of the hospital, and the staff would help me. I thanked him. Then he asked that I call my Dad and tell him what had happened.

I was too young to have a driver's license, but I had been driving the back roads since I was fourteen. If Stubby, the one and only policeman in town, saw me, I would explain. Stubby would help for sure. And I knew Dr. Herendeen thought I was old enough to drive if I were a senior. So I did as I was asked.

Phil was at a friend's house and had no idea what was happening. I knew he was spending the night at Jim Bob's, so I decided to tell him when I saw him at school the next day. I slept in Mother's room at the hospital in a straight chair that I was certain had crippled me during the night.

Dr. Herendeen arrived a little after six the next morning. He told Mother that a surgeon from South Bend was on his way and that he would perform exploratory surgery because the x-rays and blood work were abnormal. I talked with Mother for a minute, but was quickly shooed out by two nurses who were saying that they needed to "prep" Mother for surgery.

The hospital was ancient. The cracked linoleum floors were shiny clean. Everything smelled of antiseptic, and the white walls were close to a dingy pale yellow. After finding the waiting room at the front of the building, I sat in a turquoise vinyl chair with a piece of grey tape in the middle of the seat and fingered through some of last year's magazines on the table to my left. I thought of my dad. I had called the wife of one of his workers and had asked her to call her husband who was in Ohio with my dad and tell him the details of what was happening and then to relay all that to Dad. All of this was a real chore because the hospital phone was a pay phone, and I did not have money. A kind woman in the waiting room gave me a couple of dimes for the calls and said I could pay her back later. She told me that she would be there every day for a while, and I could always find her. I remember the kindness and the gratitude and wondered if Sissy had a finger in this coincidence.

Suddenly, a doctor appeared in the lobby and called my dad's name. I looked up to see a grown man that looked like a replica of Howdy Doody. The red hair and massive amount of freckles would have made me giggle except for the circumstances. Informing him that my dad was flying home and wasn't here yet, I identified myself as the daughter of his patient. He looked straight at me, took a breath and said:

"You will need to tell your dad that your mother has terminal cancer. It is throughout her entire body. There is nothing we can do. I estimate she will probably live another two months. Do you understand?"

I was riveted to my chair. I stopped breathing. And, somehow, I found enough breath to answer "yes" as the surgeon was turning to leave. The woman who graciously gave me the dimes slipped into the chair next to mine. She took my hand and patted my leg gently. I started to cry, swallowing hard to hold back the avalanche of emotions. Gripping her hand, I said that he didn't know what he was saying. I hated that man. What kind of human being walks into a room and completely destroys another human being? Then, unemotionally, he turns on his heels to run away from the devastation he caused? I continued to focus my emotions on the robotic surgeon and his actions until I had to finally take a breath. She was still holding my hand.

"Did he say my mother is going to die?"

"Sweetheart, I think he did. I am so sorry. Let's call your family, and I will stay here with you." I hugged her and said I was going to get my brother. I never saw her again, but what she did was so loving I shall never forget her.

I knew Dad was probably in the air flying home. My brother was across the street in class at the high school, and there was no other family in town.

Red-eyed and breathless, I walked into the principal's office and almost screamed at the school secretary to get my brother out of class. She rather nastily asked why I wasn't in class myself, and then, I actually did scream. The principal heard this, came out of his office, and seeing my face, asked the secretary to locate my brother.

Phil came soon. We were all escorted across the hall to an empty room. The principal, the secretary, Phil and I sat huddled as I recounted the surgery and its terrifying results, plus the impending devastation of losing our mother. My brother sat stupefied, his mouth agape and swallowing hard. We reached for each other. I had never been held tighter than at that moment.

Principal Betz asked what we would like to do. I said I thought Phil and I should go back to the hospital because our mother would be back in her room soon, and Dad should be arriving at any time. Mr. Betz said that he thought I knew best and that it was a good idea. He had a reassuring way of making one feel her own ability to be courageous, strong or insightful.

Phil and I were informed that Mother was not available to visit yet, so we settled into the turquoise chairs, waiting for Dad to arrive. A little more than two hours later, we saw him walk into the lobby. I ran to hug him. I think I did it for comfort to him and from him because the next few minutes were going to be unbearable.

The receptionist guided us to a small chapel adjacent to the lobby and left us alone.

"Daughter, what in the hell is going on here. I got a damned call that your mother was in the hospital. Is she here? Is she okay?"

"Daddy, Mother had surgery this morning. The doctor said she has terminal cancer and has two months to live," I mechanically told him.

"Well, I'll be goddammed! That can't be true. When I left she was healthy as a horse. Let me talk to this friggin' doctor."

God stepped in. At that very moment, Helen, our neighbor and best friend of Mother's, walked in. Helen was an RN and had assisted in the OR for Mother's surgery. She had just left Mother's room after staying with her in Recovery and had come searching for us. She had the most calming voice I had ever heard, other than Sissy's. She asked my Dad to sit down, and she would explain everything. She slowly described Mother's symptoms, my call to Dr. Herendeen, the arrangements to get the surgeon from South Bend, the results of the surgery, as well as what to expect in the coming two months and her personal sorrow. I remember wondering, in the midst of all this explanation and empathy, "how do nurses and doctors handle horrifying news of a friend and still do their job?"

She reached over and put her hand on his shoulder. Dad's body started to shake uncontrollably. With his head in his hands, he cried, wailed, and repeatedly bellowed "No," as he rocked, totally unaware of his world. Helen stayed steadfast and close. Phil and I held hands, spectators of an inconceivable tragedy: our Mother was dying, and our Dad was crying and out of control.

"Oh, my God!! I can't lose her. She is the love of my life. I can't live without her. She is the best thing that ever happened to me. I don't deserve her love, but she has always given it. Help me, God. This can't be true."

We were so taken aback. Dad never showed this kind of emotion. We were witnessing the collapse of our other parent. At that moment it felt like we were going to experience the loss of both parents. One was going to die and leave her physical body. The other was dying emotionally and staying in his tortured soul. Phil and I knew we felt helpless…and in some way, also hopeless. We were emotionally adrift.

We must let go of the life we had
planned, so as to accept the one
that is waiting for us.

Joseph Campbell

Dad ordered us to go home. He wanted to talk with Mother alone.
We were not to call anyone. He would do that later. I was to fix
dinner, although I was confident that none of us had an appetite.
Sometimes Mother would serve a pancake dinner with small sausages
if she were tired and not up to preparing the three course dinner
that Dad expected: salad or soup, meat entrée with fresh veggies and,
of course, dessert. Deciding I would take the chance that pancakes
might be acceptable today, I found the Bisquick and sat the waiting
batter aside until Dad arrived.

All three of us picked at our food in silence. When I was gathering
the dishes, Dad came back into the kitchen to say that we needed to
talk. Hardly ever having spent time sitting in the living room, rather
than the den where the TV was, it already felt uncomfortable and
somewhat foreboding.

"You both know your mother is dying. That is hard enough. But
it would be much worse if she knew it. I don't know how she could
handle not seeing you kids grow up, marry and have grandchildren.
So here's what we are all going to do. I am going to bring her home
from the hospital, and we will take care of her here. She needs to be
with family and familiar surroundings. I will hire a nurse who will
care for her and monitor all phone calls. Annalee, you will do the
grocery shopping, cook, clean and pay the bills. Phil, you will help
your sister and take care of the house and lawns, the vehicles and
help me at the equipment yard. Most important of all, you are NOT
to tell your mother that she is dying. It must never be mentioned.
Visitors, except for family, will not be allowed. That's about it. Do
you understand me?" Dad asked in the firmest of voice.

We shook our heads in agreement. We had no insight, no part
in decision making, no opinions. We were numb. We both wanted
to cry, to be held, to scream at the space around us. However, we
did nothing.

Dad called Mother's sister, Aunt Madge, and told her the news.

He said she should be the one to tell our grandparents and Mothers' siblings. He also informed her of his decision to keep the prognosis from her and said that if they were to visit that they had to agree to abide by his decision.

Phil drove us to school the next day, knowing that neither one of us had a driver's license. Upon entering the high school building and walking to our lockers, we became immediately aware that almost every schoolmate had heard the news. And like most kids, they did not know what to say or how to act, so they just looked down and said nothing. Teachers, at least, said a sentence or two about their sorrow and offered to be "here if you need me." I thought: "I wish to hell I knew what I needed!"

Days went by. I kept thinking about "she has about two months to live," and I counted every day. I quizzed my mother about her childhood, what it was like when she was pregnant with me during World War II, about the inventions that made life easier in her childhood and how she used a forbidden, small kerosene lamp at her bedside as a child to read. We talked about how she met my dad and stories of their courtship. I learned that she wore a great aunt's wedding dress and that at her wedding reception a guest announced that Britain had just declared war on Germany for having invaded Poland. Dad whispered to her that he was sure he would be drafted soon. Having been in ROTC at Purdue, he was already a commissioned second lieutenant, so he was certain to be called. I felt for my mother, thinking of enjoying her wedding day and, all of a sudden, knowing that her husband would soon be taken and put in harm's way. I told her my thoughts, and she smiled and touched my face.

"Annalee Grace, why are you asking all these questions? You are wearing me out, although I like to visit the memories of all those times."

"Oh, Mother, you know I will be going to Purdue in a few months, and I won't be here with you. I just thought I would ask you to share your childhood with me…and how you got to Purdue." I lied.

I was very afraid that I was not fooling her because she had told me my entire life that if I lied I had a ticker tape that ran across my forehead. I hated that. My sweet mother was living out her final days, and I was lying to her face. I excused myself to fix another meal.

45

The next week I received the mountain of material that I had requested from the University of Chicago Medical School. After reading almost all night long every other night for a week, I came to the conclusion that the medical community knew very little about cancer and its treatments. And it became crushingly clear that there was no way to save my mother. She was going to die an agonizing, painful death as her body withered each day.

The live-in nurse had a family funeral to attend, so she was going to be gone for two days. She called Dad into the bathroom to show him how to give Mother her morphine injections. Dad yelled across the house for me to come see what Nurse Elliott was demonstrating. I knew immediately that I would be the one giving the morphine shots. Dad was considerably strong physically and intellectually, but he had almost no emotional strength. Anger was easy for him, but compassion, softness, gentleness, empathy and authenticity of feelings were not his forte. As soon as it was time for the next injection, Dad hollered for me to do it. I already had it prepared, and I actually felt honored. Watching the shot take effect, I felt such gratitude that something existed to make her sleep without pain.

At the hospital, where she had returned, she passed a few minutes after midnight on my birthday. I had been watching the shallow breaths that were longer and longer in between inhalations. Death came quietly and peacefully. It seemed as if nothing had changed. The entire room full of family, one by one, touched her for a last loving good-bye and walked out as slowly as I have ever witnessed humans walk. It obviously was a walk of grief and reverence...and acceptance.

Because it was late at night, the only exit from the second floor of the hospital was down the indoor fire stairs. I was about in the middle of the group when my mother's dad, my grandfather, collapsed onto my shoulders. I caught the railing on both sides of the stairway and sat down involuntarily under the weight of my grandpa. He cried so hard that I became afraid for him. He had his own medical issues.

"No parent should ever watch a child die. I have watched two of my daughters die, helpless to prevent it. Why does God not take me. God, give my daughter back to her family and take me," he wailed, beseeching a deity of any sort that could answer his plea.

Grandma and I finally got him on his feet and down the stairs. He said nothing the entire next day. Even as family from four states trickled in for the funeral, Grandpa sat on the porch. He would answer people with a nod. I sat beside him whenever I could. Then, on the second day, he stopped moving in the rocking chair, put his hand on my arm and said it was time to do what had to be done. He was back, but never the same.

As hundreds of kind individuals came to visitation, looked at my mother in an expensive casket with horrid satin tufting that swallowed her seventy-six pound body, they each shook my hand or hugged me, said their condolences in as many different ways as possible and went home to their living families.

The funeral was exactly what it was supposed to be. It was religious, reverent, sprinkled with bits of humor, focused on the husband and children and not too long. Although it was in the middle of the week, almost the whole town turned out. Stores closed for an hour, Officer Stubby was not on duty and most of my classmates came. Both Phil and I just wanted to be alone, but that was not a possibility. Our Aunt Madge, guessing at our true feelings, whispered to us at the post-funeral luncheon that all this ceremonial stuff would be over soon, and then we could have some quiet time.

I appreciated Aunt Madge so much. Two weeks after the funeral she had insisted I go to prom. She took me to Ft. Wayne to buy a prom dress, drove fifty miles each way to help me get ready and told me that she knew she couldn't take my mother's place on special occasions like this, but she was glad I let her come. Mother's younger sister shared similarity in personality and thoughtfulness. I felt certain that our time together helped her as much as it did me, and we mutually appreciated how we were helping each other cope and heal. Those few visits set a bond in place that was to last over fifty years.

As I walked across the stage at graduation, knowing Mother was not in the audience, I held up my diploma and tipped my head toward heaven for a moment, looking upward in some sort of emotional connection. Everyone watching knew what was meant by my pause on stage. And then high school was over.

Dad's work would take him away from home for as much as five days at a time. Phil and I were grateful to have the house to ourselves. We could snack, skip meals, wear the same clothes for three or four days, not answer the phone and sleep as late as we chose. One morning as I was fixing cereal I called for him to no avail. I found that both he and the car were missing. I took my bicycle and started searching. A little over an hour later I found him at the cemetery, asleep on the fresh dirt of Mother's grave. As I touched him, he awoke, got up, put my bicycle in the Ford and drove us home. I told him as gently as possible that we could take care of each other, no matter what, but that he could not sleep at the cemetery again. He nodded. We went home and ate soggy cereal.

The new house still felt sterile to me. It was starkly empty without Mother. One day I left its hilltop perch and entered the previously unexplored woodland behind the house. There were splendid canopies of oaks, elms and maples that towered over the very thick undergrowth. Coming upon a patch that felt cool and inviting, I took off my light sweater, put it down and sat with my knees under my chin. Even though I knew she was always with me, I now felt her presence. I lifted my head from my kneecaps and said her name.

"I am here, my child. I have been with you throughout your sadness and grief. I am glad that we may talk."

"Sissy, I know you mean well, but I cannot think of a thing that you could say to me that could possibly make me feel better. My mother is gone. She is dead. DEAD!"

"No, Annalee, your mother is not dead. There is no death. I have been waiting for us to talk so that I might tell you that death does not exist. It is not real."

"Sissy Jean. Just stop! Your mumbo jumbo is ridiculous. I saw her die, I picked the clothes for her coffin attire, I saw the men lower her into the ground and I dropped a handful of dirt on her casket. So don't be telling me that she is alive. I really don't need nonsense right now. I just need comfort. I need my mother."

"I am always here loving you. You know I would never lie to you or hurt you in any way. My love for you wants to help you understand the Truth. I promise you there is no death. I will explain what happens so that you know the Truth and will be able to find peace about your mother not being physically present in your life."

"Sissy, I will listen to what you have to say. No one else has offered anything that helps. Dad won't let us talk about it. The counselor at school, Mrs. Berkebile, is of no help whatsoever. My Aunt Madge is a long distance call, and Dad would have a fit about the bill. He has to approve everything before I write the checks. So let's hear what you have to say."

"Annalee, everyone you know has a physical body. It is worthless in

the scheme of things. It carries you around on this Earth experience. It is a vehicle. That's all. Sometimes, like any other vehicle, it breaks down. So we encourage everyone to take care of it for their own comfort. But your body is not who you are. You are the Spirit Mind. Remember that I told you before that you have two minds: Ego Mind and Spirit Mind. Human mind competes, gossips, grieves, searches, complains and gets angry. Spirit mind knows that all is well. It never feels anything but peace and love, because it knows that we are all one. Everyone in the universe is connected. Everyone is your brother and sister. Everyone is incarnated with a spark of divinity from the One. And everyone is eternal. So when the physical body no longer functions, the Spirit Mind watches it take a last breath of human existence and then steps over into the realm of total peace of The One. The body is the only thing that ceases to function; all other functions continue forever. So death is stepping from one place to another, not causing one to cease being. The psychological being ends and the eternal or Spirit being continues. It is impossible for a soul to die. Your mother has taken that step that insures her peace and the continuation of her essence. She may choose to return in another time in another form, but that story is not for today."

"You know, I have to tell you that I can feel her presence. That sounds weird, but I do. And I have not told anyone that three nights after she died...her body died, I saw her. I thought I was crazy. I woke up in the middle of the night, and she was sitting at the foot of my bed. She didn't utter a word. But she had a slight smile. I called to her. She was silent and then faded away. Was I crazy?"

"No. She let her essence linger for a while to come and reassure you. I saw her, too. And then she took her final step of transition into the grid of The One."

"Sissy, you said once that all behavior has purpose to manifest an experience to learn something that our 'beingness' needs to learn. Does that mean that I have some responsibility for my mother's death?"

"You have no responsibility at all. You cannot know what the path of your mother's life was, nor what her lessons were while she was here. But you do have responsibility to learn from your experience with her and with her leaving her form. Her transition has affected you, so please recognize all your feelings and reactions, and then choose behavior that leads you to love and a greater sense of peace. This will take some time, reflection, effort and envisioning. And whenever you want, we can talk about your thoughts. I remind you to use Spirit Mind as much as possible. Ego, or human, mind will

always be bullying its way into your thoughts, and it's easy to be led astray. You have this whole lifetime to practice."

"Well, I have a few weeks left to get ready for college. I am not worried about change. I am looking forward to a new challenge. But I am very concerned about my brother who will be here alone for the most part. He is not doing well trying to cope with Mother being gone, and Dad is pretty hard on him. I just don't know how to help him. There won't be money for long distance calls, Dad could see our letters if he got the mail first at his post office box and there's no money for gas to come visit me at the university. We don't get an allowance. We have temporary, part-time summer work. We both need that money for necessities that Dad says we should pay for ourselves."

"Your brother loved your mother with all his heart. He is hurt, alone, angry and lost. But he will not tarnish her memory by getting into unusual trouble. He may focus on just staying out of sight and not saying much so that your dad will leave him alone. He is sweet and caring, but he covers his feelings by being the 'class clown.' For now, that is a role that helps him cope. Give him time to play that role and tire of it. He will join you at the university soon enough."

What would life be if we had no
courage to attempt anything?

Vincent Van Gogh

Even though I knew there would be a lot of cussing when Dad saw
the check I had written to Wile's Department Store, I bought the
twin bed sheet set, blanket, pillow and desk lamp at the last minute.
There were no twin sheets at home, and I feared taking a pillow or
blanket from my room. Knowing he would miss his desk lamp, I
bought one and rationalized I had only bought the bare necessities.
I had also "borrowed" pencils, a portable pencil sharpener, a slide
rule and yellow note pads from his office. The typewriter was a very
needed item on the college "list" I had received. I knew better than
to abscond with the one in his office.

Phil helped me get Mother's suitcase out of the attic. After
spending a good amount of energy washing the fake leather exterior
and cleaning out the dusty interior, I packed all my clothes. There
was nothing in my closet but the 4-H ball gown that was promised
to a friend for next year's prom. I packed my toiletries, a silly, old and
worn teddy bear, boots and an umbrella. I carried my winter coat
because I would need it before Christmas break, my first time home.
After the Caddy was loaded, what was left of my family headed to
Purdue.

The day before, still worried about my brother, Fippy, I spent
some time with Sissy because I had some questions I needed answered.
I desperately wanted some relief from what seemed like abandonment
of my brother. Announcing that I was going for a last walk around
the property, I left my family and sought the new sacred woods.

"Sissy Jean, I have not told anyone about you but my mother, and
she is gone. Does my brother have someone like you that is forever
with him?" Should I tell him about you?"

"*I know you love him so much and wish to protect him in any way you
can. And, of course, your brother has a non-physical being with him always.
But one must be open to and willing to accept the presence of an energy being
like me. I do not believe your sibling is open to that awareness right now. He
may discover it at some later time. It would help if he learned to meditate as*

51

you naturally learned in your special place under Grandfather Tree. So, at some peaceful time, you may wish to teach him to quiet his mind and let it be open to the awareness of his higher self. Be patient, dear one."

"Can you watch over him for me?"

"Annalee, please know that all an energy being can do is love you fully, teach you when asked and be present at your transition. I cannot protect you or change the course of your path. Neither you nor anyone else needs protection. The illusion of the situation you have chosen to manifest may look dangerous, but you have the power to change the illusion of your Ego Mind. It is precisely the illusions that will lead you to enter Spirit Mind and find peace and resolve. Earth is a hard assignment. Those who have chosen to come into form on this planet have chosen to be spiritual warriors, to open hearts and minds and change your world to one of love and prosperity of Spirit."

"What you say sounds like a lifetime of work and awareness. And I think I have a great deal to learn, indeed…a lot more than even a university can offer."

"Stay open to all possibilities. Your heart will notify you when your choices are Spirit Mind or Ego Mind. You just have to listen, dear one. The most important thing to remember is that Ego Mind is a distraction, a seductive bully and a path away from freedom and peace."

As it turned out, I was glad that Dad and Phil were with me to lug my belongings up three flights of stairs to a room that had a bunk bed, two small desks, two very narrow chests of drawers and two closets that could only be described at teensy-weensy! After walking the corridor, I discovered that the bathroom was a large room of wash basins, showers and toilet stalls, all being as far from my room as possible. A very disgruntled mother was telling her daughter that she would have to buy shower shoes to avoid getting athlete's foot and a carrying basket for her toiletries, towel and nightshirt. Dad heard this loud exclamation. In front of everyone, he handed me a twenty dollar bill, loudly saying I should get what I needed. When he wasn't looking, I gave it to Phil because I figured I could use a shoe box to carry what I needed. I'd take my chances with athlete's foot. Phil nodded his head "no," but I put it in his pocket. I knew from experience that Phil never came out ahead on money that was handed out. The guys did not stay to help put things away, but I was relieved to have some time to myself before my roommate arrived. My heart told me to choose the top bunk, but it would be hard to make the bed! By the end of the day, I was ready to start college.

A silly tradition at Purdue was that all freshmen were required to wear bright green beanies. The purpose, supposedly, was that upperclassmen would help the "newbies" navigate the concrete campus spread over many acres. The actual result of beanie-wearing was one long tease session the first day of class. I threw the beanie in the trash, and no one ever knew or said a word. My first good decision at college felt empowering.

Mrs. Berkebile was the high school Dean of Girls, lone counselor and actually the chief attendance record keeper. No girl received any instruction about applying to college, advanced placement exams or dormitory information. Actually, I think only two or three girls went to college. I was lucky to have met the Purdue recruiter. He had asked the principal for the names of students with a certain grade point average. As a result of my GPA, a scholarship was awarded to me. When filling out the application papers for advanced placement, courses and resident hall preferences, I had requested the newest residence hall. This hasty decision taught me to do research and ask questions in the future when it came to my personal comfort. The "X" was a new facility three stories high in the form of an X with a huge lobby at the intersection of the 4 arms. It was also the farthest building from the center of campus, requiring a twenty to twenty-five minute, uncomfortable walk to the library. Indiana winters often consisted of daily snow and frequently packed solid ice. My calf muscles grew daily in strength and girth as I learned to hustle across campus in the ten minutes allotted between classes. I swore that whoever did the scheduling had a mean streak or a devilish sense of humor.

Making friends was easy, but not having any family member visit me was hard. I got really clever about avoiding probing questions about family and learned to respond with questions about their own families. It worked every time. Counting the days until Christmas break, I realized I missed my brother more than I ever thought I could or would. We carried each other's history and each other's sorrow. So I was thrilled when I read the note taped to my door that said my dad had called saying when he would pick me up. He had not forgotten me!! I was going to spend the holidays at home with family and relatives. Giddy was the only description I could think of as I felt my insides aflutter.

She was a diminutive woman, my Dad's age, pleasant, widowed, childless and an unwanted visitor in our mother's home. I had a hard time catching my breath when we arrived home to find her in the living room. She sat there crocheting an afghan in Mother's favorite chair. Dad introduced her, explaining that he had met her, coincidentally, at the Yacht Club in St. Joseph, Michigan, as they were both posting a for sale notice on the club bulletin board. She was also recently widowed and, like Dad, wanted to sell the boat she had shared with her spouse. They "enjoyed each other's company," and he had invited her to spend the holidays with us since she had no children. I promise I did everything in my power to be polite, but all I wanted to do was to scream for her to leave us alone. Go away! This was the moment I began the canonization process for my late mother, which would last until a therapist confronted me years later. I desperately looked around the room for Fippy's support and comfort. I realized he had quietly disappeared.

Just before dinner at the country club, of course, I found him. He had obviously been crying. We held each other and rocked ourselves into a moment of peace.

"I hate him. He doesn't remember Mother. He doesn't care anything about me...or you. He has a girlfriend. That's all that matters. He goes to Michigan to see her almost every weekend, so I don't have to see him too often. She pretends to care about us, but she never asks one question or spends anytime with anyone but Dad. You just wait. He's gonna marry her...soon, I bet." Then my brother took a breath. He rarely said so many words at one time.

He grabbed me, then pushed me away and walked home. Dad was fuming that we were late and disrespectful to him and his "friend." I ate my first good meal in four months. Phil ate nothing. Dad didn't notice. This is not how I would have chosen to spend my Christmas. However, I cooked for the family (especially for Phil) and visited old high school friends. Many were now married and foreign to the life I was living.

I packed the pair of fur-lined gloves that Dad gave me for Christmas and a hand-knitted sweater that Mother had made years previous. I had hidden it for some unknown or unconscious reason. More pencils, pens and yellow pads were borrowed from the office. I vowed never to come to this house again. It was violated, different and had nothing to offer but unpleasantness. Phil drove me back to school. Dad said he would see me at spring break. I just waved.

Phil and I had asked a good friend, Jim Bob, if I could send letters to him, and he could give them to my brother at school. We wrote about every two weeks. Phil continued to be grateful that Dad worked away from home during the week and spent the rest of the time with Ginny, his new "friend."

At the end of the first semester, I made the decision to do whatever I could to no longer live in residence halls. That experience was not what I needed. Hungry for a feeling of belonging, of something akin to family, I decided to go through sorority rush. It turned out to be a wonderful and psyche-saving decision. I joined a sorority composed of all sorts of small town girls like myself. It was situated near mid-campus. I never quite bought into the mojo of the sorority mission statement, secret handshakes or allegiance forever, but "sisterhood" seemed real. I learned to love and appreciate those women who helped, shared, cared and laughed when needed. They became like family. I think they saved me from anger, doubt, grief and loneliness without even knowing the gifts they were offering me. Living in the sorority house I could feel my body loosen. My muscles relaxed and my sense of humor came back. I resigned from the Purdue Debate Team as it conflicted with sorority activities. Instinctively, I knew I needed a sense of belonging more than the heady and arrogant exercise of debate...and the endless weekends traveling to tournaments.

At spring break I begged off going home so I could work at a shop at the university to earn some much needed money because the scholarship did not cover the sorority house costs. I worked sixteen hour days the two weeks of break and snuck into the sorority house late so I could sleep and shower, well aware that it was closed to all residents. I got caught on the last day of spring break. The house mother had returned a day early and heard the water running. She was very gracious when I told her the truth about the entire vacation period. At that moment, she felt like a mother...not mine, but a very good substitute.

While being an illegal resident of the sorority house over spring break, I had some time, not much, to talk with Sissy Jean. I explained that I was very frustrated and could not find a comfortable and safe place to talk with her when I needed. Everything seemed so chaotic and filled with people noise. I simply wasn't able to meditate and speak with her.

"Dear one, you need not communicate with me out loud. I know it has been our custom, but if you just think the sentences, I will understand. You will hear my answer, and never again do we need voice that is audible. Please try it now with me."

"I have been thinking about what you explained about death. The more I think about your explanation, the more comfortable I become, even though I miss the physical presence of my mother every day. And I keep coming up with questions for you. So, I want to ask about the one you call The ONE. Is that the same being that I call God?"

"God and The One are the same. The One is not a being. It is 'All That Is.' It is pure Light and pure Love. We are all a particle of Its divinity, all connected, all one. It loves without condition and allows us to find our paths back to Source, or, as you say, 'God.' Just know that The One is Total Awareness.

"Sissy, I learned that if I break a commandment that I must ask forgiveness of God. Father Cochran said that if I break one of the Ten Commandments that I have sinned, must confess the sin, and ask forgiveness of God with a pure heart. Is that true?"

"Annalee, you need to know that The One never forgives because It never judges. It allows you to walk your earthly journey and learn the lessons you manifest in your illusions. The One never harms, judges, forgives or protects. It loves. And whatever you do on your path is your choice. The One waits for your enlightenment, which is nothing more than your acceptance of your own divinity, the ever-present goal of universal love, your acknowledgment of the connection of all beings with each other and that we all return to the Source."

"Well, what about religion? What about the churches of the world? Do they understand what you say?"

"My love, religion is a construct of the Ego Mind. It has been created to help teach and comfort. But it also strays to issues of control, power, punishment, misinformation and greed. Many church institutions try to help, guide, comfort and lift up the weary of your world. Others have motives that serve the darkness of ego intentions. Your heart will always know the Truth. Truth knows that all is illusion. Church is an ego construct. Be alert and gracious."

"Sissy, I really could use some helpful suggestions on dealing with my constant feelings of loss and grief. I miss my mother. When all the parents come to visit my sorority sisters, I feel self-pity and, sometimes, even anger and envy. The mothers send cookies, new clothes, extra allowance money, cards…and phone calls. I truly am happy for the other girls, but I have these dark feelings, too. And, just so you know, it really is hard to see all that as illusion. My heart hurts…often."

"*Dear one, of course you miss your mother. And I now know that you understand that there is no death…just a transition of stepping over. What you are feeling is what you have been taught to feel. You are mourning the loss of her form, her body. There can be no mourning for the loss of her essence because it is still whole and eternal. Please go deep into meditation and find the sacred dimension of Formless Form. In the depths of feeling the sacredness of the Other Side, there is a surrender that opens the door to Truth, Peace and comforting acceptance. Child, you hugged your mother a lot. Part of what you are feeling is missing the tactile connection. Her love for you is as constant as mine. Close your eyes and feel her hug, her love, her maternal embrace. I will wait.*"

Closing my eyes, I sat for a time before I felt her presence. I asked for the hug I longed to feel…and felt it immediately. Tears of unadulterated joy were streaming down my cheeks as I was immersed in the hug, the smell of her and the flow of love that seemed to fill us both. Eventually, she gently drew back, touched my cheek and was gone. It was then that I knew I would always have my mother, always be able to connect in meditation and always find the surrender needed to dissolve the illusion of her being "gone."

Feeling blessed, honored and enlightened to something unknown to me before, I said: "Sissy, that exchange has changed my life. I will never be or feel the same again. You have given me two gifts today. You returned my mother to me, and you gave me the delicious delight of talking with you without speech for the rest of my life. Thank you, my loving friend."

"*I am grateful that you feel blessed, which is a natural state, and that you now know you have not 'lost' your mother.*"

Walking around in a bit of a daze after the extraordinary experience with Sissy and my mother, I needed to do something to reconnect with the daily routine of my life. Intuitively, I was led to the Student Union Building at the center of campus. Walking the halls for several minutes, I suddenly noticed a bulletin board, and I sauntered over to see what it offered. As I perused the announcements, my eyes fixed on one near the end. An agency of the US government was soliciting applications for interns to work at their office in Mexico City for the summer. I tore off one of the info strips and jogged back to my room to fill it out. With an envelope and a stamp (begged from the house mother) in hand, I ran to the big post office bin on the corner two blocks north. Skipping back to my residence, I yelled out loud: "Sissy, I could use some help with this!" I heard her reply: "Manifest it yourself. You can!" So, right then and there I told the Universe that I was going to work in Mexico City this summer. It was a done deal!

Five weeks later a gentleman showed up at the sorority house and asked for me. My sorority sister found me and said a guy who looked like a cop wanted to see me. As I entered the living room, he stood, introduced himself as an agent of the US government and said he had some questions for me. As he sat down, I thought: "Yep, he acts like a cop!"

The questions were dull, routine and promising. It was normal, he said, to run a background check on me. And he needed to fill in a bunch of blanks. Politely answering every question with respect, I spent about forty-five minutes recounting my short life history, supplying school names, principals, pastors, family history, travel history, (non) criminal history and physical evaluation. He explained what I would be doing as an intern, and that if I passed the background check, I would be notified within the month. Holy Jesus, Joseph and Mary!

Phil called the sorority house. Since this was the first long distant call I had ever received there, I ran for the phone knowing that it must be an emergency or even some devastating news. When I heard Fippy's voice, which was cheerful and inquiring of my university life, I knew immediately that there was news. But what was he working up to?

"Fippy, I know you must be calling for a reason. What is it? Is everything okay?"

"Nothing will be okay until I can leave here. But I wanted to tell you that you will be getting an invitation in the mail to the BIG wedding! So don't be surprised."

"Whose wedding?" For a second I feared it was Fippy's because I was aware that he comforted himself with many sexual escapades. He was quite a high school "catch." I, naturally, had some concern. The high school coach, wisely, provided condoms, since no one under eighteen was allowed to purchase them at the small town drugstore.

"The Old Man's," he replied with a muffled huff.

"What? Already?" I gasped.

"When?"

When he told me the date, I said it would be impossible for me to go because I had a ticket for Mexico City. When I furnished him with all the details, he was sincerely excited for me, but said he thought all hell would break loose if I didn't show up for the wedding. He reminded me that he had a year of high school left and was going to have to live with Dad and 'her.' He would feel a whole lot better if we did this together. That hooked me for sure. I told him I would be there. Then I asked one last question:

"Fippy, does Mother have a headstone yet?" I knew he visited the cemetery on a regular basis. He would know for sure.

"Annie, I don't know if he ever even thinks about her. He has found a woman who is all giggly about him, has more money than he does and doesn't have the nuisance factor of kids. He hit his jackpot!"

"Okay, Phil, I will be at the wedding with you, but just be warned that I am putting in a collect long distance call to Dad. We need to discuss a headstone for Mom. Just in case he's mad, I suggest you head for Jim Bob's."

"Good thinking, Annie...and good luck." After a long pause, I said: "I miss her, too." I heard his swallow, and we hung up.

I called Dad within two minutes. He hesitated, but accepted the collect call.

"What in the hell is going on, Annalee? Why are you calling collect?"

"Dad, I just learned that you are getting married, and I will be receiving a wedding invitation as a surprise and that I am expected to be in Michigan two days after the semester ends. Do I have this right?"

"Oh, hell, Annalee! I meant to tell you about all this, but I have been busting my balls with work. Sorry. Yep, gonna get married. She's a fine woman. I know it's only been a year since your mother died, but fate just brought Ginny into my life."

"Well, Dad, I am happy for you. I know you are lonely and need a woman in your life. I, actually, was surprised that it was so soon, but I understand. So, congratulations."

"Well, thank you." The relief in his voice was noticeable.

"Dad, there's just one request that I have. It is an easy and necessary one. Before you take a new wife you need to buy a headstone for your dead wife."

"Dammit, Annalee. Don't you be telling me what to do. I am busy as hell, and I'll do it when I have time."

"Make the time. Our mother deserves that respect before you remarry. Let me know when it is ordered. It's the right thing to do. You get a new wife, but Phil and I never get a new mother. We're doing our best here. Please do your best. This is hard on us."

Having always had some fear as well as respect for my dad, I found myself somewhat in awe at so bravely stating my feelings. Maybe because I was not in the same room I felt emboldened. I think it was more that I just spoke my truth. And I think he knew it. The good-bye was quick.

Jim Bob's sweet mother was the second long distance call. It was about two weeks after I talked with Dad. She simply said: "Your mother's headstone was placed today." I wept into the phone, and she said: "God Bless" and hung up.

The only piece of clothing nice enough to wear to a wedding was a very light-weight wool suit I had made in 4-H. Even though it was June 3, I wore it. Thank God for a breezy, cool day in Michigan. The wedding was routine and emotionally difficult. The reception at the Yacht Club was spectacular. Great food, great music, great time.

Two days after the wedding, I took the train to Chicago and boarded an airplane for Mexico City. The tickets, as well as the advance stipend for taxis and tips, were provided for me. All instructions had been mailed weeks earlier with numerous documents for my signature. The address of my host family, the clothing needed, my passport and the address of my employment were provided with instructions and phone numbers, if needed. I would be in Mexico City for a full week (now reduced to four days due to the wedding) before reporting to my internship position. I felt very mature… with trepidation. It occurred to me that that was an oxymoron. So I decided to just push on and see what illusion showed up for my entertainment.

God had a finger in this! My host family was delightful, spoke English, were cultured and conversant on many contemporary issues. Best of all, they had two nephews that were eager to show the two interns housed with their aunt and uncle around the nightclub circuit of Mexico City. I worked hard by day and played, danced, laughed and thoroughly enjoyed myself at night. In Mexico City, works ended around seven o'clock, dinner around eight, and then nightlife began between nine and ten, returning home close to one in the morning. I certainly was busy, and drank in the adventure of being my own boss, so to speak. Mexico City was intoxicating, and I knew I would return. So I set forth a plan to expand my educational horizons. Now, reasonably fluent in Spanish, I hungered for more adventures, more challenges, more escape and, definitely, more growth.

> If the only prayer you ever say in your entire life is thank you, it will be enough.
>
> Meister Eckhart

The governmental agency was agreeable to my three month summer employment return in an expanded role of my present position. By agreement, I would be transferred to Paris for the following five months. Then I was to return to Purdue for the second semester of my junior year. Making arrangements to study at the University of Paris and live at the Cite Universitaire for a semester was an excitement that I awoke to each morning.

Reminding myself that this was an illusion that I was creating for my journey, I chided myself for the immense ego thrill that I seemed to be enjoying. I told no one for a while. My sorority house which counted on my fees and residency payments had to be informed. Also, Fippy must be told that the sister who would always be there for him would actually be across the Atlantic Ocean. Basically, unreachable.

I purposed to stay in touch with him, since I knew his senior year in high school would be a milestone year. My angst about how things were progressing at home with Dad and Ginny was ever present. Fortunately, my brother seemed to get along better with Ginny than with Dad. Hard to fathom, but I was grateful that he was not living in constant discomfort. He reported that Dad was on his very best behavior with the new wife, and I sensed that Phil was very grateful for her presence. Although he stayed at Jim Bob's house a lot, Fippy seemed to be managing well and was still entertaining himself with multiple romances. Scholastic endeavors were never, ever of primary interest to him. He was extremely capable...but lacked discipline. Having found a way to escape his grief, nothing was going to change the denial method that was working well for him. I anticipated his graduation with great joy. Even though I had vowed not to go back to "Mother's" house, I would gladly do almost anything to applaud this moment for my beloved sibling, including spending a night at home.

UGH! I had my last final exam of the semester at the same time as Phil's graduation. Since the university policy prohibited rescheduling final exams, I had to tell Phil I couldn't come. I simply didn't have the heart or the courage to tell him, and I cried into my pillow at night. I wasn't focused, and my stomach was killing me. The Universe and I were very much in disagreement. Then, I realized that it was not as much how Phil might react, but that I was selfishly grieving at not being able to be there. When I had graduated from the same high school my mother wasn't there. He would walk across the same stage without his mother OR his sister in attendance. I needed to talk to Sissy Jean.

In the middle of the afternoon, I sat cross-legged in my bunk in the dormitory room of the sorority house. It was perfect: a full-length-of-the-house third floor room full of bunk beds. Every girl had an assigned bed, according to seniority. Being a sophomore meant I had an upper bunk. It was the middle of the day, and I was totally alone in this gigantic room. As I meditated and quieted my world, I went into my heart space and called her name in my mind. Her loving presence was immediately noticeable, and she professed her willingness to help with my dilemma. As I asked how to best handle my heartbreak of not being at Phil's graduation, I knew her answer as we seemed to say it in unison: *"Love creates love. Thought begets thought. Everything in our realm begins in thought."*

Immediately, I understood that my grieving was not only creating a negative experience for Phil, but also for me. Hoping for the best experience possible for his special occasion, I envisioned calling him and telling him the truth. He should imagine Mother and me in the audience making fools of ourselves as we were overcome with joy and pride, all the while knowing that we loved him with all of our being. Present or not, love would carry his night of celebration.

"Sissy. I think he will understand when I speak the truth to him. He knows, unequivocally, that I love him dearly. Unfortunately, he is accustomed to disappointment."

"Annalee, your brother is wiser than you know and has a very understanding heart, albeit without much of a voice. Trust his acceptance of what you have to tell him. He has developed coping mechanisms of which you are unaware. All is well."

"What do you mean?" I asked.

"Your brother, at times, has a strong non-physical communication ability with your mother."

My whole being filled with love, joy and gratitude. My concern immediately abated. I knew my brother was safe and loved more than I knew. The Universe had assured me it was okay to take the exam without worry.

Fippy called me from Jim Bob's house and said he was having to work all summer in Dad's construction companies with the promise that Dad would pay for the next year at Purdue. He assured me that he could last the next three months knowing that he would escape in late August.

I told him I had a really great surprise that he would and should appreciate and accept.

Since I had dated Dave for over a year at Purdue, I had asked him if he would pledge Phil to his fraternity immediately and make him rush chairman as soon as he was no longer a pledge. Dave had already met my brother, liked him and truly wanted to help.

Arrangements were made for Phil to pay his first semester fraternity fees on a pay-back loan schedule, and then fees would be waived when he was rush chairman. Dave knew Phil's engaging personality was a tremendous asset to the fraternity house. Fippy, indeed, would bring in fine young men and needed revenue. Dad was satisfied that Phil had made lodging and meal arrangements at Purdue and asked no further questions. So...we had a workable plan.

I left for Mexico City with a lighter heart and hope for the two motherless children that had floundered about in an attempt to find our way. We shared moments of peace and some measure of preparedness for taking care of ourselves in the future. Adios Purdue, family and sorority sisters for the next eight months!

Having spent three months the previous summer enjoying the night club circuit, the mariachis and the side trips to Cuernavaca, Acapulco, Mazatlan and Guadalajara, I determined to be as fluent as I could possibly be in Spanish. I took afternoon courses at an excellent private college. Truly, one of the best decisions of my life!

After my first taxi ride to the college, I was enthralled with the architecture, sensory feel of the grounds and the loving attitude that prevailed in every class and gathering. At the end of the first day of classes, a man in a business suit walked up to me, introduced himself as Father Uribe and asked if I would visit his office the next day. Slightly nervous, but willing, I agreed. I reminded myself that clergy and nuns or monks were not allowed to wear religious garb in Mexico. So business suits, short hair and no make-up became signals to say: "Padre" or "Hermana" or "Hermano." It was never difficult to distinguish the church personnel because Mexican women tended to be very make-up conscious, and young male Mexican students certainly did not wear suits to class.

Father Uribe greeted me so very kindly. Then he asked me to sit and tell him my history and why I was attending school where I was the only American. He was curious, without judgment or expectation. To my surprise, I not only poured out my history, but I also felt a familial affection for this priest and wished he were my Dad. Father must have felt that connection too, because he said in impeccable English (with no accent whatsoever) that it would be his pleasure to take me under his wing and teach me to be a critical thinker. I asked why that was so important to him. He said that it was to be his gift to a daughter of God. Then, he added: "You will need this ability every day of your life." I felt complimented and challenged. This scholar had three doctorates, one of them in philosophy-- the roadmap-discipline for critical thinking.

Rushing to school, getting through my classes and presenting myself to Father Uribe daily, I felt myself expanding, growing, thinking, analyzing and more comfortable in every setting. On one such day I asked Father Uribe what he saw for me in the future. As he smiled, he said: "You will be a life-long healer." Then he smiled some more, leaving me in a total quandary as to what that could possibly mean.

Shortly before I was to leave for my assignment in Paris, I asked Father Uribe who God was for him. I knew that he was a very free thinker, and I was totally interested in what his answer might be. He said: "Daughter, God is all that is: Omnipotent, Omnipresent and Omniscient."

"Well, Father, that sounds like the party line, no offense."

"And, daughter, who is God for you?"

"Father, I wish I knew. I believe in God. I feel His love. But I do not yet have a description of Him. Knowing how to describe Him would give me some comfort."

"Annalee, it may not be necessary. Faith and connection may be enough. You are my daughter. I am your priest and your mentor. I know you care deeply for me. But if I ask three people who love me to describe me and give characteristics of my personality, there could be three different answers. All three would still love me, and

I would love them. Do not ever get tangled up in God's description. He does one thing, and one thing only: He loves." I heard the echo of Sissy Jean.

Before going to the airport to board Air France for the overnight flight to Paris, I asked the taxi to stop one last time at the university. I hurriedly searched for Father Uribe. I thought I would have to leave without seeing him. At that moment he walked around the corner. I embraced him, wept, and thanked him for all his mentoring and challenges that drove me crazy with the critical thinking dilemmas he presented daily. Then, I told him how much I loved him…and that he was the best ambassador of God that I had ever met. He squeezed me tightly, kissed my forehead, then blessed me with the sign of the cross and a sweet prayer. He smiled and said: "I'll count on you if I ever need a recommendation." As I was walking away, I quipped: "Already done, Padre. Rest easy!" giving him the universal thumbs up.

While nestled into my coach seat, I thought I would use the time to the New York City stop to reflect on how much education, work experience, responsibility and love I had received in the last three months. My life had been far away from everything mundane and familiar. My entire body felt filled with gratitude. My heart seemed to explode with the feelings of good fortune that had poured daily into my life experiences in Mexico City. As I thought of my mother, I wished I could spend hours with her painting a picture of my recent life. Then the lights in the coach cabin dimmed, and I rested my head back and went into meditation and communion with Sissy Jean.

"Sissy, I feel so filled with gratitude. This is such a superlative feeling, and I don't want it to come to an end. I don't want to lose this feeling! Is there a formula for extending it and holding it close?"

"Sweet one, gratitude is the result of living in joy. You have recently opened your beingness to love, compassion, reciprocity of Spirit and familial connection. You love Father Uribe as a family member…and you love without hesitation or exception. He taught you how to do that, and you soaked it up. He offered himself as a catalyst to your discovery. He lit the flame of expanded love that you are now so capable of. Remember, dear one, that your life purpose is to come to Truth and Love. At this moment, you are Heaven."

"Whoa, Sissy! What do you mean when you say I am Heaven? Isn't Heaven a reward for having lived a decent life?"

"No, Child. Heaven is a state of consciousness. On your earthly plane

you have concepts of Heaven and Hell as places of reward or punishment. Both of these concepts actually represent the extremes of the spectrum of consciousness. Everything that you manifest in your lifetime began with thought. If thought patterns develop into loving, compassionate, forgiving and caring behaviors, then your life feels heavenly. If the opposite behaviors of hate, revenge, judgment, unforgiveness and narcissistic selfishness are habits of daily living, then life is hellish, loathsome, anger-ridden and violent in nature. All of these conditions are choices. The higher the consciousness, the better the choices. And the opposite is unfortunately true for those who choose to live in an unconscious manner. Mindfulness is necessary to achieve a state of Love."

"So what I understand from what you are saying is that we must be aware, highly conscious at all times to manifest states of happiness, joy, love and peacefulness. That seems almost impossible. There is a lot that life seems to demand of us just to survive, so I don't think I can be conscious all of the time. I will be busy, tired, frustrated, sad, mad, humorous, helpful and so on. In all these circumstances I will be acting or reacting. I don't think I, realistically, will stop with each behavior to check my consciousness."

I thought I heard Sissy giggle. It could have been my imagination, but this taught me that it was possible that Sissy Jean had a sense of humor. I was beginning to feel a sensory overload with these new concepts that I needed to examine and digest.

After stopping in New York, walking a bit, and re-settling into the window seat where I thought I might rest my head against the window shade for the night, I was boldly informed by the French-accented captain that we should relax since we were 17th in line for take-off. That was mind-boggling! It also meant at least another hour of full lights in the cabin and no possibility of going to sleep under the soft blanket and pillow offered by the airline. Then, I remembered: Make the choice of love. Just the thought of it dissolved any judgment, concern or disappointment. Good lesson. I hoped I would remember it often.

Violence is the fear of other's ideals.

Mahatma Gandhi

Still hazy from sleep, I pushed up the window shade as the jet circled Paris. The Eiffel Tower! It is the most distinguishable landmark from the air in all the world. I thought of all the things I had read about that were awaiting my perusal: Montmarte, Versailles, the Champs-Elysees, Notre Dame, the Arc de Triomphe, Sacre-Coeur, the Tulleries Garden and, of course, the Louvre. Plus, the little side-walk cafes, wine-tasting, Edith Piaf, the Left Bank and the FOOD! I felt dizzy with anticipation. But first I must dispense with the airport, customs, student visa entry, luggage and taxi. At this point, I knew about twenty French words. Then, I quickly learned that the taxi drivers in Paris were multi-lingual. Thank God!

How he knew I will never know. After putting my luggage in the trunk of his Citroen, he asked: "Cite Universitaire, Mademoiselle?" With an attitude of absurd confidence, I answered a formal response of "Oui, monsieur, s'il vous plait," now having used five of the twenty French words available to me.

Upon arriving at the Cite, he asked, in slightly-accented English, to which house did I wish to go. I thought how suave and romantic his English sounded, something like Maurice Chevalier of film fame. Then catching myself in my own private embarrassment, I answered: "Maison Neerlandais."

As he acknowledged my answer, I was breathless, trying to take in the landscape of this University City. We passed houses with signs indicating at least twenty countries before arriving at my destination. I had not requested a room at the very nice Les Etats Unis because I did not want to speak English all the time in my residence. It seemed a logical decision to choose the Holland House since I was aware that most Dutch people speak multiple languages fluently, including English. I thought of my choice as an insurance policy, knowing that if I could not understand or if I needed something, I assumed I could always find someone to help me.

I marveled at the layout of this student city within a city with houses representing countries from all over the world. The concept of creating such a place for international students was a goal of visionaries to create a school of human relations to promote peace. The creative idea was that if students from all over the world came to study, learn and live together in Paris they would take that international sense of harmony back to their home countries. Many of these students were destined to be leaders in their respective provinces of the world. The idea was a spectacular experiment which was already exhibiting some success. It was a heady feeling to know that so many nationalities were residing on these dedicated grounds, all pledging openness to diversity and inclusivity. Approximately a hundred countries were lending their funds and approval to the international community created at the University of Paris and other institutes.

The taxi stopped and jolted me out of my reverie. As I exited the taxi, I used my sixth word of French and uttered "Merci." After I paid and tipped the driver, I entered the lobby of the Holland House. As I had hoped, the receptionist spoke excellent English, welcomed me, inquired about my flight and put a volume of papers in front of me to sign--all in French! I joked that I was signing my life away since I had no idea what they said. She very seriously began to explain each document. Afraid to stop her for fear of not seeming appreciative, I listened for over thirty minutes to explanations. There were no trick documents, and I felt embarrassed, but relieved. Given my room number, I proceeded up the many flights of stairs with my luggage, found the room, knocked and finally entered.

The room immediately reminded me of the residence hall room at the X at Purdue. It contained a bunk bed, the bottom one obviously taken by my absentee roommate, two small desks with chairs, two chests of drawers and a sink. Suddenly realizing there were no closets, I gave thanks to the powers that be at Purdue for the teeny closets included in our freshmen dorm rooms! The top bunk had fresh sheets for which I, at once, felt immense gratitude because I had not brought linens and certainly had no money for them. After putting my clothes in the drawers, I was ready to call the front desk to inquire about a luggage storage room when my Dutch roommate walked in. Using words seven and eight, I said: "Bon jour" to which there was no reply. I gave my first name and held out my hand. Still no response. The energy of the room was negative, uncomfortable and puzzling. Thinking it best to exit and explore the floor, I went looking for the bath and showers. Again, it reminded me of my freshman year at Purdue since the toilets and showers were the farthest possible from my room. The receptionist had given me my two weekly shower times. I was to use the sink in my room for "spot cleaning!"

Growing up, I took a bath on Saturdays unless I needed to be hosed down in the yard after a mud pie fest or gardening all day in sweat-producing heat. As I approached ten or eleven, I began to bathe every day. I became addicted to morning showers and often times evening ones too. Shaking my head, I determined to learn to bathe from a sink of soapy water.

As I was shaking my head in response to my own thoughts, the most strikingly beautiful woman I had ever seen was approaching me in the hallway. She began to mimic my head shaking action, and I began to laugh. We stopped mid-hall and introduced ourselves in French. Then the stranger began to laugh again. She poked fun at me in an exquisitely-accented English, noting that I was an American, newly arrived, hoping to learn French, enjoy Paris a lot and study a little! I answered: "Precisely!" She invited me to her room. I accepted and was amazed! Mademoiselle Jacqueline lived in the corner room which was a suite with bedroom, bath and a small conversation area. Without a roommate, she enjoyed having this spacious accommodation all to herself. As she questioned me in English, she shared as much as she requested. She was the daughter of a Vietnamese mother and a French businessman father, but, regrettably, not legitimate. I immediately responded, forcefully informing her that all children are legitimate. Illegitimacy is an issue of the parents, not of the child!

With wild exclamations in French that could easily be understood by their tones and hand gestures, Jacqueline seemed as delighted as she was delightful, and we were fast becoming friends. She asked where my room was, and if I was satisfied? Reporting my recent experience with my roommate she exclaimed: "Elle est un peu difficile!" That was easy enough to understand, and I agreed. After talking about two hours more of life and goals, she said: "You will sleep in your room, but you will spend the rest of your time in mine. Here is a key." I was now certain that my time in Paris was going to be better than I could have imagined.

Talking for the better part of the afternoon, I learned that Jacqueline sometimes modeled nylon stockings and some lingerie for the House of Dior. She was studying economics and philosophy at the Sorbonne and invited me to accompany her to two philosophy classes. She would tell me in English what the lecturer said until I could grasp it myself. Agreeing to the proposal as fast as humanly possible, I knew I had hit the proverbial jackpot. I was warmed by a new friend the very first day and would be able to escape the tortured soul in my assigned room. I confirmed to myself that I had made the right decision to come to Paris, expand my horizons and my tolerance of all things foreign. As a plus, I could learn from some international masters of their fields at the Sorbonne.

I reported early the next day to enroll in the Alliance Francaise, the French language school of accelerated learning...so proud of myself on the immediate immersion into the academic and social life of the Cite. It occurred to me that I should make the commitment to speak only French, no matter how poorly. I believed that to be the quickest way to French fluency. It was an excellent decision. My French-speaking ability grew exponentially every day. I confidently left each morning and walked to the Alliance school, stopping on the way at a bakery to order a small baguette and cheese which I ate on the way to class. Ego mind was in total control. I was ecstatic with Paris, my progress with the language and over the moon with my philosophy classes with Jacqueline.

For a night, I thought I might be in a movie scene. I had come home from buying a winter coat, something I did not have in Mexico City for obvious reasons and walked into Jacqueline's room to meet Reza face to face. He was in her room, obviously with a key, waiting for her to return. He appeared to be Middle Eastern and extremely handsome. I asked in French where he was from and how he knew Jacqueline. He, very politely and graciously, informed me he was a prince of the Saudi kingdom and that Jacqueline was his lover.

After catching my breath, not being accustomed to such calm honesty, I said: "Enchante!" and he answered, "Mon plaisir, mademoiselle." As on cue, Jacqueline entered and kissed us both on the cheeks, and we began our small social gathering with wine... my first taste of good wine, ever. I confessed that I had never tasted wine this good and spent the next hour listening to the types of wine and how they are related to their regions and productions. My brain was fried--not from wine, but from an assault of French with two different accents.

The next day Jacqueline and I discussed in French, more or less, a recent philosophy class, her relationship with Reza and the war in Algeria. Reza was the most interesting of these topics. Jacqueline informed me that he was just one of hundreds of princes, but he liked the title and had plenty of money available for fun, was amiable, polite and smart--all qualities that she found necessary in a man. She further explained that he wanted to put her into a lovely apartment in Paris. She continued to refuse his offer and explained that he would have control and not have to treat her so lavishly. Her giggles were contagious and warming to any relationship. We spent much of the late afternoon going through her enormous clothes collection, selecting a dress for her late evening rendezvous with the prince at a chic nightclub. I greatly anticipated the recital of the good times of the previous evening, often with details of meeting ambassadors or famed individuals that ran in Reza's social circle.

The first Saturday, I vowed to learn the metro system of Paris. It didn't take long. Every line was colored so one could literally say: "Take the blue line to such and such, then switch to the red line, etc." So I brought my trusty map of Paris and the surrounding areas with me, and I mapped out how to get to all the places I eventually wanted to see. Then, with time left, and not wanting to stay in a room talking, I visited Pont Neuf, the oldest bridge in Paris. It was constructed entirely of stone and spanned the Seine River. At one time it was the center of Paris. The Rive Gauche or Left Bank was intoxicating since the Sorbonne and its great historic buildings were symbolic of a history of teaching for a thousand years. A stroll along the river delighted tourists viewing the developing artwork on the many easels set up to paint the marvels of Notre Dame or the Louvre in the background. The parks were perfect for picnics, family gatherings and lovers in long embraces. This felt like a paradise to the small town girl from Indiana. With my head in the clouds, I ate at a small café with food served family style. I basked in the laughter of the men enjoying their multiple glasses of red table wine and tried to decipher much of the ongoing conversation. As it grew dark, I headed home.

Just as I came up the stairs, Jacqueline squealed and said she had been looking for me. She had two tickets for La Boheme she wanted me to have that evening. She couldn't go because of another last minute commitment with Reza. Snapping up the tickets, I gave

Jacqueline a big hug and yelled "Merci beaucoup." I ran to my room to change clothes, got a nighttime shawl, and off I scurried. I looked up the Palais Garnier on my map, found the metro routing and set off for a night at the opera in an opera house commissioned by Napoleon! When I arrived, I looked around to see if there were any students that I might invite to use the other ticket. Soon I found a young Canadian girl, Colette. She was thrilled to attend the opera with me. I broke down and spoke only English for the evening, being thoroughly exhausted from my pledge to speak only my meager French with numerous hand gestures. Colette was from McGill University in Canada and completely conversant in English and French, having grown up in Quebec. By the end of the evening, after intermissions, we felt like old sorority sisters. She lived at Canada House and had been in Paris a couple of months getting her bearings. I shared that I wished I could have done the same. After exiting the metro at the Cite Universitaire and the mandatory two-cheek air kisses, we went our separate ways to our respective houses.

The Cite is totally lighted at night, with students everywhere. As I walked I heard at least seven or eight languages that were foreign to me. They had my attention because they all sounded so happy, yet so different. As I was passing a small alleyway on my right, I was suddenly grabbed by the arm, whirled around and slammed into a brick wall. Dazed, I started to step forward, when I looked into the dark black eyes of a Mid-Eastern young man with a beard. His quickened breath was in my face, and his handhold on my arm was painful. Turning my head slightly, I saw the knife. In his free hand, the red-handled, slightly curved knife looked old and ominous. I looked back at his face. Knowing I should not look down or away, I stared at him. His eyes began to outline my face, neck, breasts, hips, finally reaching my crotch. Having no doubt about his intentions, I continued to stare at him. Finally, not being able to think in any language, let alone my own, I found the courage to scream "NO!" Tears were streaming down my cheeks, my breath was shallow, and I prayed. We stared at each other for what seemed to be an eternity. He plunged the knife into my thigh and ran. I heard noises that perhaps were approaching students out late, as was I.

My French was certainly not proficient enough for all the questions posed by the doctors and police at the hospital. A middle-aged doctor approached me in the crowd of interrogators, asked my name and where I lived. I answered and asked what had happened. He explained in English that two Austrian students with their girlfriends had found me lying in an alley with my torso on the sidewalk. They had used the ties on my wraparound denim skirt to tourniquet my leg and had gotten a policeman to get an ambulance. The doctor explained that if I had fallen the opposite direction into the alley, I probably would have lost a considerable amount of blood. He exclaimed, matter-of-factly, that I was a lucky girl.

When I recovered my wits, I asked for the names and addresses of my saviors, but was told that "policy" forbade distribution of such information. I said a quick "thank you" in my head, hoping that somehow the universe might allow them to feel my gratitude.

I was released the next day and returned with pain medications and dressing materials to my room. My roommate did not say a word. Thinking she must be crazy or blind, I said in English, "Do you see the blood all over my skirt?" She gave an ugly, dismissive sound and turned away. At that moment, I wanted my mother. I wanted to go home. I was stupid to be in Paris! Luckily, before my self-pity overcame me, the pain medications put me to sleep for about ten hours.

The last instructions of the doctor were that I was not to run or do any heavy exercise, but I was to walk several times a day. And I soon discovered that my heart beat was not located in my chest, but in my right thigh. A significant, tearing cut to the quad muscle gets one's attention...continually. Walking hurt like hell, but it kept me busy (and not screaming in my head as was the case when lying down). The English-speaking doctor had explained that his examination of the wound indicated that my assailant had, apparently, tried to retrieve his knife, could not, and, ultimately, tore more of the muscle in his effort. He concluded by saying there were no fingerprints on the knife handle, and all the blood samples matched mine. The policeman was visibly disappointed because many of the mid-Eastern students were fingerprinted for visa applications, assuming he was a student. We had made an appointment for me to look at visa applications pictures in a few days after he asked if I thought I could identify him. The flashback to the mutual stare that had taken place was enough for me to assure the gendarme that I most definitely could identify the man. He seemed pleased, but asked why I thought I had escaped the intended sexual assault. The alley was dark. There were trash cans hiding possible activity, and it seemed we were quite alone. The only explanation I could give was that I thought the man certainly meant to rape me, but the stare that lasted so long, my tears and one word I uttered paused the man's intentions. I thought, perhaps, he was sexually frustrated, with no immediate outlet, but in reality, could not carry through with the deed. The policeman smirked a bit, and then informed me that I was very fortunate and naïve. I had no argument with that! But, down deep inside my being, I felt there was more to this event…and that it was somehow for my benefit. At a loss to put it all together, I planned to meditate and talk with Sissy as soon as I could be free of medication. I again fell asleep, letting the pain drift off into undefined realms.

The greatest discovery of all time is that a person can change his future by merely changing his attitude.

Oprah Winfrey

10

"Yes, Child, I am always here. I have been with you throughout your recent illusion. And I know many of the questions you must be wanting to ask and discuss."

"Well, Sissy, it is extremely difficult to imagine that this knife wound is an illusion! This throbbing feels real, although I have stopped the medication so that I might think clearly. I feel fortunate to be alive and healing."

"Being in human form is an interesting experience. I imagine that the illusions, while somewhat frightening, can also be entertaining. However, they are of your own making for lessons that you choose to learn on the path to true spiritual love with the ultimate goal of eternal peace. So I am here to guide and inform with The Truth. What is upon your heart, or perhaps, upon the Ego Mind?"

"Sissy, I am living this 'illusion' as you call it. And then I was violently attacked at a moment that I was decidedly happy, having returned from a glorious opera house which presented a sweet Puccini masterpiece with music that transfixed me. And perhaps the best part was meeting my new friend, Colette. So the 'illusion' decides I need to be almost killed?"

"No, Annalee. You were not going to be killed. You did not choose that. You chose to remind yourself that you are here to learn. Naivete has its consequences in your environment. The classroom needs your full attention if you are to progress to the spiritual goal of love."

"So this was a punishment of sorts?" I asked bewilderedly.

"Punishment is a construct of the Ego Mind. Ego's purpose is to construct scenarios that reward, blame, punish, rationalize and lead humans to believe that they are more or less worthy than another. Such a belief is a total falsehood. Spirit Mind knows that ALL human beings are good because they were created with a spark of divinity. Ego Mind wishes to create paths of confusion, competition, warfare, violence or glamorous ribbons of praise pinned upon ego chests to differentiate the worthiness of a human soul. This is destructive and totally contradictory to the spiritual goal that holds the Truth.

Every human being is mortal, and every human's higher consciousness is immortal. All the rest of your activity is a game with no winner and serves to divert attention from Spirit Mind."

"Okay. So I get your explanation and the consequences of being controlled by Ego Mind. But I still don't understand being knifed in an alley by a man with sexual assault as his objective. Put that together for me, please!!"

"Annie, you are a woman of adventure and exploration. Your heart is open to the spirit realms and has been since you were a child. You have a moral compass, but you, as mature as you are for your time, harbor resentment, struggle with doubt, carry hurt in your heart and fight the urges of revenge. Your illusions of happy family, recognition for hard work and that philosophy and higher education are avenues to world change are deviations from your true purpose. I understand that such things seem to help the global human condition, but you are on a path to Truth. You recently learned that some souls turn from the Light and seek nefarious solutions to their human appetites for money, sex, success and fame...all illusions as you know. Being sexually assaulted was a dramatic invitation to examine the hearts of hurting individuals, particularly the ones who employ violence as the currency of their feelings of worthlessness."

"Holy Jesus, Mary and Joseph! It seems to me that there might be easier invitations to reflect on the subject of violence! You might have simply asked me to do that."

"That is not what I do. I help you decipher your illusions. I do what I can to guide you to necessary lessons and I, of course, always love and honor you. But I am not the one who CHOOSES your illusions and insights, you are. Somewhere in your higher consciousness you decided to confront the characteristic of violence in the human ego behavior. Your consciousness chose the violent encounter, and it also controlled it. So, what did you learn?"

I sat, stunned and contemplative. It was enormously difficult to switch my mind from the memory of the attack to the possibility that I engaged in this violent illusion to teach myself how to love. How could that be possible?

"Sissy, as I try to think through this, I can only step back from the event far enough to know that this man was not born violent. His life conditions, his culture, his connection or disconnection to the love or absence of love for and from others all contributed to his behavior. What I do understand most of all is that somehow he separated from his 'knowingness' of Truth, or was never connected to it, to know there were options for all his feelings that would not destroy himself or others. He had lost all hope of finding his solution to his desires in an acceptable way."

"As I think about it, I would likely believe that he was unaware that he felt so unworthy, and that the feeling of unworthiness created such pain that his reaction of desire was the choice to use violence to overpower and to, momentarily, achieve ego's goal. I suspect it was naked anger in the vehicle of violence perpetrated upon another…me."

"You, Child, are beginning to look at another as the actor in your illusion, and, in doing so, are becoming more able to see the results of Ego Mind when it is in total control, and darkness rules. Spirit Mind is always available, always curative, always exquisite in its invitation to love, but it must be primary, with the success of releasing Ego Mind to the ethers. Ego Mind is seductive, alluring, promising, exciting, endorphin-producing, creating the human body rush that accompanies conquest."

"You experienced physical violence of an ugly variety: sexual assault that has an undeniable description. There are many other forms of violence, some quite frequently used and not called as deplorable. But, I tell you all violence is the darkest of the Ego Mind."

"I guess I always thought violence was mostly physical, because one feels so overpowered, and life can certainly be at risk. But, now that you speak of violence as the darkest part of Ego Mind and a significant turn to darkness, I am beginning to see other forms DO exist in society. Prejudices that are spoken or acted upon are violent expressions of a person's own self-contempt or self-doubt. Cultural differences are not violent. The intolerance and misunderstanding of these differences are forms of violent thought and, consequently, behavior. I'm thinking about religious differences and gender preference differences in particular. And I think the genesis of violence toward such groups is from the ego's fear of what is either different or unknown feels threatening. And when threatened, ego strikes."

"Such prejudices are currently very visible and debated in your world society. Women and children are violated regularly on much of your planet. Religious leaders create guilt in cunning ways to build financial empires, many created void of Light and Love. Passive-aggressive stealing in exchange for promised salvation is a form of violence. Salvation, by definition, is something you were born with and cannot be erased or bought. Humans may turn away from their destiny of Love, but Love, as your birthright and soulright never

dissipates, never turns its back on you. It cannot be destroyed. It will be there for you when you return to the energy of the One."

As I ran through the ways that individuals are abused, I currently thought of political classes that are engaging in violent rhetoric: the irony being that the governing institutions and officers that are elected or appointed to create a better life and society often use their power in abusive and violent ways. Personal greed, quest for power, financial security and ingrown prejudices compound the darkness that seems so inherent in the political process.

"I think institutions are often, unrecognizably, violent... Merchants that gouge the most vulnerable after tragedies of hurricanes, wars and epidemics with no seeming conscience would still be profitable if they were honest."

"There seem to be a number of ways to spread and encourage violence of many varieties. So, if I examine all the roads to violence, I see that all are ego-driven by souls that seem to be slaves to immediate gratification without concern for the good of the many, or their own personal karmic journey. It feels like a motion picture of a recipe for devastation."

"Very good, my Annalee! In understanding the kinds of violence and some of the underlying motivations for such behavior, are you also beginning to see how this is a lesson in love?"

"Oh, boy! A lesson in love! A great deal of me is fighting any notion of love being part of this lesson! But because I know you are a messenger of The Truth, I will stretch as far as I know how to understand that Love is part of this recent experience and 'illusion.' Part of what I can embrace right now is that we are all brothers and sisters connected. Since we are all a spark of the Divine, The One, The Whole, we cannot be separate. I buy off on that. But as much as I know my assailant is my brother, I certainly don't like him or want to meet up with him ever again. However, I can see that Love could enable me to testify against him as an act of universal love that protects my fellow sisters from his possible violence. I can also see that Love is what is going to help me forgive him, even if he's free or in a jail cell. Love is also the guiding force that will push me forward to live my life, heal my body and be appreciative of continuing the human experience. So Love really is the answer! It is the only way forward to not walk in fear, which is the polar opposite of love."

"My dear child, there is more. Every experience in an illusion is created

for ALL those involved. Your attacker is now confronted with the memory of his unsuccessful behavior, the fear of his probable arrest, the change that would mean for his life, and he has affected his own definition of self or character."

"Your rescuers validated their concern for a stranger and did all they could to help. That has also affected their definitions of who they hoped they were, and now they have evidence that is contemporary with their ideals. The medical and law enforcement players in your illusion used their skills to help you, liking the outcome that their skills provided. The ripple effect will never be known to you because the conversations of concern that play in houses on campus that have heard of the assault are beyond your ear. All behavior has purpose. All behavior has a wide influence, to which some souls are open to include it in their knowingness, while others are closed or unaware."

"So, Sissy, if I invited this experience of violence at some level, then am I grappling with my own internal violence or violent thoughts?"

"Yes, Annie. You are. You have experienced loss and hurt at a young age without the skills to lessen your heart's burden. You have taken care of your father and brother and others without awareness of the anger you felt. Anger, dear child, is the result of unresolved hurt and loss. For some in your illusions, anger is a result of fear of hurt or fear of loss, although no evidence is supportive of the fear. Fear is a total destroyer of love, an annihilator of peaceful living and joyful adventure in your illusion experiments. Fear is manufactured. But it is a powerful tool that controls unconsciously at low vibrational levels. Fear is dark; the greater the fear, the darker the Ego Mind. At high levels of fear, violence erupts as the result of self-loathing. And this applies to individuals, institutions, countries, continents and planets; but all violence is a product of these entities turning from love."

"I understand that to progress through the undercurrents of violence in me, I have to examine my fears. That's a massive assignment."

"It is why you are on the planet in your illusionary experiment. The opposite of love, which is your ever-conscious goal, is fear, and you will confront the effects of that dichotomy ever day you are in physical form. You will spend the rest of your Earth-time trying to manage and conquer all sorts of fears that your illusions will present. It is why you chose to come to your planet. Be grateful that you are a peaceful warrior in pursuit of what is most sought in every soul: the constancy of Love and return to The One."

"If I am aware of violence in any of its many forms, do I have a duty to confront it and call it by name? Is part of my journey here to spotlight its occurrence and call forth the activators of its destruction?"

"Your heart and consciousness will notice the darkness of violence when it is present. In the illusion of the lesson, you will make the choice to expose the activity, act in a way to eradicate it, or stay silent and work for a solution that will not give birth to counter-violence. You have been well trained in higher level thought consciousness. Remember your days with Father Uribe. You will use Spirit Mind and see some movement toward elevated consciousness of those around you. If you get tangled in the arguments of Ego Mind, you will see increased violence in every discussion and behavior. Watch and be aware. You will know the difference."

"One more thing before you go, Sissy. I am getting tired. I understand the illusion of violence, its purpose and its lessons as you have explained them. But if I think of the most extreme example of rape and violent death, premeditatedly perpetrated by a dark soul, it is hard to imagine that there was some mutual invitation or benefit from such a heinous act. Help me understand."

"Every such act will bring grief and life-long moments of hurt. Families of murder victims want earth-type justice. They want to feel better and understand. They may want retribution and counter-violence. They may destroy their own planet experience by never turning to love and forgiveness so they might continue their experience and find some joy. I can assure you that the victim soul and its essence is eternal and can be connected with any heart open to the higher realms. The physical touch will never be available after one leaves the planet illusion, but the spiritual touch is always and forever available to an open and high consciousness. Earth dwellers are fond of physical touch, creative connectedness and physical verification of the relationship. As sad as losing that physical pleasure of touch may be, it was illusion. What remains is the Truth. Your loved one is real, is essence, is energy, is part of The One. That is our goal no matter how it comes about. The process in the illusion is harsh at times, and you may never know why. But the conclusion can only be that all is well."

Love is of all passions, the strongest,
for it attacks simultaneously the
head, the heart and the senses.

Lao Tzu

11

As I was healing, Colette and I would often take Friday trains to military bases in Germany and France to visit soldiers and see a movie in English. We also might ask soldiers to help us buy American candy bars and cartons of filtered cigarettes and Kentucky whiskey, all very available at the base PX. We devoured the candy bars, but sold the cigarettes and whiskey to Prince Reza. He paid us the same price as those items cost in Paris. We used the profit to travel on the weekends to Belgium, Luxembourg and Austria. And he delighted in showing off his goods to other Saudis who had to pay the luxury stamp tax on every carton or bottle. He would tease them saying: "Straight from America!" In actuality, he was telling the truth! So our profit provided him with bragging rights! Somehow, both Colette and I never felt any twinges of guilt in our single-buyer, black market operation. Reza was so often immeasurably kind by giving both of us free tickets to plays, concerts and events that we felt grateful to find some way to bring him this silly pleasure.

We two North American girls rationalized that all the walking we did in neighboring countries was just following my doctor's orders. The more walking I did, the better my quad muscle became. Lifting books tied together were weights that hurt like the devil, but did, indeed, help accomplish the building of a strong thigh muscle once again. Finding that we did not care for hostels that had used sheets and snoring occupants, we searched out very inexpensive hotels with one double bed that allowed us a good night's sleep. We got along so well that it became a running joke about when we would have our first disagreement. It didn't happen...ever. I thanked the universe every day that, in spite of a very frightening experience, I was loving everything about Paris. My philosophy classes, my exponential understanding of French (with accents from all over the world) and my time with Jacqueline and Reza brought more joy daily. The little houses with living room restaurants full of long tables with chairs for family dining delighted my palate. Most of all, my job had become a full scholarship so I had no responsibility to show up for work, and I quit the classes at the Alliance Francaise because I was learning French much faster on my own.

Returning from one such weekend excursion, I found a note on my door to check with the concierge at the front desk. After making sure I used my shower time, wet hair and all, I presented myself to the concierge and retrieved the letter. It was from my dad. I felt thrilled, anxious and hopeful. I held it between my palms for a moment and started to weep. Going to a corner of the lobby, I slowly opened it to find one small sheet of yellow, lined paper with the words: "Your grandmother died three days ago. Thought you should know."

I fell into a corner chair, stared out the window and silently wept in the same fashion I had learned to do as a child. Then the movie that started to play in my head was a perfect healing moment. "Grams" had taught me to read at age four and spent endless hours with immense patience listening to me read aloud to her. As the favored grandchild, (I believe because I was the first) I always had her attention when visiting "Gramps" and her on their farm. She would include me in the cookie-making and the home made spaghetti that we hung on chair backs covered with flour sacks. Having what I would later learn was a photographic memory, she would recite the British nursery rhyme This is the House that Jack Built, a ditty of so many verses that Grams would sometimes go hoarse before she finished. When I was about eight, I went to stay with her for two weeks. What a treat to have them all to myself for two weeks! During that time she introduced me to the novel, Ivanhoe. She read me the first chapter, and I was enchanted. I asked for a promise of a chapter a day, so Grams memorized a chapter each morning before I got up so that she could recite it to me while we did the breakfast dishes. Truly, I thought most grandmothers did the same. It was years later that I learned that she had a Ph.D. in Pedagogy. Her first job was a circuit school teacher, staying a month at each student's home where she received room and board and twenty dollars at the end of the year.

I clearly remember learning the word "nape" and marveling at the story because it seemed so foreign to anything I knew in my world. When I asked her about "the olden times," I learned that she had taught in a one room school house with about ten students total from grades 1-8. A school teacher had to be single, properly dressed (she had one dress for school and one dress for church) and had to make sure that the nape of her neck and her ankles were covered. I asked why, and she replied that that story was for a later date.

Jacqueline and Reza came in from an evening soiree and found me sitting in the corner chair. Effusive and sweet, Jacqueline asked if it was the leg pain. I handed her the letter. Her eyes filled with tears. Reza embraced me, a very rare occurrence for a Saudi. Then the two sat down, as though scripted, and did the perfect thing that good friends do. They said, almost in unison: "Tell us about your grandmother. We want to know her." It was magical as I related many of the memories that I had just been recalling, and my friends showed amazement and ask questions. Then we began to talk of all our grandparents--Saudi, French, Vietnamese and American, all beloved by grandchildren delighting in recounting their varied memories. The evening ended with nice, warm feelings of love and connection. I felt sure it was the best memorial service imaginable.

Since my leg was feeling better, and I had all my lessons read, and Collete was under the weather, I decided to fulfill a promise made to a sorority sister at Purdue. Her father had been killed in World War II when her mother was pregnant with her. Although she had been adopted by a wonderful stepfather, she wanted some connection to her biological dad. She knew he was buried in France in the Lorraine American Military Cemetery. Investigating and finding that the memorials were in St. Avold, I took a bus, my winter coat, a camera and a notepad. The ride lulled me to sleep. The bus driver nudged me awake, knowing that St. Avold was my stop from a short interchange that we had had when I mounted the bus. Thanking him for his kindness, I disembarked and asked directions to the cemetery, obviously a well-known destination for tourists. Upon arriving, I found a caretaker who asked me if I were looking for a particular marker. Taken aback for a moment, I realized he was addressing me in English. I complimented him on his expertise of the language and asked how he knew I spoke English. In the kindest, most polite manner possible, he explained that almost anyone who visits Lorraine Military Memorial Cemetery is coming because of someone they lost in the war. He was profuse in his expression of gratitude for what Americans had sacrificed for the French people. Then, after a second or two, he asked if my father had been in the war. I supposed he thought my father's memorial might be the one I was seeking. I thanked him for asking and explained that my dad was a veteran of World War II, but that he had fought in the Pacific theatre. He replied: "Oh, Mademoiselle, I am happy he is not here, but the Pacific war was much worse. You are lucky to have him."

After a moment, I agreed. Then I asked about the location of my friend's father's grave. Looking and finding it in a large record book, he immediately said he would lead me to the marker. We walked through thousands of white crosses, and I thought my heart might burst with grief. The cemetery contained over ten thousand crosses for young soldiers whose lives were cut short, who had stepped to the Other Side after an experiment in global violence. Arriving at the designated marker, I thanked him as he explained he would leave me with my thoughts, patting me on my shoulder and saying: "Merci."

I stood, lost in a sea of white crosses, turning slowly in every direction trying to absorb the immensity of what I was seeing. This wasn't a cemetery; it was a testimony to what hearts are willing to give, what agony they are willing to suffer, what sacrifice for loved ones they are willing to endure in spite of extraordinary fear...what a response to national allegiance can cost! Just showing up had to be an act of heroism.

Standing there, I wept for all the parents, siblings, spouses and children that the ripple effect of this demonstrative display had touched: orphans, widows and glassy-eyed parents who could never be able to resolve their loss. If I could have taken a picture of every cross with its sacred name, I would have. Instead, I took five pictures for my friend: Two of her father's cross, one of the caretaker's gate, one of the field of crosses, and one of a nearby tree that threw some shade on her father's cross. Then I sat down on a nearby concrete bench provided for mourners, I suppose, and began to try to reach some better state of calm.

The words of the caretaker haunted me. "Much worse" he had said. All war is horrific, so any judgment about the degree of pain and destruction certainly had to be subjective. I easily dismissed the comparison. However, I could no longer dismiss the knowledge of the horror my father had experienced in war and the lifelong effect of its devastating trauma. He was not a name on a cross in any military cemetery, but a death of a sort had occurred. Remembering the whispers when he would talk with war buddies who visited, the admonition that we never ask questions about the war, the significant spanking I had received for opening the "footlocker" and asking questions about the contents that were all Japanese except for his uniform and medals, I opened my heart to try to imagine his experience.

Mother had said that "Dad had gone through a lot in the war." As we got older she told my brother and me that his anger and gruffness was a result of the horrors of war. Once, she volunteered that she, herself, was forbidden to speak of it.

One memory is so vivid that I can recall the exact spot I was standing and the fright I felt. Dad screamed one night during the beginning of the Korean War: "I'll be goddamned if I am going to another war! I have seen enough killing for ten lifetimes! I...have...done...my...duty!! They can all go to hell if they think I will put on the uniform again." He told Mother he was quitting the reserves and didn't give a damn about retirement money. Saying "they" already had his soul, he declared they couldn't squeeze more out of him! He stomped out of the house, missed dinner and was not home by the time Phil and I went to bed. I suspected he went to the VFW bar, a local hangout for vets.

"Guadacanal changed him." That's what Grams had once said. Being in high school at the time she confessed this to me, I began to read the newspaper clippings she had kept. Yellowed, folded and stored in a Penney's shoebox, the news stories painted a horrific picture. Over seven thousand American soldiers died on that island, almost 30 ships and 600 plus aircraft were destroyed. To a teenager those numbers didn't sink in, but what did get my attention were pictures of soldiers wading through swamps, carrying comrades, and dead piled upon each other. Malaria was rampant, and Japanese war tactics were inhumane--so much so that the newspapers refused to describe the details of their accusations.

Sitting here now, cold and sad in a hallowed place in France, picturing my dad in those circumstances where his life was constantly at risk, his buddies dying and no way to bury them, thinking of all the families back home worried daily beyond description and no way to comfort or reassure them, I shivered as my thoughts overwhelmed me. Sitting back, taking a deep breath, I wanted one sweet memory, one moment that would rescue me from that war, from the destruction visited upon the personality and character of my father...just one moment of goodness. It came immediately, and I felt the relief of the smile that formed when I recalled meeting my father.

Phil and I were at Grams because Mother had gone to pick up the man whose picture sat on the upright radio in our home. Grams explained that our dad was coming home from the big war on a train to Chicago. Mother would bring him to her house. Having no recollection of him other than the picture and stories, Phil and I were excited because everybody else was. We had no concept of what a "father" was!

We heard the car, and Grams yelled to everyone that they were home. All of a sudden there was a rush of people, including his three brothers, scurrying around us. Phil and I were scared. We ran back down the long hall to hide in the dining room under a dark table, holding each other tightly. I was four, Phil just three, and we always stayed together if one was frightened. There were so many voices, slaps on backs, laughter, tears, jokes and hugs. As we peeked out from the under table, we could see down the hall. Mother caught a glimpse of us and waved us forward. We did not budge. We were hardly breathing. And then everyone in the living room began to try and coax us down the hall. Nothing was going to make us leave the safety of our sanctuary. Finally, this tall, dark-haired man in a uniform with all sorts of ribbons, unbuttoned a pocket on his shirt and reached in to pull out a pack of Juicy Fruit gum. Phil and I would have run into the arms of the Devil to get a piece of that gum. During war time there was almost no gum, and this guy had some. We ran to grab it as the stranger scooped us up into his arms, making us feel like we were suspended in air higher than we had ever been before.

As my memory ended, I reached into the pockets of my new winter coat, retrieved some borrowed gloves, put them on and called her name in my head. I needed Sissy Jean.

"Thank you for being here with me. This is certainly not something I like doing alone, but it was necessary. You are here with me so you know that I have such mixed feelings about my dad. On the one hand, I honor his military service, his hardship, his commitment to hard work and building successful companies and his wonderful sense of humor when he was in a good mood. I know absolutely that he loved my mother, even though behavior at times might belie that truth. Yet I just can't figure out my ambivalent feelings. I love him; I fear him; I don't like him; I miss him; and I think he's a lousy dad, but he's my dad. So I feel sad, mad, lonely, betrayed and confused. What am I to do with all these feelings?"

"First, Child, I am pleased that you are able to give names to your feelings. They seem so real, so impactful and so jumbled in the daily living illusions of your Earth life. These are precisely the feelings that will teach you to love, to have empathy, to care for and offer solace to others because you know the experience for yourself. These are moments meant to teach you about the breadth of humanity and the feelings that must be resolved to leave the illusions and return to the fullness of the Universal Energy of Love. What you are feeling today is precious and instructive. Embrace this moment, loved one."

"Sissy. I need to confess something, and I feel bad about it, but it sits on my heart almost everyday. The thing is that I wish my dad had died instead of my mom. Not that I want anybody to be sick and others to grieve, but life would have been so different if Mother were still here. I'm not saying that I'm wishing my dad dead, but what has happened seems so unfair, unkind, nonsensical, stupid and outrageous. I could learn to love so much better if Mother were still here."

"Annalee. Please listen to me because it is time to tell you a truth that you must integrate into your belief system. When you chose to come into form and enter a life of illusion as you have done by coming to this planet, you also chose the players that would accompany you. They would play their parts perfectly to help you through your illusions and to teach you to seek Truth and Enlightenment. Simply said, this incarnation you chose these parents, your brother and your life circumstances."

"Jiminy crickets! Why on earth would I choose my dad? I can see the wisdom of choosing my mother and brother, but Dad mostly causes fear and pain."

"Look at your life right now. You are studying in Paris, loving the friends you have made, visiting countries with traditions different from your own. And you love it. You're drinking in the illusions that bring joy and refreshing viewpoints. And you are doing this at a very young age. I invite you to take an inventory of your life now and the life you would be living with both parents alive and together. You are living inside an illusion that has a purpose: to understand and reach for the peace of Enlightened Beingness."

Stunned, I just sat in the cold, not really aware of temperature or country or much of anything. I took a breath to try to get my wits together. I chose my family as the actors in a play to experience the life events that would eventually erase my pain and bring me to peace. The concept kept shocking me as I rocked and wrapped my arms around my numb body.

After a while, I sat up straight, somewhat defiant, and said: "Sissy, so tell me why I would pick this family. That's a good one for ya... just tell me why I would choose a mother who would leave me, a dad who, essentially, would leave me and a brother I cannot protect? I must be a first class idiot."

"Annalee, look at your illusion. You are becoming an empowered soul with a voice that will speak to the necessities of human empathy, a voice that will join in the chorus for change that honors all souls, and your adventure will teach you to know what is spirit-driven and what is ego-based. You chose to do this with the players in your family and the ones you include on your journey. Bless every encounter, every moment of pain, every throb of love. It is your purpose. Even knowing that now, understanding it now, you will have moments in which you disavow your knowingness in exchange for acceptance and immediate gratification. The journey is bumpy. I am always here."

The cold was becoming bitter, the emotional pain was not dissipating, and the scenery of crosses was holding my heart with no seeming escape. Finally, I leaned forward and stood up. I walked to the caretaker's gate, thanked him with a two-handed grasp of gratitude and began to walk to the bus depot, knowing one thing for certain: I would never forget this afternoon.

When it is obvious that the goals cannot be reached, don't adjust the goals, adjust the action steps.

Confucious

12

I had visited La Maison du Mexique in the Cite several times, enjoying a couple of hours speaking Spanish and eliciting fond memories of my times in Mexico and with Father Uribe. Mexicans, well trained from childhood in courtesy and flattery, are very welcoming and focused on the comfort of others. So it was such a delight to walk into their house lobby and chat with "compadres". They were always complimentary of my Spanish, making me feel even more welcome. I had gone to several university functions with some of the guys who invited the "gringa", but there were no romances, just good fun and laughter. An American girl, studying philosophy and speaking their language, was a novelty...and to some, a bit disquieting.

One afternoon while I was talking to some former acquaintances, I was introduced to Salvador. He began to tease me, and I responded in kind. We were having fun with each other, both understanding double entendres and laughing with abandon. Time passed quickly, and hunger approached. He scooped up my purse and books, and we set off for a previously unknown (to me) family style restaurant house on the opposite side of the Cite. Chava, as his friends called him, was obviously much more accustomed to the table wine than I. At the end of the second glass, I felt tipsy. He broke into English, as eloquent as his Spanish and French, and stood me up to walk home. Fresh air and a brisk walk cleared my head sufficiently so that I avoided making a fool of myself. As we walked the Left Bank and marveled at the architecture, we finally arrived at my residence. Shaking my hand, as is the Mexican custom, he air-kissed my cheeks and walked off to his university house.

I was smitten! A polite, very bright, interesting and well-spoken man, totally masculine without bravado, had captured my complete attention. Bounding up the stairs, I knocked and was invited into Jacqueline's room. Reza was just about to leave when they both started quizzing me. "Who is he? Who is he?" Not being able to deny the excitement that I was feeling, I spilled the beans about all the events of the entire evening. There was no hiding my interest in this man. His charm was not only intoxicating, but also so very genuine. I had no idea if I would see him again. I didn't even know his last name, nor did he know mine. Reza teased me, and Jacqueline loved my excitement. My stomach would not settle down. My brain was spaghetti. This was a totally new and wonderful feeling. I understood my time with him was something special. Then I started the games of re-thinking and doubting my feelings, my knowingness, my truth about this unique experience. Only sleep quieted the exaggeration of all my senses. Seven hours later I woke up smiling.

Three days passed. I saw his face in every dark-haired student passing me on the sidewalks or on the metro. Finally, I quieted enough to try to convince myself that this experience was nothing more than a memory of a fun time with an interesting man. I was working on this resolution to my angst when the concierge said I had a note delivered by another student. Apparently, he had described me by using my first name, nationality and body characteristics. The concierge, herself a student, took note of my face as I read the note, and offered: "I got the right person!"

I now had his name, phone number and an invitation to dinner. If I was unable to accept his invitation, I was to call. Otherwise, I had a date with the most exciting illusion of my life.

We enjoyed almost every evening together for weeks. Occasionally, he had to sit for exams or prepare a paper that interfered with our daily dinners and conversations. If one lived in Paris, one walked. And did we walk! Every street was different. Architecture demanded attention. Art galleries were walls of fascinating interpretations of lives, people, moods and nature. An art gallery provoked discussions like no other activity. The Rodin Museum overwhelmed with the exquisite representation of the human body and the self-referential aesthetic. The many facets of the human creative capacity became exponential through my many introductions via Guide Chava. He had seen most of what he was now sharing with me, but his art and history mini lectures gave him pleasure as I often witnessed his passionate explanations.

The one famous piece of art that never called to me with any sense of appreciation was the Mona Lisa. We stood, staring, commenting, and both agreeing we "didn't see the need for reverence"--so it is with art and art critics!

Christmas was approaching. The university was out of session and Chava had an invitation to visit a physician friend in Casablanca. He invited me, but he informed me that he did not have funds to pay my way. He then, romantically, said he wanted me to spend the holidays with him and visit Morocco. There was no time to borrow funds from family or friends at home. I was ready to tell him how much I really wanted to go but could not when Jacqueline asked what I was doing for Christmas. Hearing that I had this spectacular opportunity to visit Morocco with Chava, she handed me the money. I refused, saying I did not know when I could pay her back. Flippantly, she assured me she had no worry with that. "We are sisters; you will do the right thing. Go. Be happy. But you must tell me everything when you get back." I hugged her so tightly. She was my family…my sister.

Chava and I departed Paris in the evening, taking a sleeper compartment on the train to Madrid. While he went for a cigar smoke with fellow passengers in the smoking lounge, I changed into my bed clothes, climbed into the lower bunk as he had instructed and was rocked to sleep by the rhythm of the train.

The twelve hour journey went quickly, and soon we were in Madrid in a taxi headed for a hotel on the city square. Madrid was enchanting, with a totally different feeling than Paris. Spaniards are infinitely polite and love to be accommodating. With both of us able to speak Spanish, we were able to get around quickly to the sites we were eager to see. The first stop had to be El Prado with its many masterpieces of Goya, Rembrandt, Rubens, El Greco, Raphael and Bosch. I found myself nearly speechless actually standing in front of an El Greco, whom I had studied rather extensively for a paper in Art Appreciation at Purdue. Many young artists had been given permission to paint in front of a masterpiece to copy the work. Looking at the student easels as I walked through the museum, I had to confess that I could not tell the difference. No wonder counterfeit art is readily bought and sold!

As in any European large city, we walked and walked. Quaint, bustling, and so very charming, Madrid became a favored city for both of us. We wearily returned to the hotel, showered and laid down for a nap before dinner and the much-anticipated flamenco show at a nightclub we had spotted earlier.

I knew I was in love with this man. His soap-scented body was next to me, and I turned to him for the kisses I had become addicted to. The comfort and opportunity of the situation was an invitation that could not be ignored. Having never been intimately physical with a boyfriend before, I always imagined it would be somewhat awkward. However, this first experience was easy, exquisite, tender, passionate and affirming. We remained embraced as we napped, knowing that we had opened the door to a new level of the relationship. I felt a quiet appreciation that my lover was not a neophyte. He was as artful in his instruction with lovemaking as he was as my Parisian tourist guide. I felt as happy at that moment as I had ever, ever been.

After one more day of poking into the side streets of Madrid, drinking sangria and Spanish wine and eating paella until we hurt, we left for Gibraltar to take the ferry to Morocco. Chava and I were easy travelers, opening conversations with strangers on boats, in hotels, restaurants and on street corners. With three languages available to us, we could usually find a common communication with anyone. Arabic was a stone wall, but we soon learned that almost all educated Arabs spoke French as well as English. The men easily joined in a conversation with us, but the veiled women only did so in private.

Dr. Caron's car and driver were waiting for us at the disembarkation wharf in Morocco. After the usual passport and customs routine, two men loaded our two pieces of luggage, and we settled in for the more than five hour trip to Casablanca. Passing through the capital, Rabat, we encountered a very overcrowded Muslim city with people approaching our car from all directions. Our driver and his front seat companion deftly maneuvered their way through the traffic to a restaurant on the southern part of the city where our lunch was outstanding. It was our first introduction to lamb and couscous. Also, MY first introduction to eating in a room separate from the rest of the party. Men and women did not eat together in public.

Then I noticed that the male passenger in our car was standing at the door during my entire lunch. Privately quizzing Chava and the driver before we continued to Casablanca, I learned that the gentleman was my assigned bodyguard. This new piece of information made me question whether I felt safer or more in danger if I needed a bodyguard.

Dr. Caron was effusive in his welcoming of us for the holidays. His home was decidedly Moroccan in style with two guest houses on the walled property. Chava was assigned one, and I, the other.

We graciously accepted these beautiful accommodations, went to our bungalows, unpacked and reported to the swimming pool and cabana for the cocktail hour. Over cocktails I learned that Henri Caron was a Frenchman, transplanted to Casablanca, a practicing obstetrician and gynecologist. He, also, did charity work with a group of global doctors dedicated to missions helping the poor and those without medical access. After dinner, we discussed a trip to Marrakesh and then an additional one up into the Rif Mountains where we could assist him with two days of surgical procedures on local women. Dilation and Curettage was a known procedure to me, but I had never seen one done or been party to assisting. Dr. Caron assured me he could teach me what I needed to do if we wanted to come along. We were all in. However, before we left we acquainted ourselves with Casablanca with the help of his driver while he was treating patients in clinic. Then we would be off to Marrakesh...city of merchants, camels and snake charmers.

Marrakesh was surrounded with high red clay walls matching many of the homes on the interior. When we arrived at the Plaza of Marrakesh, I thought we were in the center of a movie. Stall after stall of spices, crafts, clothing, silk veils and pottery. The Berber tribes had long settled this region, and their carpets were on display in all directions. Such beauty and color were delightful to all the senses. The odors of the various restaurants enchanted. As we approached the very center of the plaza I saw it: a real snake charmer with the basket home for the cobra, the flute and the long-haired, messy-looking snake charmer. Turning to Henri and Chava, I asked if it were real! Henri laughed, approached the disheveled man, gave him some money, and his flute began to play its coaxing tune. Soon enough, a cobra rose from the basket with flared head appendages, looked up for about twenty seconds and then descended down into his curled position. I was thrilled, hoping I had taken enough pictures.

Once again, I enjoyed dinner in the company of other lovely women, all chatting in Arabic as we sat on large cushions on the floor and passed food family style. Quietly and respectfully, the woman across from me asked in French if I were visiting from France. I answered that I was, but that I was a student at the Sorbonne and was an American. She immediately responded in English, informing me that it would be better for her so she could practice English. Her British-accented English was not only impeccable, but also was engaging, and her manner regal. We spoke of countries, customs, classic books and women's rights. As both of us were veiled, as was required after eating, we watched the flutter of the silk across our faces and giggled. Thoroughly enjoying our conversation, I was reluctant to leave when my bodyguard came to collect me and escort me to our transportation back to Casablanca. I asked her what was an appropriate way to say good bye to a new friend I would probably never see again. She lifted her arms in praise to Allah and shook my hand. I won't forget such an interesting and noble conversation with a woman so talented, yet so restricted from using that talent. I felt joy and regret, but I was immensely thankful. There are moments in life that are recorded indelibly…and for our blessed journey to embrace the significance of the experience. I didn't know her name, but I was an intimate acquaintance of her soul.

It was almost prayer-call time as we approached Casablanca. Henri took us to a minaret tower with its conical crown where we climbed to the top for a view of the city during the call to prayer. Indeed, all over the city, men dropped to their knees and bent in reverence, rocking up and then down, in a rhythmic adoration exercise that was lovely and respectful. I stood watching such devotion, such allegiance and such routine daily commitment to a belief that brought them solace and conviction.

Early the next morning we left for the Rif Mountains to help Henri with his mission medical practice. As we arrived at the village, many showed their excitement about Henri's arrival and promptly volunteered to round up the patients we needed to see. As Henri prepared the surgery room, he instructed me in everything I was to do. He inquired if I had an aversion to blood or smells, and I assured him that I was fine on all accounts. Blood had never bothered me, but I had no idea about the smells that I was about to encounter. Many times I swallowed hard and quickly to keep my tummy in check because rotting flesh and long-disregarded female infections have a nauseating and repugnant odor not to be forgotten. I was being initiated to all this within the first hour of my physician assistant role.

After a long and arduous day doing something I so much enjoyed, I reveled in my new learning. Henri informed us that he had told the villagers that it was our Christian New Year, so they had prepared a celebration. He was also quick to inform us that the smallest of reasons was a mandate for celebration in the mountain villages. We were to be wined and dined, village style. With precautionary warnings from Henri, we chose the foods he suggested, and liberally partook of the wine. Morocco had oranges that were as large or larger than the grapefruit on American breakfast tables. From these extraordinary oranges wine was made and graciously shared. It tasted exactly like orange juice, a favorite beverage my entire life, so I gulped a lot of the sweetness down during the early part of the evening. Needless to say, I had no recollection of events when quizzed the next morning by the unending teasing of Henri and Chava. I was certain that they greatly exaggerated my inebriated behavior. Both promised never to tell on me, and that they would destroy the damning photographs!! Then…the realization that I had another day of tummy-challenging work. Karma!!

When time came to return to Paris, we both slowly packed our luggage. We dreaded the necessity of re-engaging in college life. Henri had been the best of hosts, always gracious and exquisite in his planning of activities he thought would delight, inform, surprise or mystify. I, as a developing world traveler, often paused in gratitude for the unique experiences with people I would probably never see again, but whom I so enjoyed and connected with energetically. They were all gifts that, once opened and discovered, I did not want to kiss good bye. I would never forget!

Our return trip to Paris was accompanied by some melancholy in both of us. Our vacation had been beyond what we had expected. We fell in love with Henri and his work. It is always hard to leave people whom you genuinely care for. Added to the emotion of leaving Morocco and returning to tiny university housing rooms and studies was the knowledge that in one week I would be leaving for Southampton, England to sail on the SS Rotterdam to New York, then fly to Chicago where Fippy would meet me. My studies abroad were over, and Purdue expected me to resume my scholarship studies in late January. Indeed, I had missed my family of sorority sisters and my sweet brother. Since I had only received about one letter a month from him, I knew there was a lot to catch up on, and I suspected that it was not at all uncommon for young men in college to forget to write their sister more often. Dave, my one-time boyfriend who had helped secure housing and meals for Phil, was a man good for his word, so I truly did not worry about Phil. I knew one thing for sure: he was much better off at Purdue than at home.

But I was in love. A part of me wanted to forsake everything to stay in Paris and be with Chava. Trying to imagine a day without seeing him, I would choke up, and my chest would hurt. He was a bit more stoic and sensible. We were students, not just star-crossed lovers with no responsibility. After all, I needed to finish my degree, and he was just a year away from his finishing his studies. Somehow, we would make this work, albeit long distance and a year's worth of life in between. As one in love, I had no doubt we would overcome all these obstacles and find our way to life-long happiness. If life were an illusion, I certainly was picking this one. For the first time in my life I felt completely loved, cherished, wanted and protected. All these feelings were being soaked up to the maximum so that when I was gone from their sensory affirmation I would be able to recall the finery of touch, smell, taste and vision of the man who had begun to define a large part of my world.

I would meet him in New York a year from now, introduce him to my brother, grandparents and Aunt Madge and then accompany him to Mexico City for the holidays to meet his family. He teased that his sisters had a bet on him coming home with a French "cookie," but they never would have placed a bet on an American he met in Paris! We laughed as we often did, teased, kissed, held each other in a long embrace, each trying to make sure that we had captured every sense of the other to carry in our memory.

On the train and ferry ride to England, I was partly unconscious, or, at least, it felt that way. The long lines at the ferry dock on the French side of the Channel were moving slowly. The drizzle was dirty and cold, cars were loaded and passengers were demanding coffee as fast as it could be served. I felt no interest in any of the activities being mentioned in the brochures handed out by the Holland-American line personnel. They were marketing onboard the ferry, trying to entertain the many passengers headed for the SS Rotterdam. What was obviously a trip anticipated with excitement and joy for others felt like a bucketful of sadness and loneliness for me.

> Resilience is distinct from mere survival,
> and more than mere endurance.
> Resilience is often endurance with direction.
>
> Eric Greitens

13

The English Channel is not always calm. The ferry ride to Southhampton was crowded, cold, damp and extremely bumpy. I had to sit a while to get my nausea to abate. Since childhood I had been embarrassed many times with motion sickness. I found England to be dreary, depressing and not at all the lovely place I had always envisioned in the many novels whose backdrops were English country sides and acres of gardens. The ship port was dirty, bustling and an industrial hub of freight, cranes and crass men. Knowing I had no choice but to board a vessel that was taking me far away from where I wanted to be, I forced myself to shuffle forward, stand in one queue after another, checking passport, student visa, health certificate, all with close examination because I had a Moroccan entry stamp in my passport. At length, I was allowed to board this luxurious ship filled with salons of chandeliers and deep carpets that lent an air of regality as I descended to the lowest fare level of staterooms. Satisfied that it was clean, I unpacked some of my clothes, stowed the suitcase under the bunk and went for a self-guided tour of the ship. I took notice of all the entertainment and eating venues, the grandness of the mid-ship stairway, reminiscent of the dramatic scene of Rhett and Scarlett and the outside decks for walking and lounging. The swimming pool seemed an absurd amenity for a North Atlantic crossing in January. We left early in the evening. The passengers enjoyed culinary fare of every sort, not noticing the vessel silently slipping its moorings to begin the trans-oceanic voyage. I missed the customary bottle of red wine on the table, but settled for salmon and fresh vegetables as my heart whined for the companionship of Chava and non-stop conversation that had some depth and satisfaction. Aware of how pathetic I must have appeared, I started innocuous conversation and felt no connection to anything. I decided to seek out Sissy Jean on deck the next morning, as I needed her and missed her. My heart had been so full of joy and adventure that I had not taken time to meditate or self-reflect. Now I felt lonely, apologetic and slightly nauseous. I promised myself the next morning would bring a sweet and loving conversation with Sissy.

During the night the nausea increased, and by morning I was intimately acquainted with the bathroom. I so wished to be able to go to the outer deck, catch some fresh sea air and meditate. But at the moment, vomiting took priority over any thought of meditation. I was so sea-sick I could not crawl! The kindness of my Swedish roomies intervened when they called the ship doctor to help with the American girl who was hogging the bathroom, albeit without intent. The Dutch doctor gave me some meds that ameliorated the constant vomiting and made me go to his onboard clinic for an IV for dehydration. All of this attention was difficult for me, but I was weak enough that I knew I could not protest. By day five of the voyage I was able to stand and walk a few yards. I also noticed my clothes were a bit loose. After weighing myself before checking out of the clinic, I commented to the nurse that this was one hell of a diet, telling her that I had lost nine and one half pounds in five days. She smiled and said: "I don't doubt it. Happens all the time on winter crossings!" Sissy would have to wait.

We docked in Newark, New Jersey, waited for our luggage to be loaded for New York City or one of the airports. Finding the bus for La Guardia, I checked to see that my luggage was loaded, found a seat and took note of all the scenery on the way to the airport. The country and the nation had a totally different feel from where I had been living. Paris is a beautiful, charming, arrogant and a semi anti-American city, but its energy is vibrant, old world and uplifting. Newark to New York was energy-draining, unkind and unforgiving. I just wanted to get to Chicago and hug on my baby brother for a long time. Knowing that once I was checked in at LaGuardia, I could call Fippy and check on details of meeting at O'Hare, I noted that the temperature at that airport was stated at minus 12 degrees.

Making the phone call to the fraternity house at Purdue and asking for Phil, I waited an eternity until I heard his upbeat voice. I was giddy with excitement at the sound of his "hi, Sis" greeting and immediately spilled out all the information needed for the flight so he could pick me up at O'Hare. Noting the pause, I asked if something was the matter. Phil, hesitantly, offered that he had sold his "jalopy," so he couldn't pick me up, but Dad and Ginny would be there. He continued that they would take me to campus, meet up with him, and he would get me settled into my sorority house. Sadly, I would have to wait several more hours to see my brother. I reluctantly accepted what was inevitable and graciously accepted the situation before hanging up. The underlying anger I felt about having to meet Dad, the man who had communicated a mere ten words total to me in nine months, in spite of my newsy letters, was quite unsettling. I never mentioned the knife attack and the trip to North Africa in my letters because I would catch grief and hear about it for a long time. As I thought about Dad waiting at O'Hare, my stomach tightened, feeling the meeting would be awkward and unnatural. I had no choice, and I would be able to endure anything for a short time.

My "land legs" were almost normal as I walked the ugliness of La Guardia airport searching for the United Airlines terminal. A bit of a smile crept over me as I realized that my lifetime curse seemed to be that wherever I was headed was usually the furthest away. However, once in my economy seat, I settled in and put my head back to try to relax and think about the latest events, sadly relegating meditation and Sissy until later in a more peaceful environment.

Leaving Colette was endurable. She was from Canada, and a future meeting was entirely possible. But not being able to say good-bye to Jacqueline and Reza hurt my heart. They were such dear friends and kind individuals, always seeing the bright side of things, joking and laughing, while equally compassionate at appropriate times. Reza had left for Saudia Arabia for religious holidays and had not yet returned to Paris. Jacqueline was a different story. The concierge told me that she had received a report that her mother was wounded in Vietnam, and she had left immediately. No one had any information on her whereabouts or her plans. Wanting to offer emotional support and be the friend she had always been to me, I left all my contact information with the concierge so she could inform me when she knew something. Chava had also promised to check from time to time to see if there was news. I not only wanted and needed to honor my dear friend, but the money I had asked Phil for before my holiday trip had arrived the day after I left for Madrid. I so wanted to repay Jacqueline's kindness to me. Chava said I should keep the funds for travel emergencies, and I could wire funds later when she returned. As it turned out, I did need some well-deserved tip money for porters and ship attendants.

So here I was on a plane to Chicago to meet a dad who was

difficult and judgmental and a stepmother whom I had no connection to. While feeling bereft at leaving Chava, Colette and Jacqueline and a city I loved, I so anticipated my reunion with Fippy. Feeling still somewhat weak from the Atlantic crossing, I tried to imagine the re-acclimation to Purdue life. I felt down and pitiful. Using denial mechanisms to deal with what would be only temporary circumstances, I jolted upright in my seat! It just occurred to me Phil had said he didn't have his "jalopy" anymore. At the time I thought it probably had stopped working since it was rather old. Now I was certain I knew the truth. Phil had sold it to send me the hundred and fifty dollars I needed for the Moroccan trip. The nausea returned. My guilt was palpable, and my selfishness appalling. Phil had worked hard to try to cover expenses and save enough to care for his dilapidated vehicle. We needed to talk and figure all this out because we were always each other's touchstone and support. I would find a way…as soon as I could catch my breath and walk the maze of impending events.

After surveying the arrival area while carrying a heavy suitcase, I searched for Dad. I finally went outside to see if maybe he was late or waiting curbside. Indeed, he was definitely upset that I had kept him waiting curbside in the cold weather with airport police telling him to move. I don't think it ever occurred to him to park and meet me at the gate. With a slight sigh, I said "Welcome home, Annalee" to myself, put my suitcase in the back seat, scooted in and took a breath. O'Hare was a fertile traffic environment for Dad's well-known rants and expletives, which of course accompanied our exit from Chicago.

Traveling southward to Purdue, Ginny asked about Paris, my classes and the weather in Europe, with seeming interest. We were having a polite interchange when Dad asked if I had "found me a boyfriend" in Paris. Hesitating, I finally told him that I had indeed. Surely, there would be no more questions. But Dad then asked if he were French. I answered that, in fact, he was Mexican, to which my father said: "Oh, for God's sake, Annalee. You can do better than that!"

We sat in silence until we arrived at Phil's fraternity house. I needed to lay hands on him, hold him and thank him. It didn't take long for Dad to leave and for us to begin talking non-stop. He borrowed a car from a fraternity brother, and we headed to my sorority house.

I cherished these young women and was hugged and kissed by almost all of them, trying to answer questions and be responsive to each sweet inquiry. While the climate was not alien at all, it certainly did not feel as comfortable as a year ago. It would take some concerted effort to fit in again, feel at home and be a team member. Within the hour, I was settled in and went out to dinner with Phil. Everyone accepted this as totally understandable. We went to a drive-in restaurant so we could talk, and I ate my first hamburger in nine months!

After telling him about my studies, my love for Chava, my friends and many experiences, I paused to reiterate that I wanted to know how college was for him. How life was for him? He became teary-eyed, abandoning the lighthearted manner that he had been playing so well. I took his hand: "Tell me," I begged.

"I hate him. I miss Mother so much. Sometimes I'm glad she's gone and doesn't have to put up with him. He never should have had kids. We're in the way. We're not even important enough for a phone call. It would be so different if she were here. She'd be at every college event we invited her to. We'd get phone calls and packages in the mail, and she would sneak us some money every once in a while. Do you know what that bastard has done?" he wailed.

Holding my breath unintentionally, I found enough wind to ask what Dad had done. Phil then explained that while we were trying to survive on a pittance of a college allowance, Dad and Ginny had bought several lots on a small Bahamian island and recently built a three bedroom, three bath home for their winter months away from Indiana. He confessed they were irritated that I was returning from Europe after the New Year just in the middle of their planned return to Paradise. My jaw was slack in shock. Certainly Dad had every right to his decisions, but Phil was right. We were an interference with his new life. I cried with my brother. We held each other and rocked ourselves to an eventual calm and a decision to take a breath and move forward. We knew we were essentially on our own. The venting helped because we were with each other. But we knew, at the end of the day, our future and daily living was up to us to figure out and provide for ourselves. I assured him I would have a plan by morning. He always trusted me. I had to think fast.

Exhausted, I lay down on my upperclassmen, bottom bunk in the dark and started to sort through these dilemmas. We could not go to Dad. That route had never proven successful. So how could I come up with some funds relatively quickly. Getting a part-time job was essential no matter what, but we needed funds more quickly. Then, from the far reaches of my mind I recalled that a guy I knew on the debate team had told me my freshman year that when his scholarship stipend was late that he appealed to financial aid and received a low-interest government loan. He had said it saved his first year of college.

Arriving at the financial aid office at eight o'clock the next morning, I filled out the appropriate papers for a government loan at three percent interest with the first payment due at the end of my education. It also included a waiver for years of graduate school. I prayed, beseeched, begged and hoped. Phil and I were not aware of any safety nets. Aunts, uncles and grandparents were lower middle class with month to month struggles of their own.

Since the semester was beginning in two days, bills needed to be paid at both our residences, and Phil's tuition payment was due before classes began. Using the emergency money from the sale of his car, we managed to pay the tuition bill so that he could enroll. My scholarship automatically covered tuition, fees and books. We were discussing telling both our residences that money would be forthcoming when I got the phone call. The University Financial Aid office was informing me that I was to report for an interview at 9:30 the next morning. Phil smugly suggested we postpone the "poverty speech" to our residences until we had news. Since Phil was still rush chairman, his expenses were fewer than mine. Exceptions were rarely made for late payments because residence buildings constantly existed pretty close to the financial edge.

Not having slept well, I was quite unsettled about having no alternative plan. I missed Chava like crazy! I was tired and grumpy the next morning as I walked in the falling snow on sidewalks lined with grey-stained, previously plowed snow so high that it impeded my view. I asked the universe to help in any way possible as I entered a room with eight seated men. One empty seat was at the near end for the applicant: me. Inhaling and composing myself, I slowly removed my coat and hat and sat down. Addressing me immediately from the far end of the table, the chairman of the committee asked bluntly why I needed the money since I was just returning home from a nice semester abroad. The tone was unmistakably semi-sarcastic. Looking around the table, I made a decision to respond full force with the truth. I was going for broke. Take it or leave it, but I put my folded hands on the table and began:

"Gentlemen, I am appreciative and grateful to be here and be able to make my case to you. You are correct that I have just returned from a very instructive semester of hard work and real rewards for my studies at the Sorbonne. I was able to accomplish that through the generosity of a scholarship and some part-time work for a while. Now that I am back to continue my studies here and graduate next year, I find I have no funds for lodging and meals. My father paid some of those previously, but has not offered to contribute to mine or my brother's education this semester. He is well-to-do, but since my mother's death and his remarriage, his interests and funds are used elsewhere. Without your help I am relatively certain that my brother and I will not be able to be at Purdue this semester. It is a dire situation for us."

Then I choked. Nothing more would come out my mouth, and I felt my eyes welling up with tears. I was going to be a pathetic girl and embarrass myself. So I coughed and grabbed a Kleenex. Not fooling anyone about my emotions, I thanked them again for their careful consideration.

I was a mess: no money, no Chava, no emotional self-control. On top of that I was mad. Mad that Phil and I had no parent whom we could count on, no parent that seemed to give a damn about his children, their needs, their accomplishments, their grief or their well-being. Fuming for about four blocks, I talked to myself the rest of the way to the sorority house, accepting that if we both had to drop out of school we would work, save and get our degrees later than originally anticipated. It wasn't the end of the world. And, just before opening the door to the sorority house, I laughed. Everything I owned I could carry in one suitcase. Moving would not be hard.

The universe answered in a double way. Later that afternoon the Financial Aid office called to inform me that I had been approved for a government loan in the amount I had requested. Phil and I would stay in school! Just as that gratitude was sinking in, I got another call. Phil said that an envelope had arrived at his fraternity house which was mailed to me at his address. He was sure it was Dad's handwriting.

"For God's sake, Fippy! Open it! It could be money or a disinheritance notice!"

"Annalee! It's a check to you for five hundred dollars!"

"Fippy, that will almost cover your tuition AND our room and board for the semester. Oh my God!"

"You know, Annie, the old man can't even get our addresses

straight. And he certainly wouldn't trust me with the money. I'll let it go in a while, but I am glad we can survive 'til summer."

"Fippy, I am so relieved, but I don't get Dad. Education has always been so over-the-top important. You'd think he would want to make sure we're okay here."

"Annie, that talk was all when Mother was alive. It's way different now. And I got a feelin' that repayment is on the horizon. Wait and see."

"Fippy...for now we can breathe. We'll never hear from him all semester, so go celebrate. And, oh, by the way, I'll give you what's left of the money you sent me."

"Nope. Keep it to send to your friend when she's back."

Able to breathe and enter Purdue campus life, I determined to do two things immediately: write a letter to Chava and talk with Sissy. Sissy came first for a change.

Lying in my bunk in the large third floor dormitory room all by myself, I finally entered deep meditation and relaxation. The all encompassing feeling of reverence, love and acceptance that I was so accustomed to when going inward came once again and enveloped my being. I felt aligned with Source. And her voice was as soft and warm as ever.

"Hello, dear one. It is good to see you take some time to relax and enter conscious awareness. Your earth-bound illusions have been multiple and entertaining. It is interesting that you create illusions with so much color, energy and intrigue. I can feel at times that you miss me, but you are assured that I am always present, always available, always loving you and whatever you are experiencing. What is on your heart today?"

"Sissy, I have to apologize to you. You are always here for me, and I know that I am not reciprocal, but I am so appreciative. You are the only guide I have and I trust. Just that is so important to me."

"Dear heart, there is never a need for apology. You have not misbehaved. You have simply behaved with no judgment attached. Your life events are illusions, so they appear only to you. Remember that you invite and create them for learning purposes. They all eventually lead to a need to extend love, feel love, be love. Throughout life your illusions will intermingle perfectly with others' illusions to create an experience. Lately, you have had many!"

"Sissy Jean, I am in love, and I love being in love. I never want this feeling to go away. It carries me to levels of joy that I have never known before. I love you. I love beauty and nature and beautiful things. I love my brother. I love some family members and friends, but I have never felt this kind of love. My body aches, my brain goes haywire and nothing else in the world seems to matter as much as the love I feel for Chava. Is this normal? I think my parents loved each other, but I never ever got a sense that they felt like I do when I am thinking of or with Chava."

"*Sweet Annie, this is a new love, an erotic love that has been unknown to you before. It is sweet and exciting in the illusion the two of you have created. It is good to feel this experience. There are many types of love shown in your human experiment. You know familial love, agape love, spiritual love… and now, erotic love. All but spiritual love are creations of your earth-bound environments and experiences. And all of these are temporal and appear or vanish according to the illusion you are having at any given time. Sometimes they are necessary for the lesson at hand. At other times they are absent to lend meaning to an illusion. The erotic love you are feeling for your boyfriend is pheromoned love, fueled by your human body's response system and hormonal capabilities. It cannot sustain this heightened level for more than about six months, so enjoy, and be in gratitude for the discovery of another pleasure.*"

"Oh my goodness, Sissy, what happens when this pheromone-fueled love abates? Does this exciting feeling also go away?"

"*Sometimes it does. In fact, most of the time it evaporates, and humans create new illusions. If the connection between the lovers is strong, then they may develop abiding love, a love that promises to endure everything together. You need to know that that is the kind of love your parents and grandparents had. Behaviors may not always seem kind and faithful, but you nor anyone knows the heart and spirit of another. Humans only guess. They often times miss the mark. For instance, are you aware that the very word 'sin' means 'missing the mark?' Be gentle with yourself. You are just beginning many of your illusions that will bring important and life-changing lessons. Stay open. Love what is good with all your heart. Be in conscious awareness as often as possible. Meditate. Own all your human feelings, and know that the ultimate purpose is to bring peace to your world and return to love…The One.*"

As I slowly exited my meditation, I felt an overwhelming love for this non-physical being who shared her knowingness. She loved me like no other had. I knew I could get through anything in life knowing my purpose and having this spiritual connection with her. I reverently said "thank you," arose and within the hour began my lengthy letter to my pheromoned love.

Love is whatever you can still betray. Betrayal can only happen if you love.

John Le Carre

My adjustment to college life again was my usual: sign up for lots of activities and stay busy. Within two weeks I was totally involved in sorority committees and enrolled in a heavy course load. Phil and I talked on the phone every week, but he was on the other side of campus with no transportation. We said we would get together soon to talk about our options for spring break. Phil said he had an idea, but would tell me later. We both knew going home was not an option unless we heard from Dad. That was not our first choice anyway, and we were reasonably certain that Dad didn't know when spring break occurred. Therefore, we were fully prepared to take care of ourselves in our creative ways.

At Purdue there were 9x12 manila envelopes with lines on the front and a string on the back to wrap around a grommet sort of connection. One's name was written on the front with a university address. Purdue's version of inter-office mail was then to be delivered to the last name and address listed. It was actually kind of exciting to receive one of these, and I presumed it was most likely from one of the activity chairmen. Whoa! Was I wrong! The Dean of Women, Dr. Beverly Stone, infamous for her mandate that female students were not allowed to wear slacks on campus or in class unless the temperature was below freezing, and then only under the skirt, informed (not invited) me I was to report to her office at 9:00a.m. two days hence. There was no mention of the reason or even a "sincerely yours." Knowing I had done nothing that would merit a disciplinary audience with Dean Stone, I thought perhaps it might be to welcome me back from my studies abroad. My grades were above average, I had no record of unacceptable behavior, and I had paid all my university bills.

I arrived at her reception area at the appointed time. Soon her secretary said the Dean would see me and escorted me into a dark office with all shades drawn on the tall windows. The energy and décor were dismal, as I soon learned was equally true of Dr. Stone's personality.

"Sit," she ordered.

"Dean Stone, you asked to see me?"

"Yes, I did. You are recently returned from your studies in Paris, France and re-enrolled at Purdue. Is that correct?"

"Yes, ma'am," I answered

"And I see that you studied philosophy. Quite a deviation from your Purdue courses."

"Yes, ma'am."

"Well, the reason that I have called you here this morning is that I want you to understand that this is Indiana, not Paris, France. We are provincial and appropriate, and I will not allow any deviate behavior from the women of Purdue. Do you understand?"

Dumbfounded, I sat silent. What on earth was this woman talking about? I was not about to ask. This was her show, and I would listen.

"I asked you if you understand?"

"Dean Stone, I am confused. I do not know what you are talking about or what you expect of me here today. Are you saying that I have done something wrong?"

"Young woman, what I am saying is that people in France do things differently than we do. You are in Indiana. Just make sure you behave yourself. I don't want to see you in my office again. You may go."

I left her den of darkness without a word and walked to the sorority house, knowing that I would have to share this absurd encounter at dinner with my sisters. And, indeed, we had a great laugh. It was our custom while waiting to be served dessert by the waiters to tell something funny that happened that day. It, for sure, was my turn!! For the next year and a half I would often hear "Annie, you behavin' today?" as a sweet tease.

Finally able to see Phil at the Union Building at the center of campus, I bear-hugged him with both of us in big, wooly winter coats. Asking if he was buying cokes, he said: "Only if we go Dutch!" I punched him in the ribs and asked what his big plan was for spring break. He explained that a fraternity brother that had an apartment off campus that was within walking distance and was going home to Wisconsin for spring break. He generously offered the apartment to Phil and me, knowing we were not allowed to stay in our Greek houses over mid-term vacation. Unfortunately, just about everyone in our respective houses knew that our dad wasn't around or to be counted on. We didn't talk about it, but it became very evident at every Parent Weekend, any vacation or beginning or ending of school time when all other parents were loading, unloading and being a family. Phil and I never talked about it with others; we knew the situation, and it never surprised or haunted us. It was what it was.

The book stores at Purdue often hired temporary help between semesters and over spring break because they could hire students who were still on campus. Phil (his great idea!) and I signed up, got the jobs, worked eight hours a day and four hours overtime six days a week during the break. Since we would need money for the next year and never knowing our circumstances, we worked our butts off. The book store owners bought us lunch and dinner which we ate at the warehouse and were very appreciative of our good nature and good work. They also told us that we were welcome back two weeks before fall semester for book sales as cashiers or pullers (pulling a student's list of books for all his classes) if we continued the good job we had done this mid-term. We took them up on the offer, pledging to report at the appointed time. So...we had some money now, summer work money would come and a two week part time job promised for fall. We both felt a little lighter and joked more than usual, knowing this time together was our version of family.

About a month before the semester ended I received another lined, yellow notepad memo from Dad, addressed to Phil with the sorority house address. Geez. The mail delivery pledge teased that if my brother was getting mail at our sorority house she would like to know which room he was in because she would come "knockin." Another teased that she would have to stand in line, and, besides, pledges came last! All this sure sounded like the family fun we saw on TV. I secretly like the attention.

After calling Phil who told me to open the gold-plated envelope, I read him the following message:

"You and your sister will work for me in Elizabethtown, Kentucky this summer. Ginny and I have a three bedroom trailer there, so you will stay with us. The job needs me there--Phil will work construction with me, and Annalee will man the office, do payroll, taxes, phone etc. At the end of the summer you will receive your tuition and room and board for the next year. Enclosed is a hundred dollars to get here. Address on envelope. Dad"

"Oh, my God!" Phil said. "Just what I always wanted to do. Spend every day in the heat doing construction along side my beloved Papa! And, Annie, you'll go stir crazy sitting in a room all day. The price tag on education just went up. Have we sold our souls yet?"

"Maybe so, Fippy, but just for a couple of months. And if we don't do as he ordered, there will never be another dime to help us. We've got each other to help us get through this. We've had worse times."

Hearing him swallow hard on the other end of the phone, I said I would call the next day, and I could almost hear him nodding his head in agreement. Before the phone call, I wrote a letter to Chava, but I always avoided any mention of family issues because of feelings of embarrassment, shame and drama.

The semester ended with nice grades and accolades. The conversations of what my sorority sisters were planning for summer vacation were the topics of the day. Exotic trips, engagement parties, planning for weddings and shopping were the most common. A few had summer jobs, but most were anticipating a vacation from course work.

Phil and I took our one suitcase each and my mother's sewing machine that was stored at the sorority house and a bag of Good Will clothes that I could cut into patterns for skirts and tops. I had yarn for a new sweater and found four new pairs of jeans for Phil. At fifteen cents each, they looked relatively new. I had noticed his jeans were cutting him in the crotch (what we called "high water") because he had grown almost seven inches his freshman and sophomore year! It was my suspicion that Mother's death stunted his growth in high school. When he graduated he was five feet one inch, and now he was five feet eight inches. As buxom as I was, Phil was slight, wiry and athletic. We were polar opposites in physical build and in personality, but totally bonded in our hearts.

Thanks to Greyhound, we were on a bus headed for E-town, Kentucky. When we called Dad from the bus station his response was: "Goddamn time you two got here!"

Actually, the accommodations in their trailer were not bad. We could shower, eat dinner and breakfast and sleep. Ginny was a decent cook who needed a lot of praise for her culinary efforts, so we made sure to never leave the table without the mandatory compliments as we headed to the kitchen to do the dishes.

Talking with Ginny was pleasant and shallow. We were grateful for conversation that was not filled with expletives and not at a decibel level that eventually wore you out. After dishes and showers, we often watched their favorite TV programs and were comfortable for the evening. Once Dad caught me writing to Chava, saying: "That still going on?" I did not respond and took a book to bed.

After constructing four new skirts, three blouses and still working on the sweater at my one room office, I felt I was ready clothes-wise for my senior year. All I had left was to paint my senior "cords" for my final Purdue year. I felt empowered, accomplished and excited for this chapter. This would be my best year. Phil, on the other hand, was pretty well spent with the hardest, dirtiest and most disgusting of construction assignments. We bolstered each other with jokes, teased and impersonated Dad.

There was no warning. Dad picked me up from the one room office with Phil already in the car and announced that we would be staying in a different trailer. After living with Ginny and Dad for six weeks, we were to move into a trailer catty-corner from theirs. We were in shock; what was the matter? Why were we not living together?

Dad fumbled and said that Ginny never had children and was finding it difficult to acclimate to a family situation. She felt crowded.

Phil and I looked at each other. We spent only dinner and evenings together and were never aware that we were "crowded." Just as we were perplexing over this new development and trying to catch our breaths, we arrived at our new digs: A camper trailer older than both of us put together, with one double bed made from a sleeper couch, a cooler for ice and a bathroom with toilet and sink. No kitchen, no shower, no air-conditioning, no TV or radio, no sheets and no privacy. Dad hurriedly explained that it was rented for one month. We could tough it out. And now we knew Ginny was a "snake in the grass." "Nice goin," Dad!"

It was a weekend, and we were hot, cramped, mad, hurt and going crazy. I knew we had to leave. This arrangement was untenable, and the betrayal was shattering to our bones. Talking to Dad about it was not a viable option, so we sat down on the old, old couch and began to see what we could do. Both of us agreed immediately that, in view of the present betrayal, we were not at all certain that we would get the promised payments at the end of the summer. Thus far, we had not received a dime for toiletries or other minor necessities that all human beings need. I started asking questions.

"Fippy, do we have any money?"

"Annie, I have five twenties that I brought for an emergency. I didn't tell you because I thought you would be afraid that I would spend them. But they are under the inner lining of my work boots."

"God bless you, brother! Is that enough money for gas to get us to Indiana to our grandparents?"

After Phil affirmed that it was, I asked if we could get the fifteen year old Buick from the worksite that Dad had promised us at the end of the summer and drive it to Indiana. He thought and was silent for a long time. Then he said that he had to get the keys, but that meant going to the worksite, getting the keys and the car. Dad would see it at our trailer. Then, we exclaimed in unison: "Not after they go to bed!" So the plan was hatched, and we couldn't wait to escape to Indiana and to people who loved us: our mother's parents.

A little before dark Phil left for the two mile hike to the worksite as I sat and thought about our lives. I would be okay no matter what, but Phil was so tenderhearted, so easily abused, so needful of acceptance and love that I worried about his future. He had been conceived on the night before Dad had shipped out of San Francisco for war in the Pacific. Mother had gone to the West Coast with him to say good-bye, leaving me with her mother. Phil was born nine months later, a son that Dad did not see until the war was over. Bonding never took place, and Phil was nick-named 'eightball' by Dad ever since I could remember. My brother never really had a chance at being accepted; he was small, not interested in school, although very bright, disorganized and an attention-grabbing clown. He was the opposite of his father. I was witness to the ongoing fact that Phil never caught a break, and I often wondered why he didn't hate me as the favored child. He didn't ever show me anything but true love! We were a year apart, but treated as twins by Mother and our cousins. We were always together, sticking up for one another and so close in age. Many family members would ask about the "twins" and treated us as such. We became used to this characterization until we left our home town and began to sprout really different personalities and preferences.

Since it was the weekend, Dad did not miss us, nor did he know, of course, that we had driven straight through the night to our grandparents home near Ft. Wayne. We took turns driving and drinking lots of coffee. Our sweet grandparents met us at their back door, as usual, and were surprised and excited that both of us were there. Grandpa was a six foot three gentle man while Grandma was not quite five feet tall. Mutt and Jeff. They were certainly two of the kindest souls Phil and I were privileged to know, love and go to for help. Grandma wanted to know immediately if we were hungry. YES! We were starved. Grandpa knew something was amiss, but, always a patient man, he waited until we had some food in our bellies and then asked why we were at their house together and hungry. He mentioned that he thought we were in Kentucky working with Dad.

I started by saying I thought they should sit down because this would not be a short story. Looking at Phil, he waved me on to continue our saga of the summer. We both expressed how sorry we were to interrupt their lives, but we felt safest coming to their house. We said we just needed a place to land, think and put a plan together for returning to Purdue. I was doing fine until Grandpa asked if this was my senior year which I am certain was a question meant to affirm what he well knew already...one of those tactics that one uses to buy some time while they're thinking. The mention of my senior year, though, brought tears to my eyes, and I excused myself to the bathroom for a few minutes.

By afternoon, Grandpa said he had a plan. Assuring him that all we wanted was a place to stay where we could think and figure our lives out, we soon learned our Grandpa wasn't having any of that. We were the kids, and they were the grownups, he informed us. Then he offered his plan. We were to inherit Mother's part of their estate which would be about two thousand dollars apiece. He would give each of us that money now, contingent on talking with his other three children and explaining the circumstances. My brother and I became misty-eyed immediately. It sounded like pure love, not money.

Sunday morning Grandpa informed us that he was going to call our dad and needed the phone number. He said it was only right to let Dad know where we were and why. One did NOT argue with this kind man when he became firm on a subject. Offering the number, I listened with Phil while Grandpa made the long distance call on the rotary phone. We heard Dad's booming voice as Grandpa identified himself. There was a lot of rhetoric about unappreciative kids and how hard life was and how soft his kids were. Grandpa stayed calm. He explained that his children were safe and preparing for college. He hoped this could be worked out. Dad was irate, to say the least. He informed Grandpa that we had stolen his car, taken it across state lines, and that if it was not delivered to his Indiana home within twenty four hours that he would file charges for our arrest. Calmly, Grandpa agreed, thanked our dad for talking with him. We didn't have the slightest idea what to say. Grandma obviously knew that Grandpa needed to speak first.

Grandpa finally said that tomorrow morning after breakfast we would go see his friend at the used car lot and get a car for us to use and get to school. He further informed us that he would withdraw the money from his savings account to give us our inheritance, minus the cost of the car. Then…he said the most beautiful sentence in the world: "Grandma and I will come to visit you once during the semester, if that's all right." We may have hurt them when we both hugged them so hard and long, knowing that they were giving us one quarter of their whole life savings to help us…AND would come to visit.

The next day Grandpa and Phil drove to our house an hour away, deposited the car and drove our new (used) Chevy back together to the little two bedroom, one bath house, fully-paid-for home of our loving grandparents.

We eventually thought to tell them that we had two weeks of work waiting for us at a Purdue bookstore, so we must leave in another two weeks to be there to start our jobs. I asked Phil where we were going to stay. He teased me with stories of sleeping in our car before he informed me that he still had the key to his fraternity brother's apartment, and that the guy probably wouldn't return for another week. That left me with a week to figure something out for myself for the week before school opened.

I had no doubt that the sorority house mother was an appointed angel from heaven. She agreed to let me move into the house four days before the others moved in, with the proviso that it was "our secret." No one will ever convince me that there aren't angels in our paths.

Love all, trust a few and do
wrong to none.

William Shakespeare

While we spent time with our grandparents, I painted the classic "senior cords," thereby officially ready for my final year. Chava was coming in November for five days to meet my grandparents and Aunt Madge and her family. I, in turn, would meet him in Mexico City for the Christmas holidays and have a chance to meet his entire family. Having so much to look forward to, plus all the senior activities, I found myself feeling some relief that Phil and I were on our own and no longer hoping, wondering, guessing and feeling stressed about our financial situation and Dad's angry moods.

Phil kept the Chevy at his fraternity house which was the right thing to do. He needed it for his dates and his part-time job. Because he was a guy I thought it would help him feel more like a man. As it turned out, I really never needed it. There were plenty of senior sisters with cars, and I had no business or affairs to conduct off campus. All I really had on my mind was counting days until Chava's arrival. My heart didn't race as much as it did last year because letters were not a good substitute for being held by someone you love and feeling the palpitations that signal the closeness and shared excitement. But still the remembrances of so many things we had shared together in Paris created videos that ran through my head so often.

I had the tickets in hand that he had sent me so that I could meet him in New York City, see some sights and then fly to Chicago where Phil would pick us up. We were all looking forward to this fall break time with a family that was dying to meet the guy that I couldn't stop talking about. In fact, my relatives were all so cute trying to be on their best behavior. They teased him about stealing me from my homeland. As is true with so many Mid-Westerners, my family took him in as one of their own. They fed him a good Indiana fare of fried chicken, mashed potatoes and skillet gravy served with their garden veggies and homemade sugar cream pie. Accepting seconds, or better yet, asking for them, was a proper thank you. Chava had listened well as Phil and I had prepared him for family customs. Time never passed so quickly as those five days, but Chava had not seen his family in three years and was eager to lay eyes on them as well. I was so grateful that he came to see me first, I didn't whine about his leaving for Mexico City. I would see him at Christmas!

Even though it was starting to get really cold on campus, I was packing lighter weight clothes for the two weeks in Mexico City. Phil and I were having dinner together at our favorite hamburger joint and making plans about plane departures and arrivals because he had wheels. He was to spend the holidays with our relatives and spend some time in our hometown with his high school friend, Jim Bob. At one point he laughed awkwardly, asking what I thought the "old man" was doing for Christmas. I told him if I had money, I would bet that Dad and Ginny were at their home in the Bahamas. We cheerfully raised our cokes, and I toasted "Merry Christmas, a time for family and peace." Phil choked on his coke.

We were both sure that I would miss my flight due to a massive snowstorm that had traffic backed up forever. Multiple vehicles were off the road, wreckers were traveling on the gravel edges trying to remove impediments to traffic as quickly as possible. Phil borrowed a few of Dad's over-used expletives, which I happened to agree with. We were both grateful that the old man had taught us both how to drive on snow and ice, an art much needed in Indiana winters. When we finally arrived at O'Hare we were beyond relieved that my plane was delayed due to de-icing procedures. Phil hugged me good-bye and warned me not to get married while I was gone. He assured me he would be the one walking me down an aisle. Then he admonished me to be sure to catch the return flight home.

I was so familiar with Mexico City that it felt a bit like I was coming home. And there could not ever have been a more gracious family in all of Mexico than Chava's mom and sisters. Their patriarch, son and brother, was a star for them, and they treated me as an honored guest. Talking non-stop for days, spending enchanted evenings at restaurants in the Zona Rosa, the tony section of Mexico City and attending holiday parties was beyond fun, but extremely exhausting. At each fiesta a beautiful and long-time friend of Chava's made sure that she approached me. She politely quizzed me and recited years of activities with Chava. One of his sisters noticed this ritual and explained that the senorita had always expected to marry her brother. Asking if they were engaged, I was quickly assured that that was not the case, but definitely a presumption on the young woman's part that one day they would be. His sister patted my shoulder and informed me it was obvious to everyone that I had the inside lane. Chava interrupted the conversation to say that our hosts, some German-Mexicans, were clearing the dance floor for a polka. Being raised in northern Indiana, a haven for German-Americans, I grew up dancing the polka until we were totally drenched in perspiration. Chava mentioned he had a slight headache, but wasn't about to miss the fun. After telling him I had a long history of polka dancing, he grabbed me and we went swinging and clicking and dancing until we became breathless, and we were one of the few couples still left on the dance floor.

Just as I was about to suggest that we join the saner folks on the sidelines, he stumbled and lurched forward while dragging me with him. I knew I would fall if I didn't let go. As I disengaged from his forward thrust, I saw him fall. As I rushed forward, so did many others. A number of physicians were guests at the party. All of them rushed to help. With a fervent request that we all stand back, a doctor ordered him rolled over, holding his neck carefully, asked for an ambulance and began to examine him. When he put his ear to Chava's chest and mouth I became very concerned. I was usually excellent in emergency situations. But now my respirations were shallow. I became lightheaded and talked to myself, using "he'll be fine, Annie" as a mantra that I kind of sang in my head to steady my growing fears. I could not see him for the five or more physicians surrounding him. At one point a small viewpoint opened. And I saw his face. I thought that he looked lifeless. He was probably just unconscious. I gasped and squeezed my burning eyes.

The ambulance arrived and took him away accompanied by two of the doctors, his mom and older sister. The party obviously ended abruptly. I remember people leaving, going to the restroom and, eventually, sitting in Chava's living room. I have no recollection of the missing parts that connected those scenarios.

His younger sister excused herself to take a phone call. Unexpectedly, she screamed a primal scream that remains forever unforgettable, and she collapsed. The kind people that had brought us home rushed to help her. Tears were pouring from me; nausea was in full force. I swallowed hard. One of the gentlemen picked up the phone. As he hung up, he slowly announced to the small assembled group that, tragically, Chava had suffered a massive rupture of a brain aneurysm followed by a fatal stroke. The only word I heard was "fatal," which is basically the same in Spanish as English. I remember thinking if "fatal" meant "dead."

Shock and grief are an insane mixture. Unable to sort things out in my brain as the entire room was erupting in screams and gasps and "Dios Mio," I sat...paralyzed. All that ran through my head was that this was impossible. We were dancing, planning to announce our engagement, having fun picturing a life together, working on logistics, feeling so in love and so incredibly blessed.

In Mexico, when death occurs, the wake is almost immediate, and the funeral follows. This happens all in 24 hours. Sitting at the wake, I removed myself to the back of the room. My heart and head could not begin to translate all that was being said to me. I so needed to be alone and not pretend that I could survive this loss. Having moments of lucidity, I felt annihilating grief, raging anger, homicidal and suicidal momentary thoughts, questions about my own sanity, hatred for doctors, shame at some of my thoughts, and, most of all, profound, overwhelming sadness. I found I could not cry. One breath at a time was hard enough.

His poor family was destroyed. Understandably, they had almost no awareness of me. I knew I was suffocating there and unable to help in their massive grief. I packed my bag and left the best-written note I could manage. I went to the airport, cashed in my return ticket and bought a train ticket all the way to W. Lafayette, Indiana. This would allow me time to think, pray, absorb, cry, and find some direction. Really, I wanted the time of the extended train ride to try to gather my thoughts into some kind of order that I could live with and walk in daily. Life for me had totally changed.

When Mother died, we sat watching every breath, knowing death was imminent. This sudden, unexpected death was cruel, savage and destructive. It meant the evisceration of my future, my beloved and my life. Fleeting thoughts of our unborn children, of our wedding anniversaries, the weddings of our children, grandchildren and life together visited my insanity.

Somewhere between the border and St. Louis, I sat staring out the train window, oblivious to passing scenery, except for the entrance into a long and beautiful forest. My spirit awakened a bit. I sat up, took a deep breath and shut my eyes with my feet flat on the floor instead of curled under me. As I called her name in my head, her essence appeared through the softness of her answer.

"Sissy, I don't know where to begin, what to do, what to ask or how to feel. I need help to hold onto myself. I am floating, and I see no where to land. I am not making sense to myself. I go from self-pity to anger to beseeching someone/anyone to fix this, change the tape and then back to self-pity. I feel shame, blame and total loss. It's hard to imagine my life has meaning now."

"From all our conversations, I believe life's events are illusions of our making to learn precise lessons that will lead us to the feelings and behavior that bring us closer to love. But I swear to you there is no way I would have attracted this illusion or this lesson. I was fully in love for the first time in my life, bringing forth greater happiness that I had ever imagined. I know the lesson of loss: I learned that well with my mother's passing to the Other Side. But Chava's leaving and passing over makes no sense whatsoever to me."

"*Dear one, this illusion was indeed a beautifully crafted courtship and eventual union of two souls so open to adventure, learning and personal growth. Every soul has its unique journey to fulfill its chosen purpose, and Chava's passing over was no mistake. However, I do not have the answer of why his journey took that turn. His goodness stays with you and also goes with him. He gave you the gift of learning how to accept love, something you did not know how to do before. You are exquisitely adept at gifting love to others, but love always hopes to be a reciprocal act. Perhaps he came only for that purpose; one will never know on this plane.*"

"How do I retrieve my selfhood and my beingness when I feel so empty, so gutted and so abandoned by what I believed in and trusted. Something in me is closed. Whatever it is has made me feel different, almost not alive...just kind of mechanical and robotic."

"*Annalee, you are choosing to suffer. Suffering is a hiding place where one may easily choose unhappiness, using a myriad of self-pitying stories to create a narrative to justify the act of turning from spiritual love. EgoMind creates a mayhem of all the perceived wrongs, slights, broken promises, unfair happenings and convinces you that you have no choice but to suffer and are justified in escaping into the darkness of hopelessness. On this darkened path, one will practice forgetting their true nature, their true legacy from Spirit, their ability to open to the healing powers of love. True spiritual love accepts the illusion, sees beyond the story created around it, and it lets all negativity flow through without depositing the sediment of ego's destructive forces. Breathe in love, exhale fear! Let the sensation of perfect love and protection flow in, around, through and beyond you. You can use your visualizations powers to create the process for you to exit the devastating grief and lift yourself into the higher realm of knowingness that affirms all is well. This illusion is a story lesson which creates more need for you to find more portals to higher consciousness. It is a process. I recommend you do this: fully live this moment, then knowing it is gone, fully live the next moment. You only have the moment...there is nothing more. It is, however, the vehicle that carries you on your journey with purpose. Moment by moment in high consciousness brings the awareness and experience of pure Truth which is pure Love. Choose, dear one, to purpose to live consciously. That is the only path."*

As I slowly opened my eyes, I noticed the forest was no longer beside the train, and my breathing was easier. The black hole in the middle of my chest was still there, but the need to cry or wail had passed for now. As I thought over what Sissy Jean had just said to me, I felt an urgency to put some kind of formula to her words so that in times of returning grief I would not forget the healing process she had shared. The formula that developed was: 1) invite the feeling of the experience, 2) observe what story or meaning I am was assigning to the experience/illusion, 3) after the recitation of story, let the experience FLOW through me and outward into the universe and 4) give thanks for the lesson and know that all is well. I realized that in doing what the formula outlined I would be recognizing, embracing and blessing my hard lessons on the path to Love. I realized for the first time that Spirit and Spirit Mind are, genuinely, my TRUE nature. How that popped into my awareness I will never really know. But now that I knew it, it could not be erased. It would be possible to IGNORE the Truth, but I could never again DENY the Truth. I felt a moment of peace.

Phil was waiting at the train station in W. Lafayette, Indiana, the home of the university. I almost lost my balance and my breath when I saw him. How did he know I was arriving on this train? How could he be here to meet me? I considered that I might be losing it. When I ran to him, he hugged me and grabbed my suitcase.

"You don't look so good, Annie. Did the trip go okay?"

"Fippy, how did you know to meet me here?"

"You called me, silly. I thought I would be going to O'Hare. And I bet it cost a pretty penny to call me from Mexico City."

"I don't remember calling you. I'm sorry. I was very distraught."

"Well, I don't blame you. I don't have the slightest idea why that guy would break up with you. You're the best there is. So sorry about your broken heart."

"Phil, what did I tell you. I don't remember."

"Well, yeah. You said Chava was gone. That your life was ruined, that you needed to come home."

"That was it? Nothing else?"

"Well, you told me about the train and the schedule. I'm not a mind reader, I promise. Otherwise, I'd have an office on campus selling exam answers. Come on, it's cold."

I don't know why I didn't correct his misconception. As I thought about it, I kind of relaxed into the idea. I would not lie to him. However, I could say that it didn't work out, that he was gone or that sometimes life really takes a turn that hurts like hell. Knowing there was some deception at base, I relished the idea of having some absorption time, some time of my own without having to explain things…and most of all, I was not ready to deal with condolences and sympathy. Put simply, I was not ready or willing to be engaged with my world in a fashion that worked for me yet.

Phil and I stayed at his buddy's apartment until the day when I could legally move back into the sorority house. Sisters were all abuzz with stories of the holidays and questions about my trip. Using the deception I had discovered shut down any more questions, I accepted their sweet of expressions of "I'm sorry" or "Geez, I've been there. It hurts like hell" or "Time will help" along with their sincere quick hugs. I also knew that news of his death would put a pall over the sorority house, and the girls might treat me differently. Most people don't know what to say or do with the passing of a loved one. Everything could be awkward. In my heart I knew I was protecting myself and was not ready to fully embrace the truth of the events or my unknown future. I felt safe, but also alone, guilty and tired.

My melancholy the last semester of school was evident, but everyone chalked it up to the loss of my love relationship. It became such an accepted fact that I gave up trying to figure out ways to correct the misconception. I let it stand. And I spent the entire semester practicing the Sissy formula for the mitigation of suffering, with growing success.

Graduation was coming as evidenced by all the bulletins sent to seniors regarding gown rental, diploma fees, family accommodations, tickets for the ceremony and photographer stations. I tossed all of them in the trash but for the one that was a request for a mailed diploma, which required a real address. My grandparents gladly gave me permission to use their home address. They would have been front and center at a ceremony but for the recent stroke my grandma had suffered. They had visited Phil and me the first semester of that final year, while staying at a suite in the Union Building and walking slowly around campus with us. We doted on them, teased, shared dinner at the hamburger joint and thanked them a zillion times. It was the first time any family had actually come for a weekend visit. We informed everyone we knew, like it was an international event. Our friends nodded nonchalantly! Some things in life are everything to some and nothing to others. Illusion at work!

As an assistant in the French and Spanish language labs, I was in the Romance Language building almost every day and enjoyed my part-time job. When I applied for the job I had a great time with the interviewers. They asked in English if I had much experience or had taken many courses in these two languages. I, rather haughtily answered, using colloquialisms in both languages, demonstrating an ease with the interview. They affirmed my employment on the spot. I apologized to the universe for my behavior…with ever so slight a smile.

I walked out of the office of the chairman of foreign languages after collecting my paycheck. I turned the wrong way in the hall and happen to see a large bulletin board. As I turned to head the opposite way, I stopped to read the postings under Graduate School Assistantships. The University of Virginia and the University of Washington were seeking applications for teaching assistantships for their graduate program in Romance Languages (Spanish, French, Italian and Portuguese) for the coming year. The requirements were a two year commitment to the university to teach two classes each semester, one summer session, a university transcript proving a B average or better and a letter of interest. Taking down the information, I went directly to the sorority house typewriter, filled out the applications, wrote the letters and ordered my transcript sent. Both Virginia and Washington received identical applications.

Slowly recovering from my Mexico City trauma and slowly exiting my grief, I began to realize I had no idea what I was doing the day after graduation. Many sorority sisters were getting married that summer, planning wedding showers, shopping for gowns and ordering invitations. I needed to consider my options for life post-Purdue. Going to my grandparents would be a burden and going home was not an option. Working all summer saving for whatever was in my future was obligatory.

Almost a month to the day later I had three letters in my mail cubby. Accustomed to nothing but flyers and advertisements, I was in no way excited. The first was an acceptance letter from the University of Washington, awarding me a teaching assistantship which included a waiver of all fees and tuition and a stipend of $140.00 a month, a livable wage to cover rent and food and maybe books.

The second letter was from Chava's older sister, kindly expressing her sorrow for my loss. Her understanding and consideration were extraordinary. She included apologies for their behavior at the time I left, and news of their life and their mother's progress in handling his passing. The note was sweet, considerate, but wound-opening. I quickly folded it and put it away. I would re-read it later.

The third letter had a French stamp that I was so familiar with from all Chava's letters. Not recognizing the name, I wondered at its purpose. Soon, it became evident it was from the student concierge at my Cite Universitaire residence in Paris. She had been requested to inform me of news about Jacqueline, my special sister-friend. The kind concierge reported that Jacqueline had never returned to the Cite. Her belongings were still in her room paid for by her French father, and no correspondence had been received from Jacqueline in this past year. Further, her father had hired investigators in Vietnam to try to track them and help them. No success had been reported to date.

Contrary to what Sissy had sweetly taught me, I engaged in the pathetic narrative of suffering: Mother and Chava were dead. Jacqueline was missing in action. Dad was AWOL to family. My grandma was the victim of a stroke, probably caused by the stress of Phil and me. I was essentially broke, and I desperately needed to find a job and quarters for the summer. The trajectory of my life did not look especially promising, and I still nurtured an aching heart.

Tell me and I forget. Teach me and
I remember. Involve me and I learn.

Benjamin Franklin

Momsy and Popsy, parents of a sorority sister, approached me on their monthly weekend visit and asked if we could talk in the corner of the living room of the sorority house. Hardly anyone ever went into the formal living room except with parents or for interviews. I was so delighted to have some time with them. Everyone loved Linda's parents and their fun names. I nodded yes. We all had waited for the dress-size box of homemade chocolate chip and oatmeal raisin cookies that Popsy carried up the long walk while Momsy opened the door and promptly deposited them on the vestibule table so every passerby could grab one. After grabbing one for myself, we scooted into the corner with its three elegant chairs, sat and talked a minute about graduation. Then, Popsy said outright: "We all want you to spend the summer with us. We have the room and would love for you to come." I was totally taken by surprise! I finally found a proper response of thanking them for their kindness and would love to accept. I knew they lived in the country outside Indianapolis, and I needed to work. Before I could finish any explanation, Momsy said that they had thought about all that. If I found an evening job I could use her car. Protesting that this was all too much, Popsy admonished me to hush. He said: "Annalee, we know you have no parents and no place to go. Our place is as good as any. So consider it done."

When the semester ended, Popsy loaded my stuff in the car, and we all headed for their place in the woods. The universe knew that I needed nature and the company of loving people. I quickly found a waitress job in a bar across from the Indianapolis Speedway. I memorized the names of cocktails, and made sure I wore eye shadow and lipstick to work every day. An hour before leaving for work, I would play a game of Hearts with Linda and her dad. Popsy finally guessed mid-summer that I counted cards. He teased that I should let him win more often, and I should have because the kind, sweet nature of this couple was a memory I would keep forever. Not only did they give me food and lodging as a courtesy, but they also showed me by their example the everyday workings of a loving relationship. As I soaked it up, my melancholy began to dissipate. There were so many times I wanted to tell them about Chava, but the daily life was so idyllic, I refrained from my selfishness. I was so grateful for a summer of the best psychiatric care one could ever receive.

When they dropped me off at the Indianapolis airport for my two leg trip to Seattle, I hugged my three family hosts for a very long time, not knowing when the next hug might come. I was going across country to study languages I already knew so that I could get a master's degree without any idea of how to use it was inexplicable. All I knew was that I was good at languages and wanted desperately to find someplace new. Of course, my brother was my one regret. He would be on his own. I was not sure that he would tend to himself and his needs appropriately, knowing that he often displayed large gaps in maturity and wisdom. Knowing that he needed guidance, love, acceptance and a sense of belonging, I hoped his fraternity brothers would be a safety net for him. He had assured me that he "always landed on his feet." Despite my concern, that was actually true.

I knew the minute I took the bus from SeaTac airport to the University that I had made the right decision. Turning down the second letter of acceptance to Virginia was more of a geographical decision that an academic evaluation of programs. The Pacific Northwest was full of national forests and year-long evergreens with mountains in the background and the Puget Sound in the foreground. The San Juan Islands decorated the waters off the coast, and Vancouver was a small distance to the north, just across the border with its world-wide reputation for arts, culture, architecture, gardens and diversity. Paris and my travels in Europe and North Africa had erased any trepidation about new places or concern of acclimation. I not only was ready for Seattle, but I was excited for the experience.

After renting a room from a widow who offered her two vacant bedrooms for female graduate students, I treated myself to a walkabout of the beautiful grounds of the University. The Medical School, Law School, Engineering and so much more were all situated around a center focal point of a large plaza filled with cherry trees. I walked the "Ave," the nickname for the avenue adjacent to campus where one could find book stores, t-shirt and sweatshirt shops and the best French Dip sandwich ever.

The next day I reported for teaching assistant orientation at the School of Romance Languages and Linguistics at Denny Hall, the oldest building on campus. I sat in a room of mostly men with the exception of fellow classmates, Angela (Angie) and Isabel (Izzy). The lone female faculty member sat with her head down and never looked up the entire period. As soon as the protracted and repetitive meeting was concluded, I turned to Angie and Izzy and motioned that we should leave together and have a coke. They were in lock step with me as we exited to the eternal drizzle of Seattle and headed for the "Ave." Within an hour we decided to cancel any previous living arrangements and live together. We soon became the "Three Musketeers." The guys knew better than to play us off one another.

Our two bedroom, one bath house sitting on a hillside, as almost every house in Seattle does, was ten blocks from campus. This seemed to be nothing of a hike to class after walking miles around and across Purdue. So I approved of our choice and volunteered to share a room with Izzy. Angie had her own room. It was fun learning that Izzy had spent one year teaching at a poverty-level salary and was returning to graduate school for a master's degree to up her pay category, while Angie had just graduated from the University of Montana and was a beauty queen using her scholarship winnings to come to UW. I volunteered that I thought I was getting married, but when that didn't work out I decided to try graduate school on a whim. Izzy teased that it appeared she was the only one with a purpose, and that she envied our freedom to casually decide to continue our schooling. Assuring her I was at the poverty level too, I noticed that Angie said little. Later, we learned her family was multi-generationally well-heeled, with multiple homes and large safety nets. Fortunately, we got along extremely well and were protective of our group.

My studies were interesting and relatively easy the first semester. Much like Paris, I spent time in art galleries, museums and book stores, places that gave me pleasure. This cost me nothing and allowed me time to contemplate, wonder and investigate. On one such outing, I was standing in a narrow aisle in a bookstore looking through the philosophy section. A big man bumped into me, politely asked my pardon, and started a conversation. Pleasant, sort of jolly and with an extensive vocabulary, he engaged me in a conversation about existentialism because I was holding a book by Jean-Paul Sartre in French. He remarked that I might want to exchange it for a copy in English. I smugly retorted that I would prefer to read it in the original, having attended a lecture by the author. He roared, said "touche" and asked if I would like a cup of coffee as an apology for his erroneous assumption. Having a rush of guilt about my earlier "smartass" retort, I assented.

Sissy had instructed me numerous times to practice awareness, mindfulness and to always take an inventory of my intuitions. Her motto was indelibly etched on my every day thoughts: "The Universe wants the best experience for me, but I must choose according to my knowingness." It was just this precise intuitive feeling that I knew my conversation with Arval, the bookstore bump guy, would probably be entertaining and, perhaps, enlightening. Way to go, Sissy!!

Within a short time of mutual quizzing of each other's history, I learned that Arval was a former college football player and looked the part! Additionally, he was a full professor of law, specializing in constitutional law, was well-published and had won the famous loyalty oath case in the U.S. Supreme Court. There was no bragging or haughtiness in his disclosure. I had intentionally pushed the issue, wanting to know what he was proud of in his life.

It was time for me to do my new part-time job tutoring football players. I stood up to thank him and said that I hoped we might run into each other again. He responded with: "How about coming to my house for dinner tonight?"

"I don't think that is wise. I don't really know you."

"I am inviting you to my dining room, not my bedroom. And my wife's name is Wendy. We always cook together," he laughed.

"You win. We're even: Sartre faux pas and wife faux pas."

He wrote his address on a napkin. As he was doing so, I simply explained that I had no car and did not know the bus system of Seattle. True to the attitude of a law professor, he instructed me where he would pick me up and at what time. He continued, "And don't be late. It will be raining."

Wendy put an apron on me as we were being introduced. I inquired if her husband often brought vagabond women home with him. She answered that he was very discriminating so she was eager to know what tantalizing wiles merited sharing dinner with them. I liked her immediately.

As I was preparing the salad, she asked if I liked artichokes. That was followed by another inquiry about avocados to which I informed her that I loved them but was, however, allergic. As she handed me a large Haas, she squealed with delight that she would have my share. My hosts were well matched and sparred with double entendres, inside jokes and bawdy humor. It was the first of many dinners with great table conversations.

I learned that Wendy was pursuing a master's degree in Slavic languages and spoke Russian well. I confessed that I knew not two words of any Slavic language and that I had not been drawn to it because of its guttural sound. Then I remember her teasing me, saying that I had taken the easy route with the seductive musicality of the romance languages. Perhaps she had a point.

As the semester marched toward the holidays, I secretly became a bit melancholy once again. I had our little house and an invitation to Arval and Wendy's home for Christmas dinner with all of Wendy's family in attendance. Shortly before the holiday break began, Wendy asked one night at dinner if I would like to bring a date. Without thinking, I told her that I wasn't ready to date yet. She looked up from her prime rib and said: "Bad break-up?" I easily said: "Really bad. He died."

She stared at me with tears in her eyes, expressed profound sorrow and asked me to tell her about it sometime. I slowly agreed. Had I finally broken through my wall of secrecy and protection? I was grateful for having had the time and wisdom to do the necessary grief in my own way. But I wish I had found an equally soothing way to grieve my mother. I always felt guilty for not allowing my sorority sisters to assist in my grief, but I had protected myself believing I was protecting them. When one feels alone, she is alone. I had not yet learned to trust anyone, even those who cared for me. I had a lot to learn.

Wendy's family wrapped me up in friendship, attention and humor, creating a memorable holiday dinner and Christmas celebration. At one point her mother casually asked if I were religious. I answered that I was on the path of trying to figure that out. She laughed and retorted: "Aren't we all!" A few nights later, after a hasty phone call from Arval telling me they would pick me up in fifteen minutes, we sat down to dinner with the guest that Arval had been chatting with in the living room.

The male guest named Doug was sort of rough looking, rumpled and scruffy, donning a Gilligan hat decorated with numerous fishing lures. The hat never came off. However, that was of no concern once the dinner table conversation started. Arval made a habit of presenting me with an ethical dilemma problem for dinner discussion, saying that one always had to hone his critical thinking skills. Actually, we just enjoyed the banter. Due to my honed debating skills and my Father Uribe education in critical thinking, I didn't embarrass myself. Wendy would often groan that it made her brain hurt. But that night, with Doug and Arval easily discussing the most erudite of topics, Wendy and I remained absolutely quiet and mesmerized for the two hour discussion. Finally, Doug announced that he needed to be going because he had some fish to catch early the next morning. As Arval was taking me home, avoiding the dirty dishes, I commented on how fascinating the evening had been and asked if the other lawyer practiced in Seattle. Arval laughed and informed me that Doug was a jurist in Washington, D.C. When I inquired for which court, he said: "That would be the big one!' Geez, I had just spent the evening with William O. Douglas, youngest ever Associate Justice of the United States Supreme Court!

Izzy and Angie had gone to see their respective families for the holidays, and I was feeling lonely and envious for some of the same family togetherness. Having no idea where Phil might be, I skipped over the possibility of hearing his voice. And, of course, I never found the courage or especially the inclination to see if Dad was home. I called Momsy and Popsy and got the much-needed warm fuzzies.

Second semester was so much easier. We three gals knew the ropes, had side jobs tutoring linebackers in a foreign language (that got more foreign weekly) and had our group of friends. The only down side was that Angie was dating Eddie, a "bad boy," that gave me the creeps. Izzy and I usually left when Eddie came around, knowing that Angie needed some privacy for her intimate relationship. Izzy disapproved on moral grounds and I, on intuition. Eddie was a local artist and perpetual part-time graduate student hoping for a MFA degree one day. He was a major mooch, which Angie could afford, but Izzy and I could not.

Very early on a Sunday morning in late April, the house began to shake like we were in a blender. The crash in the kitchen was deafening, and Izzy was losing it. When the calm came, I tiptoed to the kitchen to find the breakfast nook that was on stilts on the hill part of the house was gone…just gone! We had an open air kitchen with booze everywhere. The bottles left from the BYOB party the previous night had walked themselves off the counter, breaking and splashing all over the floor. The landlord showed up about an hour later, announced the house was condemned, and informed us we were to leave immediately and kept our deposit.

Housing near the university was hard to come by and even harder after an earthquake. Fortunately, we found a two bedroom apartment on the bus line that a married couple had just vacated for non-payment of rent. For once, we were grateful to Eddie and his car that we could move the same day. When the three of us reported for class the next day, we found Denny Hall was now condemned and uninhabitable. It felt like a Chinese fire drill trying to find classrooms spread all over campus. Of course, the aftershocks were hard to get used to. We soon learned to hold onto our purses and anything nailed down so we would not fall, just bobble.

At one point the local newspaper advised everyone to put a piece of paper with their name on it in their pocket in case they were caught under rubble. For a while it felt like a third world country. When the bulldozers came onto campus, the clean up went quickly.

The end of the semester came, and my world changed. Izzy failed to make the grade average necessary to continue as a teaching assistant and left for home. She had received a failing grade in transformational linguistics, a formidable, required course that had one three hour exam at the end. I, personally, have always disliked "all or nothing" situations because it can be a roll of the dice.

Arval called my apartment the afternoon after the semester ended and said that Wendy had moved out. She left a note and had moved in with a fellow grad student. She wanted a divorce! He was heartbroken and lost, and inquired repeatedly if I had any inkling of this. Of course, I didn't. That totally surprised me. My intuition was usually on high alert. I could see that keeping up with Arval was arduous work and maybe difficult for a good marriage. To compound matters, Arval was to leave the country soon for a sabbatical in London and Geneva, teaching constitutional law, American style. So my two best buds that I so enjoyed were going to be AWOL.

Angie had gone home for a week between the end of second semester and summer term. I was left alone in the apartment after

Izzy packed and left. After a dinner with Arval who was still trying to come to grips with his life changes, I wanted to get in bed early, do a meditation and just enjoy solitude. At the end of that thought, the doorbell rang. The peep hole revealed that Eddie was outside and wanted to talk. I said that Angie was gone and that I was tired. However, he was relentless and begged to talk to me because he was lonely. Against my intuition, I acquiesced and let him in. He had a half empty bottle of whiskey in one hand. He plopped down on the sofa, took a swig of Jack Daniels and whined about missing his gal as he got drunker by the moment. After unloading the dish rack and putting china away, I looked over to discover that he was passed out on the couch. No amount of poking and prodding would arouse him. After about an hour, I covered him with a blanket from Angie's room, put on my nightshirt and went to bed.

In the middle of the night I totally lost my breath when Eddie landed full force on top of me, holding my wrists tightly against the bed and pushing his knees into my inner thighs. Screaming and thrashing and calling his name to stop, I was in serious pain and feared the strength he used to hold me down. At the pitch of one of my "Nooooo" screams, he fell hard onto the floor next to the twin bed. His sexual assault was unsuccessful. I lay still, barely breathing, fearful he would attack again. As I heard snoring, I inched my way silently down to the end of the bed, walked to the front door, put on my long trench coat, boots (always in Seattle), grabbed my purse and hurried out the door and down to the front steps of the building.

Darkness and drizzle were my companions as I sat on the steps, embracing myself, rocking back and forth and taking deep breaths. This was the second sexual assault in three years and the second escape from the brutality that I could have endured. I was so mad, so scared, so ashamed that I had let this monster into my apartment because of my affection for Angie. I should have listened to my intuition and was so grateful I was alive. As I contemplated asking for help or going to the police, I considered it was my word against his, and I had voluntarily let him into the apartment. The bruises on my thighs were not yet evident. Eventually, I just decided to be quiet until Angie got back. At that point I would fully describe the event to her with a zero tolerance mandate prohibiting Eddie from ever coming to visit again.

At about six-thirty in the morning Eddie walked past me on the steps and went to his parked car. Obviously still somewhat drunk, he drove off never having noticed my presence. Certain that he was gone, I entered my apartment and left the door open. After checking every room and closet, I closed and double locked the door. I sat down to take stock of my life, my environment, my goals and my boundaries. I felt absolutely violated and alone. I would access Sissy as soon as I was calm enough to meditate.

17

If you wish to succeed in life, make
perseverance your bosom friend,
experience your wise counselor, caution
your brother, and hope your guardian.

Joseph Addison

I walked aimlessly in the drizzle until I found a park where I could quietly sit in meditation and feel safe. My apartment felt like an instant replay video of yesterday's unsettling event. I had been traumatized and knew the answer was to become present in the here and now. I stayed on the course of present awareness. The bench appeared near some azalea bushes whose dead blooms were now scattered on the nearby lawn. The cessation of the drizzle encouraged me to sit down and close my eyes. I called her name very softy. She answered with her customary warm signature of love I had experienced for many years. Her loving voice brought a sense of relief and assurance, quelling some of my anxiety.

"You are very present and open to me at this calling. We are united in love's healing balm to enter the classroom and resolve the situations that have brought you pain and beckoned Ego Mind to exert influence and control. You are in a battle with angry and unconscious people--those of low vibratory resonance, unaware and controlled by Ego. You have been drawn in. Consider them your blessings and greatest gifts of your recent life experience."

"Sissy, I have so enjoyed Arval and Wendy. I was compatible with my roomies, but I agree I was not in awareness with Eddie. I am trying to stay out of judgment and trust a bit more. I am not being particularly successful, and I feel my neophyte status in awareness is failing me when I need it most."

"Child, I repeat that you are in the classroom to learn to deal with the challenges that unconscious (unaware) friends, family or others present. Challenges may often draw you off balance and trap you in the clutches of Ego. Earth school often focuses so much on the intellect and its production that one easily slides into un-awareness and into power struggles that produce reactivity and low vibratory responses such as arguments, rationalizations, denial, hurt and competitiveness. Students are expected to follow the example of the teacher. If the teaching is high vibratory stimulus, that is to say of a high awareness and consciousness, you will easily float along. However, those

of low vibratory energy and unawareness will challenge or try to destroy your peace. If your teacher is of low vibratory energy it is often easy to be absorbed into that energy. You must be conscious at all times."

"Sissy, I truly loved Arval and Wendy. Their kindness and inclusiveness were extraordinary and appreciated. How can that have ended so sadly?"

"I cannot answer for their paths, but I know they are blessed. Your precious friends have their own challenges and lessons to learn which they have manifested for that purpose. Your reception of love by the two of them was a mutual giving of high vibratory moments. You felt it profoundly. However, their non- awareness or unconsciousness of other issues were not being addressed in their daily lives. They will be good students on the path to enlightenment. Thank them. Please remember that nothing is ever ruined, just postponed."

"And the sexual assault and rape attempt by Eddie? Another challenge I manifested for some higher purpose?" I asked in a slightly sarcastic tone and then immediately felt apologetic.

"Annie, there are no accidents in life. All behavior has purpose. It is no accident that you escaped rape twice. It is also no accident that you somehow manifested this trauma twice. These two challenges have significance--no more, however, than any other lesson. You so whole-heartedly wish to access and live in conscious awareness that your personality proposes extreme challenges to make the point for you. You may want to look at your need for the extreme. That is an Ego construct. Consciousness has no degrees. You are accustomed to being at the head of the class. That is not appropriate or possible on your road to ongoing consciousness. If you stay aware and remember this, you will not manifest assault again."

As I returned to the apartment, I had a new understanding and new purpose for my life journey. I felt a liberation in this knowingness as well as an obligation to live my awareness. Second year graduate school would be different and purpose-driven with a hint of low vibratory rebellion and the excitement of awakening.

When Angie returned, we immediately had our necessary conversation about Eddie. After listening to me, she informed me that Eddie had called her at her parent's home. He reported he was over-wrought. He told her he had gone to our apartment where I sexually came on to him, and he had to push me away. Hearing this, I made clear in a very firm and declarative manner that if she believed that, she should find separate quarters today. She had one hour to consider her options. I left for a walk on a rare sun-shiney day. Upon returning, I was assured that she was breaking up with Eddie and would not ever let him into our quarters again. Since she would probably see him again, my intuition said he would not be re-visiting our apartment. I was never sure that she believed me, but that did not matter. I knew the truth in vivid color. And I would not soon forget. But I would be vigilant and conscious.

In addition to the usual course load required of a teaching assistant, I was required to write a master's thesis after successfully passing a three day written exam over all course material covered in the first three semesters. During the third semester, the student candidate must present a thesis topic for approval and defend the proposal before a committee of three faculty members. Being a bit obsessive-compulsive, I checked the exam and proposal off my to-do list as soon as possible and started writing the thesis outline. Research and organization were paramount to be able to complete everything on time that was required. I began to see it as a job deadline with my focus being to keep checking off boxes.

My intense focus on organization and production culminated in freed-up time so that I could participate in some of the things that higher consciousness had recently made aware to me.

My previous travels had not only broadened my tolerance and acceptance of all sorts of differing world views and behaviors, but also had heightened my awareness of discrimination, social injustice, political manipulation and gender inequality. I might not be able to change the world, but I felt a need to be a party to focusing a spotlight on these issues in loving and appropriate ways. This began my life-long participation in peaceful protest. I marched the "Ave" in support of the freedom marches of Martin Luther King, Jr. on his Selma to Montgomery March in the South. Segregation and discrimination are void of love, compassion and the concept that we are all one. I marched again against the war in Vietnam. We marched to honor the brave soldiers, but the American Presidency needed to be held accountable for lying to its citizenry. This war was not necessary. As I was finishing the anti-war march, a woman walked up to me and spat on my face. As I allowed the spittle to run onto my dress, she screamed "Peacenik" with high vitriol. I marched on without a hint of recognition, staying a course of consciousness that I hoped echoed some meaning to those watching. Kindness, caring, involvement and patience taught a lesson better than a classroom lecture or reactivity ever could. And lastly, I volunteered at the Medical School to give speeches in the community speaking out about female genital mutilation. While assisting Dr. Henri Caron in the Rif Mountains in Morocco, I had witnessed the results of this mutilation on every female patient. It is extremely painful to girls and often times caused harmful, ongoing infections and, sometimes, even death. My speeches highlighting awareness brought gasps from audiences made up, primarily, of university personnel. However, it also brought donations to the World Health Organization for world-wide education to help eliminate the horrendous practice upon female children, helpless victims of tradition and male insecurity. I frequently caught flack for the speeches because the subject matter "did not concern Seattle."

My message was clear. "We are one." "We are one." "We are not separate." These words have to be said to an unconscious world that is full of people with hearts that have a remembrance of knowingness and deep inside know that love is curative. We do not turn our heads away from suffering; we reach out in a myriad of ways.

At Christmas break every friend I had went home. I called Phil, and he said he had some news that I probably wouldn't like. Holding my breath, I waited while at least ten scenarios sped through my head. He announced that he was getting married! Stunned, I asked who, why and when. He confessed that he was not cut out for college, wanted love and a family and he had met the right girl. It seemed right to him. He knew that I could not come to Indiana for the wedding, but he would send pictures.

Catching my breath again, I asked if he had a job. The answer broke my heart when he said he was going to work for Dad as a foreman on one of the many construction jobs Dad had in a five-state area. Hearing my groan, he tried to assure me that he knew how to handle the old man now. He would just let him blow and verbally abuse him because he knew how to let it roll off his back. This was pure nonsense. My sweet, kind-hearted brother could never survive Dad's daily barrage of put-downs and insults. I was afraid he was going to be damaged, and I couldn't stop it. Although I begged him to look for other work, I was soon convinced that he was set on this course of self-destruction and was unwilling to be convinced otherwise. With all my heart I wanted to hitch-hike home, kidnap my brother and teach him about mindfulness and consciousness, but the same heart knew he had his path, his discoveries, his sufferings and joys and his growth timeline. I said a very explicit prayer for his sweet, sweet soul. I felt I had lost a part of my brother.

It was a miserable Christmas holiday due to a full-blown winter cold with all the accompanying chills, fever, cough and self-pity. Seattle was always damp, and respiratory bugs were not only prevalent a lot but were also my nemesis. Dragging myself out of bed and down to the little grocery store on the "Ave," I headed for the soup aisle to buy what Mother always gave us when we had a cold: Campbell Chicken Noodle Soup. Feeling awful and remembering Mother's kindness and care when we were sick, I started to weep. As I tried to control myself, an older woman with the face of an angel patted my arm and asked what was wrong and if she could help me. I blurted out that my mother had died. It had been over six years, and I told this lady those words like it was yesterday! I will never forget her response.

"Darlin', you need to cry a lot. We all want and need our mamas. Let's get your soup, and I will walk you home."

I have often thought that my mother visited that day in the form of this "grandma persona" that showed such genuine love to me. As the woman walked me to my door, she reached out to hug me. I stepped back, warning her I had a bad cold. She stepped forward, hugged me warmly and ordered me to drink the broth of the soup. She told me she never caught colds and wished me "Merry Christmas." I became less miserable and decided to spend some time doing a feeling inventory.

New Year's Day was fast approaching, and never having made resolutions at the beginning of the year, I thought I would fill a rainy day by making a list:

1) I want to be open to romantic love again, but not so fiercely.
2) I want more adventure, doing things differently, but appropriately.
3) I want to do more service volunteer work.
4) I want to talk with Sissy about a possible relationship with my father.
5) I want to be less competitive with myself.

I looked at the list and smiled. This might take a while, and I wanted to be honest with the discipline to try to fulfill these goals. It was usually best to start with the easiest and work up to the hardest because I knew you built self-confidence on the way up. I decided that volunteer work was the easiest. Therefore, I approached the Med School, offering my services as a translator for pre-procedure immigrants. However, when they saw my resume, they asked that I work in the Sexual Transmitted Disease clinic as an intake interviewer for females. I assumed they thought my experience in Morocco might qualify me as someone accustomed to seeing and dealing with STD patients. I, also, quickly got the impression that they had had some difficulty in filling the position because they offered to hire me. The director was over the moon when I informed her that this was my volunteer commitment. She expressed her gratitude, explained that it was mostly evening work and made me promise not to quit after a week. The fact was that I really liked the interaction with the sex workers. There were frightened teenage girls that wanted to be assured that I would promise not to notify their families (the exception being disease via incest), wives that had had sexual contact outside the marriage, rape victims that didn't want the police involved and women who could not count the number of sexual encounters and wanted to check if they were "safe." Compassion and tolerance had always been my long suit, resulting in good and not-so-good consequences. In the clinic the patients sensed the good part, which helped the process immensely. I worked three nights a week on Tuesdays, Thursdays and Sundays and was able to do something I felt really good about, and I could write on my thesis if work was slow. The director said, repeatedly, that I should be a counselor. I responded that I had zero training and waved her off.

Sitting in Dr. Panuelos class in Spanish poetry, I came upon an idea for an adventure of sorts. He had assigned a paper in which we were to do a stylistic comparison of a Spanish-speaking poet and an American poet of somewhat the same period. Pablo Neruda of Chile was a favorite of mine, and every student of this particular professor knew Dr. Panuelos loved T.S. Eliot. It was also universally known that everyone made a B or C in his class. An A was, unfortunately, impossible. The adventure that I was to set upon in his class would qualify for one of the things on my resolution list, but also cause trouble with self-competitiveness. Oh, well. It was too much fun to take a pass.

I wrote a decent paper to present in the one hour allotted time frame for an assignment in front of Dr. Panuelos' class. I also memorized the entire Lovesong of J. Alfred Prufrock by Eliot and included some of the drama training from my high school performances at the Lions and Kiwanis Club of my hometown. Having time at the clinic, I would practice until I knew it perfectly, without difficulty. At the actual class presentation, when Dr. Panuelos realized I was reciting totally from memory, he relaxed in his chair at the back of the room, closed his eyes and enjoyed the recitation. I got the A and had fun. An adventure!!

Before the final thesis approval, I had to pass the qualifying exams. Studying hard, memorizing for short term recall and taking the exams before the other candidates, I felt prepared and eager to check off the box. All worked well. I finished writing the thesis and setting a date for the graduate committee grilling to defend my writing, assertions and conclusions.

The spring day was soul-feeding with plenty of rare sunshine, balmy breezes and perfect temperature. I thanked the universe for this wonderful gift as I walked to my thesis defense, feeling invulnerable. As the committee started the session, they were kind enough to ask how I was feeling. I easily commented on the gorgeous day and my delight in being able to defend my work and start interviewing for jobs. They smiled, grilled, complimented and stood up to shake my hand, and said that it was a pleasure. I imagined that was probably pretty routine by the time one had passed all required courses, qualifying exams, thesis topic approval and the final thesis defense in two years.

On the way out, I ran into a fellow graduate student who volunteered that he had just finished an interview with the Vice-Chancellor of the Dallas County Community College District. He really liked the guy and would take the job if offered, but he lived in the Rio Grande Valley and wanted to return there. Noting that I was all dressed up because of my thesis defense, he suggested that I hurry over to the Union Building where interviews were conducted to meet the guy and get some experience. I did as he suggested, caught the guy on his way down the hall, interviewed and three weeks later was notified I was hired. A contract, including a full description of the job, benefits and facts about Dallas would follow if I still was interested. I threw kisses to the universe! I had a real job and would start in late August as a college instructor.

I kept my new job secretly to myself since there were others struggling to find a job in the location they preferred. Now I must seek full time summer work. I needed a car, gas money, luggage, rent deposit and funds for necessities in a Dallas apartment. Once again a bulletin board in the Language Department, now located near the Library, had a posting asking for applicants for two summer sessions teaching Peace Corps volunteers. Applicants needed to be fluent in Spanish and males were going to teach re-forestation in Chile, while female volunteers would teach nutrition and midwifery. I thought to myself: "I'm your gal!"

My languages skills and my Moroccan medical assistant work were just the ticket. Government pay was better than university pay. I could do something I liked and not have to give up my apartment. Angie left a few weeks early after the semester ended, but had paid her share on the lease. I had time to myself to read what I chose and cook vegetables, which I rarely ate after Arval left because they were expensive...but most of all, breathe a little.

My summer was filled with young, enthusiastic Peace Corps workers who were total delights. They were prohibited from speaking English in their dorms or classes. Total immersion in the language was necessary to grasp enough linguistic ability to leave five weeks later. The Medical School provided the midwifery training, which would really be assisting women in Chile who had been birthing babies themselves for centuries. Our main goal was to convince Chilean mothers not to wrap and bind the legs of newborns, which caused deformed limbs and crippled toddlers.

There were ten days between summer sessions in which time I could accept an invitation from an LA businessman who had been asking for two years that I go to French Polynesia with him as an interpreter to get permits to export processed foods (ham, sausages, pepperoni, etc) to Tahiti. I called and informed him I could do it then if he still wanted to go. All arrangements were made. We flew to Honolulu, stayed the night and continued on the next day to Papeete. He had made all the necessary appointments with government officials, not realizing that nothing in Papeete happens on time. The population was fun, happy, relaxed and easy-going. I had appointments lined up all day long for three days which ended up taking almost six days. With permits and sales orders finally in hand, I managed to rent a skiff to Moorea to enjoy a day on the beach. But Bora Bora would have to wait, and I needed to get back to Seattle. As I boarded the plane in L.A., the CEO of the food company handed me an envelope and thanked me for my hard work as a translator, negotiator and social hostess. I thanked him as I stuffed the envelope in my purse, ran down the jetway and plopped down in an aisle seat.

Getting ready to return to Peace Corps classes for survival training in the woods, I dumped out my purse to get some essentials and head for the training field. I had forgotten about the envelope with jet lag and excitement intervening. I took a second to tear it open. Five one hundred dollar bills with a short note saying it was a bonus for work well done. Oh my God! I had the down payment on the Karmann Ghia I was dying to buy. It was only a year old with a price tag of sixteen hundred dollars.

Showing up for the Peace Corps training in the woods with an orchid lei around my neck caused a commotion of fun. At the end of the day, I gifted it to the only other female instructor who was overjoyed. As soon as I was at my apartment, I phoned the local bank and asked for an appointment for late afternoon the next day. Degree in one hand and a job contract in the other, I was ready to provide evidence that I was a good loan risk for twelve hundred dollars. The loan officer looked at both documents, my driver's license and the car VIN number. Leaving me sitting while he talked to his "boss," I told Sissy that she could help on this one. She silently told me that was not her job! He shook my hand, returned my documents and told me I was granted the loan. I was now legally in debt, having a car loan and a government education loan on which to make monthly payments. I began to pack a nice piece of Samsonite luggage I had found at St. Vincent de Paul thrift store to replace the one that had served me for several trips to Mexico, Paris, Madrid, Africa, New York, Chicago, Seattle, LA, Honolulu and Tahiti before the clasp just gave out! Good-bye Washington with its magnificent forests and hello Texas, a new state and a new adventure.

Remember that children, marriages
and flower gardens reflect the
kind of care they get.

R. Jackson Brown, Jr.

18

There was very little time to get to Dallas in my new car. It was packed full with one suitcase, a box of books in the back, kitchen utensils and some towels in the front seat. I drove straight through, sleeping every now and then at a safe rest stop. Long-haul truckers seemed to be my friends as I settled into the cradle of several convoys and felt well cared for. Approaching Dallas, I drove to the address of the college so I would know how to get there the next morning for orientation. After a much needed, much appreciated, long, hot shower, I laid my only nice outfit on the motel bed, smoothed the wrinkles and then hung it in the bathroom steam.

Deceptively fresh and relaxed, I reported to the new faculty orientation on time and mixed with colleagues from all over the nation. The community college was brand new and the first of seven planned for Dallas County. The press and city fathers were all present with Texas-size welcoming handshakes and proud comments about their city and this new educational project. Thank God lunch was served since I was down to less than ten dollars and my checkbook. I needed to find a bank where I could cash an out- of- town check. No bank would open an account for me without waiting seven days to clear the transfer check from the Seattle bank. I approached the president of the college district school board who was also the president of a Dallas bank and informed him of my problem. He walked me and several others to his bank where he told his employees to give us VIP treatment. I felt good that I was an extrovert and a take-charge kind of woman, and thanked the universe again that right thought creates right action.

After a long day or orientation, I searched for an apartment and found one in a nice neighborhood. It was fully furnished with all bills paid. I signed the lease, found the nearest Sears store, applied for a credit card, bought my very first TV and some respectable clothes for teaching. My sewing machine was in the trunk, but I needed materials. That would have to wait until the weekend. Double bed sheets, TV and a small plant went on the new credit card. Now I had four monthly payments: car, student loan, rent and Sears. I felt I was very All-American and a full-fledged member of the working class.

Saturday morning my new car got an oil change, and I visited the Dallas Teachers Credit Union to set up a savings account. Conveniently, a block down from the Credit Union I spotted a fabric shop and bought enough yard goods for three skirts and jackets. Back at the apartment, I put the books on a shelf, the TV on an end table, the kitchen stuff where it belonged, some groceries in the fridge, made the bed, hung a towel and settled in. Dallas was now my new hometown.

Monday morning the secretary of the division chairman's office asked for my phone number. Having totally forgotten about needing a phone, I informed her I would let her know as soon as it was installed. After a hefty phone deposit, I realized I now had five monthly payments, and that I was fast building a credit score.

Since I had never lived in the South, I needed to acclimate fast. The twang was very distinct, the manners always cordial, the pace somewhat slower and the culture much different from Seattle. I was a liberal, free-thinking female in a conservative, male-dominated city, and I felt I needed to recalibrate my behavior if I wished to fit in and be able to do my job. Not easily playing the role of the sheep, I operated with caution and learned quickly. And a fellow female English instructor colleague willingly shared her opinions on what I needed to know. Becoming fast friends, we made this new experience much easier for each other. The students were delightful. Half of them were older than me and returning to school after raising families or retiring. The mixture of ages, as well as cultural and socio-economic backgrounds, were intriguing and interesting to navigate. Being the youngest faculty member, I got teased a lot and hit on frequently. It always surprised me when I found out that a married faculty member was asking me out. I quickly learned to ask if the suitor was married. I smilingly shook my index finger when the answer was: "Not today!"

As a newly-graduated member of the faculty, I had the lowest salary possible because pay was based upon years of teaching experience and degree level. Even so, I still was hoping I could afford a ticket to the symphony or a live play every so often. Season tickets had millionaire prices, but, perhaps, there were individual performances that I could attend. In Seattle I often attended a coffee house with live music, such as early performances of Janis Joplin and Bonnie Raitt before they became well known. Much to my delight, Dallas was beginning to focus on performance art and cultural events.

At the beginning of November, a polite and well-spoken colleague, a government and social science instructor, was seated next to me at the monthly faculty function at a local restaurant. His ability to discuss current events and debate either side of an issue impressed me, and I liked his Mid-Western accent which matched my own. Before the evening ended, I had learned he also was from Indiana, had done his graduate work at the rival Indiana University and that his mother still lived in his hometown. My dad's company had recently replaced the town's decrepit sewer system and sewage disposal plant. He was appropriately quiet about his liberal points of view, but was an avid student of FDR. He smiled when I told him that one of my heroines was Eleanor, and I was committed to naming a daughter after her. By the time he walked me to the car, I had accepted his dinner invitation for Saturday night.

His silver Oldsmobile convertible was parked in front of my apartment exactly on time. Punctuality was a paramount characteristic I desired in anyone, especially a date arriving for the first time. Thoughtful and polite, he asked what food I might be craving, and Italian cuisine of any kind was my quick answer. He must have had a place in mind for all options because he drove directly to a quaint Italian restaurant with fewer than ten tables. We enjoyed verifiable home-cooked Italian. This guy was punctual and organized and planned ahead. He had my attention. Good conversation without sensationalism was the dessert that tipped the decision to accept a second date invitation.

Prior to Joe, I had squelched all romantic endeavors post-Chava. I had good male and female friends, all interesting people, but my chest had been cracked open when I lost Chava. The healing was slow. Aggressive men were boorish. Recently divorced men were needy. Popular men felt a bit ego-maniacal. Chastising myself for such judgments, I blessed them in my mind and stayed away. Joe, however, was easy-going, goal-oriented and kind. I grew continually more comfortable around him, planned weekend time to accommodate Friday and Saturday night dates and looked forward to our get-togethers with a relish that was interesting, though not intoxicating.

Aware that I certainly was not falling in love, but I was in major "like," I continued seeing him for most of the first semester. Both of us were private by nature, so the faculty was not aware that we were becoming a couple, which gave us more freedom to get to know each other.

Sissy and I had our times together, but I needed to be more aware of my situation and my feelings, so I set aside some early Sunday morning time for our meditation visit. I had been thinking about going home over Christmas to see Phil...and Dad. It had been a while, and I was muting the historical, vocal ugliness, creating illusions of sweet family reunions and wanting desperately to know that my brother was loved, cherished and happy.

On the sofa with the morning sun warming my face from the nearby large living room window, I closed my eyes, fell into deep meditation where consciousness is at its highest, and whispered. She spoke and loved, all in one sound.

"My child, we are here to love and learn. I know that your heart is weighing many egoical illusions that are so well-defined that you experience them as real. They are not your truth. However, I recognize that you are open to acknowledge your need to establish a relationship with your dad. So, maybe we can begin there."

"Sissy, I need help understanding him so that I can tolerate his personality and not be absorbed into his dynamic hostility, overriding pessimism and hurtful judgment. It is extremely difficult to stay in high consciousness when I feel barraged by emotional bullets. I need tools, insight and an openness to try to love him without fear."

"Dear one, thank you for asking to learn a lesson that will accompany you your entire earth plane experience. Your dad is an excellent example of a perfect soul who does not know his goodness or believe he could find it and live it. He believes his existence is a war of 'us' versus 'them', where he has to be perpetually on guard and totally in control. That is the abnormal way he has found to feel safe with his fear. His illusions are that the world is harsh, rewards are few, others are not trustworthy and happiness is illusive. Almost everything he feels is projection, which is the practice of assigning to others that which one actually feels himself. He doesn't trust others because he feels untrustworthy; he sees his business partners as cheaters because he would like to cheat (or does, in fact, cheat) as he assumes they do, or he tries to control others before they have a chance to control him because he greatly fears loss of control."

"Whoa, girl! That's a lot to put my head around. I have always been afraid of him. Does that mean my fear of him equates to me being afraid myself?"

"Exactly. So, my child, look inside to your knowingness to give definition to what you are afraid of, which, of course, is an illusion to teach a lesson."

"The first sensation that arises is that I am afraid that he does not love me because he doesn't treat me lovingly or say that he loves me. I have always felt that I was on probation, and that as soon as I proved I was good enough, I might get some sign of approval or acceptance."

"I know, sweet love, that you have worked very hard to deserve his approval, when, ultimately, all this illusion is to show you that HE needs approval, acceptance, recognition and the freedom to finally accept himself. You both have played your parts well in trying to achieve the acceptance that was already yours, absolutely holy and free of charge."

"Sissy, I feel trapped in action/reaction scenarios every time I am with him. His ego is his identity. He is angry, has to always be right, speaks righteous indignation and is a bully. If I see that in him, are you saying that is also in me?"

"Child, what is in you when you interact with your dad is ego identity. You allow yourself to be dragged into the battle, the unholy definitions that are the result of accepting his illusions that he holds dear. You both have a common divinity. Don't let go of yours. Do not mistake your ego identity for who you really are. You must stay conscious and aligned with Spirit. Have faith that you can do this and see your dad's divinity."

As I sat mulling over everything Sissy had said, I kept hearing the words "see your dad's divinity." Nothing about the combination of those words was anything I had ever thought about or could believe, at least for the moment. Dad and divinity...dad and divinity. After a while I stopped thinking of him as Dad. I changed the focus to think of him as a brother human being, knowing that we are all one on the planet living our contrived illusions thinking that they produce survival or some sort of insurance to combat our fears. Then I saw him as a little boy, scared and hungry in the Great Depression, a young man with academic and track scholarships to Purdue because he was valedictorian and ran cross-country to get to school and back, a newly-married soldier going through unspeakable battles, a father way before he was prepared for the role or the responsibility, an entrepreneur who always thought he was going broke, an older brother to three others who had no vision or goals except to survive, caretaker of a father who expected it without contributing or gratitude, a man exhausted and who felt cheated in life no matter how much he gave or did. Dad lived on a diet of fear and self-pity, but he got up every day to pay homage to his suffering and destructive illusions.

All of a sudden I realized that I knew who he was and that I had a leg up knowing that we were divine and stuck in our family struggle illusion that would continue without my intervention. To intervene, I knew that I had to stay in high consciousness, know when to keep quiet and not confront anything unless to not do so would do harm. I should give love the best I could and know that the illusion is not the Truth. I felt a bit of confidence, but not a whole lot! Having spent twenty-five years afraid of him, trying to please him, hoping for some even ground, I took a deep breath and picked up my phone.

When he answered my call, I started with pleasantries, trying to set some sort of cordial stage for the conversation. Rather abruptly, he said: "So to what do I owe the pleasure of this call?" With more than a touch of sarcasm, he continued with some hesitancy since we had not spoken since Phil and I had skipped town in Kentucky. I lovingly replied that Christmas was coming, and I thought about coming home for a visit if they were going to be in town. There was a long pause as if to say that it would be a tremendous stretch on his part to allow me into their plans. Chastising myself for this thought, I waited for an answer. I almost giggled when he said that a lot of plans would have to be re-arranged, but I could come for a few days. I recited my plans, dates and desire to see him, his wife and Phil, his wife and new baby girl and that I was looking forward to the reunion. I remember questioning if lying was okay in an illusion. Guilty as charged?

Joe was also going home to Indiana and asked if I would like to ride with him. I was not ready for that much time together, so I informed him of my intention to fly to Indianapolis, but thanked him for his offer and kindness.

I found all sorts of little packages on my office desk before Christmas: baked goods, Christmas tree ornaments, sweet hand-made cards (some written in deplorable Spanish!), a Christmas wreath with Mexican decorations, a sarape and other gifts of utter kindness. Feeling a bit like the first grade teacher getting all sorts of goodies sent by the parents, I thanked my classes for making my first full semester of teaching so "damn much fun," to which there was a whooping and hollering reaction. I choked up at feeling the blessing of being with these students at this time in Dallas, Texas. What an adventure! Living on my own while doing something I loved felt light, wholesome, mending and somewhat healing.

Phil picked me up in Indianapolis. He looked not only older, but actually looked old. His wife and my niece did not accompany him so I had a two hour window to learn everything I could. It soon became apparent that the marriage was not what he thought it would be. Affection and emotional support were lacking. He loved his baby with all his heart. Dad was a bear and demanded so much that I thought I heard innuendos of self-destruction and suicidal ideation in some of Fippy's remarks. When I confronted him and affirmed that he did not have to work for Dad or live near him, I heard feeble excuses from a broken man. I ached to the point that I felt homicidal toward a man whom I had traveled to interact with in higher consciousness. That was not happening in my heart or head. He had a responsibility to be human to his son that he always degraded to "make a man out of him."

My niece was beyond cute, and as I held her I understood my brother's loyalty to family and his sacrifice to come home to his sweet bundle every day. His life was rote and unforgiving, putting one foot in front of the other to get to the next day. Then, I got a hint of some of Dad's behavior exhibited in Phil's interaction with others. I began to understand that he must, at least unconsciously, feel that if he were to be successful and accepted as a son he would have to imitate the behaviors of his father, employer and demagogue. My feelings were in a centrifuge, whirling in full-blown ego reactions, and my willingness to be fully conscious and view the illusion from afar was evaporating rapidly.

As I slept in my childhood bed, I felt angry, vengeful, spiteful, protective, guilty and as uncomfortable as I could ever remember. Walking around my bedroom, remembering Mother sitting at the end of that very bed after she passed, wishing to see that faint smile for even a second, feeling much more like a child than an adult, I sat down to try to put some order and plan to this moment. Higher consciousness or good acting? My knowingness begged for honesty and acknowledgement of this painful illusion, but my whole being told me I could not survive the ongoing encounter with my father if I didn't put on a good act. I really wanted to get the heck out of there, but Phil had no room at his house, so I stayed in my room, slept very little and showed up for Christmas dinner.

As I was feeding baby Kim, Dad starting asking questions.

"So...you still seeing that Mexican kid?"

"No, I'm not," I replied without elaboration.

"Good. Just as well," he volunteered.

"You dating fellas in Dallas?" he inquired.

"Sometimes," I answered flatly.

"You're not liking girls, are ya?" he half-heartedly asked.

"Nope."

"Well, when ya pick one out, let me know cause I'll be walking you down the aisle! And you'd better hurry up cause you're getting up there, and I deserve grandbabies."

Taking a deep breath, I mentioned that I thought he had a very cute one that was asleep in my arms. He waved me off, rose from his chair and left to go read. As I gave Baby Kim to her mother, I held back all manner of screams and went to help with dishes.

I visited high school friends, held their babies and felt like a foreigner in my home town. I had come home to embrace my brother who I could now see was visibly uncomfortable with himself and his situation. Sadness filled my heart. Dad was unapproachable and insufferable. I, above all, was full of judgment and unease. I needed to leave.

> Man cannot discover new oceans
> unless he has the courage to
> lose sight of the shore.
>
> Andre Gide

19

Grateful to be on a jet back to Dallas, I thought of Sissy Jean and her teaching that all perception is illusion created to serve the cause of the lessons we came into form to learn. I truly did not like my perceptions or present experiences, but knew I needed to look at why I was creating them. Was I supposed to see that I never would have a real family to enjoy, feel the support of, or have fun with? Did I still carry the fear of my dad's wrath because I thought I deserved it? Was its purpose for me to learn to stand up to it? Was all family an illusion, and not even my brother and his pain were real? Was I to help Phil, bless his path, teach him what I knew, rescue him or just love him? The picture in my head of a Fippy as a beaten down kid in his youth broke my heart. I vowed to call him more often and remind him of the good in him and in his world, especially his precious Baby Kim.

As I sat back to close my eyes and think, I thought about Dad admonishing me to hurry up and get married and have babies. Being in no hurry, I dismissed any thought of an obsessive search for a husband, however. I did entertain illusions of a family of my own someday. Many women have marriage and family as a goal. I did not. I rather liked living life and seeing what happened rather than encouraging the illusion to happen so that I could meet some cultural expectation set for twenty-four year olds. There was also the haunting, hurtful memory of the loss of a fierce love that unconsciously warned me against trusting a long-term relationship. I opened a book to read, put aside thoughts of the future, and escaped into someone else's illusions on written pages.

The Dallas winter didn't have snow, but it did have ice storms. Very few on the road could navigate driving on ice except Yankees. Schools, courts and many offices simply closed on icy-road days with good reason. They didn't want their inexperienced drivers to lose life or limb trying to brave the weather conditions. When I showed up at the college on the first ice day, I was laughed at. Lesson learned!

Joe and I continued to see each other, cook together, go to

cultural events and talk about life goals. He wanted to go to law school, so I encouraged him to take the LSAT, the first necessary step in the application process. We went to Southern Methodist University to tour the campus and meet with the Dean for further information. SMU was inordinately expensive, and law books were several hundred dollars apiece. The secretary to the Dean told us that one out of three freshmen would graduate and that the first year was the toughest. None of this deterred Joe from wanting to apply.

After receiving a high LSAT score, he navigated all the other necessary hoops, including our joint effort in writing an essay with the application. He was notified of his acceptance.

Shortly after his acceptance, we attended a major community college conference in Houston. As our elevator descended, Joe produced a small, blue velvet box from his pocket. He opened it revealing a solitaire diamond ring and, affectionately, asked me to marry him. Before I could think or answer, he grabbed me and kissed me and said we would have a wonderful life together. I never said "yes," but I didn't say "no." He put the ring on my finger and announced to the crowd of colleagues outside elevator that we were engaged. Everyone started congratulations and celebratory comments. It was a heady situation, fun and surprising, so I went along. I wish I had made a decision, but I just went along...just went along.

I became caught up in the excitement, and I began to think of myself as engaged and "in love." It was definitely not what I had known before as "in love," but I convinced myself that respect and compatibility counted for love. I knew I loved this kind man. Unfortunately, I doubt I was ever "in love" with him...or he with me. We simply met each other's purposes in life at that time.

There are no mistakes, just decisions that one should or would not make the same way again. I tried to believe we had a purpose together. Also, I stayed away from my meditations and my conversations with Sissy, not wanting to confront this illusion and the consequences of not going through with all our plans. I wanted to be normal... NORMAL...normal. What in the hell was normal? Right now, it seemed like normal was getting married, putting my husband through law school and starting a life and family together.

Our students were so excited for the two of us, as we were two of the favorite faculty members. It was Hollywoodesque romantic that we were getting married. Students who lived in mansions in Highland Park were planning wedding showers for us, and one student approached me to offer one of the two wedding gowns worn by her same-size-as-me daughters only a year ago. I gladly took her up on her generous offer but had a hard time deciding between the two gowns. The champagne satin and lace one with a drop- pearl-on-the-forehead veil won.

Calling Dad to share the news was not a stellar moment. I told him that Joe was an Indiana boy going to law school in the fall, and we were planning an early August wedding. He congratulated me and said that I should write him all the details. As he told Ginny the good news, I heard her say that that was not a good time for the wedding because they had a trip to Canada planned. Trying to explain that we needed some time for a honeymoon and to get ready for law school, I was rebuked with: "Well, that doesn't work for us, so you need to change the date." I soon found out that the only date suitable to Ginny was the last weekend in August which was two days before Joe had to start law school at SMU. That meant no honeymoon, no preparation time for school and no consideration by my dad or his wife. I asked one more time if we couldn't negotiate something better. He firmly informed that this was the best he could do and that I should stop being selfish. Wanting to get off the phone as fast as possible, I hesitantly asked one more question.

"Dad, would you think about what kind of budget I can have so I can plan the wedding accordingly."

"Well, daughter, that's easy! You're a grown woman with a full time job. You can afford your own wedding. It should be enough that Ginny and I will have to buy airplane tickets and hotel rooms. Your Ole Dad isn't Fort Knox, you know."

I hated myself at that moment. I knew better. I was an idiot to think I could have a wedding like any other daughter. I didn't want him to come. I missed my mother. I hated Ginny. I wanted my brother. I wanted to run away. I was stupid not to recall that I had always been on my own since I left home. I felt so abnormal not to have a family. I cried myself to sleep.

I had to tell Joe that Dad was not going to help with the wedding, so the reception would have to be very minimal. He was extremely supportive, sympathetic and helpful. Confessing that when he told his mother that we were getting married, her response was: "Well, what's going to happen to me?" Recounting the reactions of both his mother and my father, we started to laugh and joke about our "great family support!" I knew Joe's dad had taken his own life when Joe was thirteen, and his mom was emotionally dependent on her sons, particularly Joe. We agreed to invite his mom to Dallas once a year, and also try to visit Indiana each summer for a week or so. The "parents" were an issue that seemed to bring us closer together, and there was a certain amount of comfort in standing together in our decisions regarding them.

Our wedding was beautiful. The flowers donated by a bride who had gotten married in the church in the morning were graciously left for our Saturday afternoon ceremony. The mother of that bride was so charitable and helpful that I felt like a member of her family. The aisle of Christ the King Catholic church is the longest in Dallas. Of course, Dad complained about it as we walked down to the altar. Joe's mother was in a full-length dusty burgundy gown with lace sleeves and looked very elegant. Ginny wore a turquoise blue, strapless, sequined evening gown. The contrast was as stark as it was painful to me. Dad refused to rent a tux, but he looked nice in his dark suit. I was successful in rising above all the illusions of the day, truly giving my heart and making a life-long commitment.

My three attendants looked wonderful in the tailored, gold gowns I had sewn for them, so I felt a sense of pride in being able to have a somewhat normal wedding. The reception was punch and pimento cheese, crustless sandwich wedges with nut dishes. I'm pretty sure it was the most streamed down wedding reception ever attended by most of the guests. Glowing and happy, Joe and I made most attendees feel our joy, and all were comfortable. My heart ached so much for my brother to be in attendance, but I knew he was with me in spirit. I knew that it had not occurred to Dad to invite him along.

Monday morning I accompanied Joe to SMU Law School orientation after receiving an invitation as the spouse of a law student. As I surveyed the auditorium, I counted three female law students and two hundred and ninety-plus male students. I couldn't help but wonder if few females applied or few females were accepted. I determined at that moment to study law along side Joe just to prove to myself that females were as competent as males! So much for the resolution of committing to not competing with myself!!

Joe and I made a big error in judgment when I committed to

working a full time day job and four nights a week to pay for law school. He committed to studying hard enough to survive the two-thirds cut after the first year. The result was that we had no time for each other. There were no casual conversations or even small decisions, let alone major ones. We were the proverbial two ships passing in the night. At the end of the second year of law school, I ended up in the hospital. The internist told me bluntly that I was suffering from extreme exhaustion, and that if I didn't stop the pace I was running that I would become seriously ill. I listened with skepticism. However, when released from the hospital, I went to the Dallas Teachers Credit Union and borrowed enough money to make up for the night classes that I would surrender at the end of the semester. After teaching straight through the summer sessions, I could see the end in sight. One more year of law school and then I could slow down. Then we could have a marriage. The fatal errors were compounding. Once again, I wanted normalcy, however that was defined.

Not having taken time for myself and certainly not feeling connected to Source, I sat down in our bedroom one Saturday afternoon to see if I could still find her. I really needed guidance and support. Meditation did not come easily. I was so out of practice and accompanied by doubt as to whether I was deserving after so long an absence. Eventually, I heard her voice. Feeling like a family member had embraced me, I poured my heart out to this loving entity. I told her I desperately needed help with my propensity to judge the actions of others and the overwhelming feelings of victimization and loneliness. Her lesson that day again changed my life. I remember every word, every nuance, every connection to Love and Truth. Source entered every part of me, and I listened.

"You, dear one, are encountering the Ego Mind of judgment. Let me emphasize that judgment is weaponized thought. It is a process of Ego Mind that experiences events or words of others and then places a valence factor of goodness or badness upon the event. Power Mind, the adolescent fiction of the Ego, feels empowered through judgment, using evaluation as a weapon for or against its immediate challenge.

I announce to you that all judgment is without merit and ego-created. Simply put, we judge in others that which we fear most in ourselves…so judgment, ultimately, is a revealing statement about our own personality construct and insecurities. Judgment is the crown jewel of Ego Mind because the illusion is that it creates power, a currency of evaluation, a feeling of superiority and a personal verdict visited upon the vulnerable or challenging opponent. Nothing, absolutely nothing, destroys the higher consciousness and connection to Love and Peace more than judgment."

"So what you're saying, Sissy, is that all judgment ever does is encourage Ego Mind to act against self and others and come to erroneous conclusions inside the created illusion that called forth the judgment in the first place?"

"Exactly. And there's more. Do not fool the self into thinking that negative judgments are the Ego Mind's only naughty and destructive thoughts. Judgments that are complimentary, feel good to others or received from others are STILL judgments. Those, too, can remove us from the peace of higher consciousness. Judgments can never be justified. Anger or attack as a result of judgments is never justifiable. The illusion will draw you into the sludge of judgment unless you remain aware and conscious. Always, always dismiss judgmental thoughts. They serve the illusion, not the Truth."

"Sissy, I have to think that what you are saying is almost impossible. Every day we are judged in this world by our behaviors, our opinions, our personalities and our skills. People are promoted or demoted, win or lose, fail or succeed, keep their job or get fired, make marriage work or get divorced and feel happy or sad all according to the judgments of others or themselves. It's how the world operates, and I see no chance of changing that."

"Dear heart, you are right. Your world does work that way inside the illusions of the multitudes that live outside awareness, outside the constant goal of peace and connection. You will navigate these illusions your whole life in the Earth experience. However, you know something you can never forget and will be unable to put aside or dismiss: You are a seeker of Truth. Truth does not exist inside the illusion. Only a shift in consciousness is the path to enlightenment, peace, love and re-connection with Source. You already have learned the lesson that Ego truth is a self-serving illusion. Spirit Truth gives peace. If you do not feel at peace, shift your consciousness immediately."

I knew Sissy was right. There are certain things one encounters in life that make such an impact that one is unable to forget the insight learned because it resonates as Truth down to rattling one's bones. Somewhere inside, you just know it's the Truth. Her lesson on judgment was one such resonating experience, and I was certain I would fail and succeed at dealing with this daily for all the days of this incarnation. It is a major, major part of managing the illusions.

My dad, mother-in-law, political blowhards, religious zealots, church leaders, Madison Avenue fashionistas, racists and prejudiced groups, xenophobes, homophobes and a thousand or more other irritating and anti-love, anti-oneness individuals were all possible recipients of my judgment or anger. After my meditation with Sissy, I became hyper-vigilant about my behavior and that of others. Was I observing or judging? It rapidly became a crazy-inducing exercise. I needed something that was soothing and helpful. I found it in the Buddhist practice of mindfulness and the practice of living in the moment. The "newness" of our life is all we really have. Each moment comes, we are mindful, the moment passes and we enter the next one. It is a useful and successful path to moments of peace in a hectic world of illusions.

Joe and I stood in the Rotunda under the dome of the Texas State Capitol Building as he was sworn in as a licensed member of the Texas Bar. The exams were behind us, the debts were almost paid and the job offer from a respected Dallas law firm specializing in personal injury and workman compensation law had been accepted. Now we could start our life for real.

As a "baby" lawyer, Joe spent at least 80 hours a week at the law firm and was exhausted most of the time. He assured me that this wouldn't last forever. While he worked long hours, I started studying other things to challenge myself and learn something new. I regretted not taking the bar exam because we simply did not have the money, and I could not take off summer school teaching to go to the law review course and study for the exam. Who knows if I would have passed it, but there was a likelihood that I would have. Soon after, the law was changed and only law school graduates could take the exam. Therefore, I dismissed that option and looked for new interests.

I found that I enjoyed studying investments: real estate, the stock market and arbitrage. Soon I was playing with a small make-believe portfolio that was doing rather well for a neophyte investor. We agreed to use a small bit of savings to see if I could manage it and make it grow. I felt a growing sense of maturity and confidence in being debt-free and investing in a home and some income-producing properties in the future. Making a defined plan for the implementation of these new ideas, I received a super boost to the plan when I was offered a promotion to become the division chairman of the English, foreign language, speech, drama and business communication department of a new college in the Dallas district. Opening a new campus was labor-intensive, especially since the planning work was in addition to my regular teaching schedule. Being busy, developing a new project and feeling productive were rewarding, juxtaposed to an otherwise mundane life at home.

I thought about my life. There existed a lack of passion that was insidiously becoming acceptable, a psychic numbing to the reality that Joe and I were good at being friends, but neither one of us felt passionate about the other. We were respectful, good citizens in the community, moral leaders and interesting participants in current event conversations. Regrettably, we were not bonded with one another in any way. The bonding time had been erased with our decisions to prioritize law school, work and rationalizations coupled with denial. Neither one of us wanted a divorce or even brought up the subject. Joe was comfortable with our life. I was eager for more. So I filled my free time with other passions: cooking, investments, dinner parties, speeches and seeking out interesting people who liked to use critical thinking to discuss a variety of things. In urging Joe to join these socializations, I believe that I was more shrew than persuasive partner. My frustration with his reluctance to create excitement of some manner in our lives was beginning to show, and I did not like that part of me whatsoever. So I re-doubled my efforts to find common ground.

For a couple of years I had secretly been yearning to have a family. I had been informed that I needed an exploratory surgery to ascertain if there was a reproductive system problem that inhibited or prohibited conception. The doctor was apologetic when he told me that my Fallopian tubes were like wet Kleenex, and an egg would not travel though them. It would be impossible to have children. Joe was kind, understanding and empathic. I was sad, forlorn and even more committed to having a family. When I mentioned adoption, Joe was very accepting of the prospect and began immediately to help with the process. For the first time we were totally doing something together.

The Edna Gladney Home in Fort Worth had accepted our application, and we both were ecstatic at the prospect of welcoming a baby and becoming a family. Being warned that the process would probably be about two years, we settled into family mode and easy-going preparations. Simultaneously, the Chancellor of the college district, Dr. Priest, called and asked to see me when convenient. Being called to the office of the Chancellor was a bit scary, but I reported as requested, and was informed that if I were willing to get a doctorate in higher education administration that I would be considered for the presidency of one of the future campuses in the planned seven-campus development. Not yet thirty years old, I suspected he knew it would take a few years to complete the degree while working and going to school part time. Still, it was a heady and complimentary offer. I even bantered with him a bit when he said: "I would like to consider making you the first woman president of a campus," to which I retorted that I would prefer he leave out the "woman" part and find a less discriminatory word. He laughed good-naturedly and said he was glad I was not afraid of the challenge. We began a trusted friendship, and from time to time, we sat in his office discussing options and ideas. I liked his gruff manner and his active brain.

I enrolled in the University of North Texas, the closest institution that offered the degree required, and loved being back in school again. However, the classes were less than satisfying because I was already a college administrator and knew from actual experience much of the subject matter. Secondly, a colleague of mine informed me that he knew a young University of Texas female student that was pregnant and was looking to put her baby up for adoption. We put my colleague in touch with an independent lawyer that could facilitate the adoption with all of us remaining anonymous. It was all that Joe and I could think about: a baby…our baby…our family. By the time that Eleanor arrived in December, we were prepared with nursery, books on parenting, a pediatrician and expectant love.

The lawyer and his wife walked up to our front door two days before Christmas with an infant carrier with a big red bow tied around it. A blanket covered the top of the carrier so the baby was not visible. I had been a nervous wreck waiting three days for the official documents to be executed and was eager to meet our new daughter. The lawyer put the carrier on the kitchen table and his wife removed the baby blanket. I looked at our beautiful daughter and felt a kind of love I had never felt before. Instantaneously, I loved her, would protect her against anything in the world, would die for her and would do everything in my power to make sure she felt loved and safe all her life. Life now had more meaning than ever, new direction and new goals. We stared at her for two days, totally missed Christmas and checked on her obsessively. We were giddy, overwhelmed with gratitude and felt a new weight of responsibility that commanded our attention. Eleanor was the only child in the universe. We needed to slow down and get a grip!

I found a nanny that would mother us all, arranged my schedule so that I could be home by four and took only one night course for my doctorate. I felt in control of my life once again, was more comfortable in my marriage and, ironically, became less judgmental of my dad and Ginny. When I told Dad that Eleanor had arrived, he actually made a trip down to Dallas to meet her. Now having two granddaughters, he seemed more relaxed and appreciative of his own two children. I liked the new attitude of my father, but I would proceed with caution. He would never, ever have an opportunity to hurt the little being I now loved more than anything in the world.

Doubt is not a pleasant condition,
but certainty is absurd.

Voltaire

It was difficult telling Dr. Priest that I was resigning my job at the community college and pursuing a doctorate in a field other than education. I thanked him for his faith in me and the opportunity that he had offered for the possibility of a future presidency. He shared his disappointment, but also mentioned that it was apparent that I was not one to be bought or have her head turned by promotion or power. Until that moment it had not occurred to me that I might agree to do a job that did not feel like the right place for me.

Having been at the Chairman post for two years, I knew I did not want to be an administrator or to work for anyone but myself. I certainly did not want to spend time evaluating others on subjective criteria and, definitely, did not want to take another course in educational administration. As it happened, one semester I enrolled in a required elective and chose abnormal psychology because its description in the course catalog sounded interesting. Within weeks I was enchanted with what I was learning. As I continued to enroll in courses in treatment modalities, psychometrics, group dynamics and psychopathology, I knew I was "home." Everything I studied was interesting, applicable to real lives and had treatment and healing as honored goals. I could genuinely focus on helping human beings understand, change and enjoy better behaviors and viewpoints. Psychology, as a field of study, is rich in options: social, experimental, clinical, neuro, behavioral, educational and community and many others. My preference quickly became counseling psychology where the emphasis was on the counselor/patient interaction. My personality, belief system and world view were a good fit for hourly counseling sessions with individuals or groups. So after completing the necessary deficiencies (18 credit hours in undergraduate and master level required courses), I proceeded to apply for acceptance to the doctoral program. Women were not especially welcome! However, that was beginning to change, and I had a straight A average in all the required courses. I felt I had an edge. My GRE (required Graduate Record Exam) scores were more than acceptable, and my attitude was appropriate with the interviewing committee, but not deferential.

Joe was understanding and helpful, saying the least he could do was to support my doctoral studies since I had put him through law school. He also left his initial employment with the Dallas law firm and formed a firm of his own with a retired Army colonel who had recently received his law degree from George Washington University while working in the Pentagon after Vietnam. Don was just what Joe needed: an extrovert who would be the rainmaker of the two man firm, and Joe, the introvert, would prepare all the legal work while Don showed off in the courtroom. As a result, Joe could support our family of three while I completed the doctorate. I gave speeches and administered IQ tests to school children as supplemental income which we agreed to invest in rental properties. I liked the diversity of our income and building equity for financial security and retirement. I was never, if I could help it, going to be without savings and feel the dread I had seen in my dad when I was a kid or need the supplemental financial support of our children. Since I was not one to have much of a need for immediate gratification, it was easy for me to save. I was not a minimalist, but I was never one to spend much on clothes, non-necessities, jewelry or impetuous shopping. Joe, however, liked his ten custom-made suits, shirts and Italian shoes. Micro-managing a household was not my style or job, but we did have some heated discussions about our different tastes and priorities.

As I was finishing a long day as an intern in my final year, Fippy called. Distraught, depressed and beside himself, he recounted some recent events and said he had to get a divorce. His marriage was not salvageable, and his dreams were shattered. To make matters worse, the apartment he rented separate from his wife, had burned down, and he had lost everything.

Joe and I immediately went to Indiana, thinking he might need legal advice. Phil was so grateful to be alive. He had made it out a bedroom window as his car exploded in the adjacent garage. And he was so grateful that his daughter was not with him. He talked a great deal, became more accepting of the reality of his situation and assured us he would be able to move forward with his life. I rested a bit more easily because I could see the shift in his energy. He would make it!

It was very unusual for an intern to complete the research, the dissertation proposal before the university graduate committee, the pre-and post testing and actually write the dissertation during the same year. However, I made an outline of deadlines, met them and defended my dissertation before all faculty members who wished to attend and question my research. Enjoying the defense of my dissertation was a memorable, fun day. No one in the world knew more about my research than I did. It is sad that so many candidates never finish the degree because of the final hurdle of the dissertation. For me, it was MY day. I knew my research!!

Having already ordered my shingle with my degree letters on it, I hung it at my newly leased office and opened my practice in psychotherapy. Graduation for the degree was not for two more months, so I had requested the degree be sent to me as was my Bachelor's and Master's. I had no thought of going to the University in the heat of a Texas August to sit through a graduation…until my dad called and said that he wanted to see me hooded!

It had a dual purpose: he wanted to see me hooded (the act of placing a satin scarf around the neck with a hooded sash that extends down the back of the doctoral gown. The sleeves are emblazoned with three velvet stripes to indicate the doctor's degree, and the hood is satin and velvet with the colors of the university and the color representing the Ph.D.). Second, he wanted to see Emma, our second daughter.

After being amazed at the love one feels for a child as I was when Eleanor arrived, I was thrilled that the arrival of Emma brought the same thrill and protective feeling. Emma had been born prematurely of an alcoholic, drug-addicted, brittle diabetic mother in her forties and was a ward of the state. A nun, whom I knew previously, had called and asked that I come see this infant and pray for her. Sister Monica knew what she was doing because the minute I saw this fragile, precious being with tubes and wires everywhere, I was in love. And, Joe, being a lawyer, filed in court to intervene with any social agency looking for other parents. Emma was half Hispanic, of a Catholic mother, and was supposed to be placed in an Hispanic home. We convinced the judge that we were acceptable parents since we were Catholic, and I spoke fluent Spanish. We waited almost two months for her to weigh five pounds, exit the incubator and be able to come home with us.

Even though I was totally busy building my practice and caring for our young daughters, I went through the ordeal of ordering a gown and making reservations for auditorium seats for Dad and Ginny. If my dad thought this was significant enough to buy two plane tickets, it was something I must do to please him. It was an interesting feeling to have him request a favor because I had long past given up on needing his approval. I had my own family with my own responsibilities to export love, acceptance, praise, comfort and a peaceful environment.

The psychotherapy practice grew rapidly with hours from six in the morning to two in the afternoon. Joe did the morning duties, and I did the afternoon and evening duties. The nanny was beloved by all of us, as she made the household run smoothly, always having dinner ready, a clean house, groceries in the cupboard and happy kiddos who loved her dearly.

Dad loved his granddaughters and began to call more regularly. He invited me to visit Treetops, the island home he had built after Mother died, and he married Ginny. Needing a break, I met him in West Palm Beach and flew to Marsh Harbour in the Abacos, Bahamas. We enjoyed the clearest blue water imaginable as we took the ferry to Hope Town, a settlement on Elbow Cay. It was an out island three miles long and a half mile wide at its widest point and 500 feet at its narrowest point. The candy striped lighthouse overlooking a protected hurricane harbor just inside the barrier reef was enchanting.

For the first time in years, I relaxed down to my core. The house was, indeed, in the treetops with a two hundred seventy degree view of the Atlantic Ocean and the Bay of Abaco. I walked the wraparound balcony and inspected the living quarters upstairs with the view and the guest quarters downstairs. Dad told me the tale of buying the land. An architect who was living on a boat in the harbor had approached him with an offer of designing a home for free and overseeing the construction in exchange for living in it when it was not occupied. My father's research revealed that Ralph Zimmerman, the architect in question, was a protégé of Frank Lloyd Wright and, supposedly, had been the number two man in the firm. It was a great deal because everybody would win in the bargain.

The house was very modern with angles everywhere. I loved being there in the middle of the jungle, yet, above it all. The sun shone into the bedroom to wake me up. Then it followed into the kitchen and deck area in the morning and afternoon. Finally, it set beautifully over the living room. As I rested in this island paradise, I fell in love with the house and how I felt there. And...Dad was a fun, respectful, engaging and an entertaining human being. Treetops transformed him! I grew to like him, talk with him, joke with him, challenge him and enjoy him. I was astounded and gleeful. This was our new family home.

One balmy afternoon, I got a wild idea and asked Dad if he would join me for a walk on the beach, just the two of us--kind of a father/daughter outing. Seeming pleased that I asked, he agreed, grabbed a baseball hat, and off we went. We walked at the edge of the waves rolling easily upon the sand, jumping every so often to avoid the inevitable splash. We were having fun together, and we both knew it. Eventually, I asked to sit at one of my favorite spots because I had some questions for him. Looking a bit trepidatious, he sat down, patted my knee and asked if I needed some advice from the Old Man. After assuring him I was just curious about some things in his past and that I wanted to get to know parts of his history which I had no knowledge of, he encouraged the questions. Feeling thankful that we were finally going to talk, I asked him if he ever missed Mother in spite of being happily married to Ginny. Immediately, he said he missed her every day. It was not mourning, just thinking through memories and wishing she could have seen her children grow, mature, succeed and have grandbabies.

We both laughed thinking of how Mother would have been the stereotypical, doting grandmother and would have spoiled all three of her granddaughters rotten!

Then, he surprised me! He asked how I coped with missing her. Explaining that I often talked to her, I reported many of my feelings so that I could work through her not being present for all the wonderful events of our lives. He nodded, patted my knee again and said: "Well, you're the shrink; you should know!" I retorted with: "Well, Dad, shrinks do pretty well looking at other people's lives, but not always as well with their own." He snorted, slightly.

"Dad, you did something that I cannot fathom ever having to endure. You were required to leave your pregnant wife and infant daughter, go to places that were totally alien and fight for your country and your life in horrific circumstances. I cannot begin to imagine the fear, the courage and the faith it took to do that. I want to thank you."

He quickly said that he was just doing his duty. He was never able to accept compliments or praise with grace. I asked him if he could tell me how his war experiences felt, how he coped and how he recovered. I added that I wanted to know that part of him that happened before I had memory.

It was easy to tell that he wanted to honor my request. He sat for a long time, then put his head in his hands, rocked back and forth and cried, saying, "I can't, I can't!" The emotional pain was palpable, stabbing at his chest and, clearly, impossible to contain. This time, I patted his knee, assuring him that I did not want to cause pain and that I was sorry, but gratitude still was the message I wanted to convey. I reached over and hugged his neck as he buried his tears in my shoulder. I will never forget that moment, not for the emotional breakdown of my father, but for the validation that he was a real, feeling and loving person who could be vulnerable.

Joe and I began to go to Treetops every year, usually for two weeks. Joe worked with Dad to do necessary repairs. We bought a golf cart, built a garage for it, renovated the house, replaced balcony dry rot and, essentially, saved the house from total deterioration. So when Dad wanted to sell it, Joe and I bought it for money expended and a remainder paid to support Dad. We absolutely loved having Treetops as an escape.

Now a family of four, we needed a bigger house in Dallas and more yard for a trampoline, pool and outdoor activities. We found an old Cape Cod that was charming and near the school that we wanted the children to attend. The many large oaks made my heart sing and shaded the large back porch with a swing for daydreaming. One day-dreamy Saturday afternoon when the kids were at soccer practice where Joe was the assistant coach, I relaxed on the swing and started a meditation. I had put children, husband, my practice and my community speeches before any time for myself. With no intention of being sacrificial or excessively caregiving, I, indeed, was doing just that. Sissy Jean could help me sort this out.

"Sissy, I am tired, and I'm hungry for my own company. I know that I am hypocritical in my daily life when I teach others to care for themselves in a healthy manner when I do not give myself the gift of self-reflection and deep honesty. I am pretty sure that I know what is real for me and what is pretend. And even knowing that my life is a self-created illusion, I live it daily and feel the consequences. My children are everything, every joy I had hoped for, every challenge that is normal in bringing up a family. My practice is more than I had anticipated in enjoying the interactions with patients and seeing them grow exponentially. My side interests in investments and community service are pleasant and infrequent so as to not interfere, but my relationship with Joe is stagnant and unsatisfying. I have had no success in changing it or breathing new life into it. We have these beautiful children that need to grow up in a loving and healthy home. I feel like a fake wife."

"Dear heart, it is helpful that you take a feeling inventory of your daily activities. You are troubled because you are living the self-serving illusion that you created to feel normal and to experience marriage and motherhood. At times, you think Truth is what one decides to believe, and that reality is the illusion acceptable in the moment. These ego illusions give momentary comfort and acceptance of your life events, but Spirit Truth always brings peace. You are telling me that you are not at peace and don't know how to get there without hurting others."

"Exactly. Our children deserve the best chance possible at growing up in a normal family without major difficulties. I want that for them. I owe them that."

"No, my love, you do not owe your children anything but pure love. Inside such love, you will teach them to think for themselves, honor their creations, illusions and ideas and support their journey as they experiment with life. You can help them find their own definition of love and peace, their own enlightenment, and their own alignment with Source. When you see peace in each other, you will know that alignment has happened in a harmonious and a perfectly suited manner. They will find unique ways to access Spirit, probably different from yours. Teach them to honor all paths to Source. If you embrace what I am saying, you may give yourself more permission to be authentic... and stay in your marriage or not. That is your journey."

Somehow, I exited that meditation with a lightness not felt for several years. Knowing I had options, that I would not ruin others if I chose authenticity, I accepted that life could change for me, and I would be all right. But...I was not ready for family change. I was only ready to become more honest about how I was going to live with my feelings.

Dad and Ginny showed up, as planned, made appropriate

exclamations of happiness when introduced to Emma and seemed to enjoy our home. Dad and I were early risers, giving ourselves a head start on the day. And so it was that the next morning we found ourselves in the kitchen, far from the sleeping family in another part of the house, with our coffee and elbows on the kitchen table.

"So tell me, daughter, about this counseling degree. That's not some crystal ball kind of mojo, is it?"

"No, Dad, it isn't. Actually, psychology is the study of the personality, its development and its ensuing experiences and behaviors. It is fascinating and rewarding to use what I have learned to help others with situational difficulties in their lives or with their families of origin."

"Well, speaking about families of origin, did you ever have to discuss your own family?"

"Absolutely," I said at the end of taking a breath.

"Well, so how did we measure up?"

"Dad, what are you asking me? Whether there were things in my family that I would have changed?"

"Yeah," he answered hesitantly.

"You know, Dad, the one thing I really wanted as a kid was for you to tell me you loved me."

"Goddammit, Annalee, I worked my ass off to take care of my family, went to war to preserve their freedom, made it through the death of a wife, and you all never went hungry. And you have the gall to say I didn't love you," as he pounded the tabletop so hard that the cups jumped out of their saucers.

"Dad, I am grateful for all you did to serve your country, support a family, deal with great difficulties and work hard every day. I thoroughly recognize all your efforts. And I know now you love me. I'm just saying that, as a kid, I needed to hear the words."

"Well, dammit, I never heard those words as a kid!"

"Would you have liked to hear them?"

"Well, there were seven of us, the Great Depression, lots of stuff going on, so we just worked together to make ends meet."

"Dad, that had to be hard, and you all survived except Baby Dickie who died of the Spanish Flu. I'm just asking if, as a little boy, would you have liked to have heard those words: 'I love you'?"

"Yeah, daughter, I guess so."

"I would like to hear them."

"Annalee, you are my daughter, and I love you and am proud of you."

"Thanks, Dad. I love you, too."

It was a seminal moment, and I shall never forget the energy that surrounded the exposure of our familial love. It was transformative. It was a beginning.

The next day was graduation day. Dad, Ginny, Joe and I went to lunch before the afternoon ceremony. We were all enjoying ourselves when Dad proposed a toast: "Here's to Dr. Annalee. I'm just sorry it's not my son!" Joe took hold of my knee under the table and patted it as if to express his condolences. I was shocked and discounted, but, mostly, I hated that my talented brother was even more discounted. It was apparent that Dad had no idea how he had belittled his son, and on the other hand, he was expressing a truth. His world view preferred the son to shine, and the daughter to do well at her female role. The moment was sad and defining. Graduation was methodical.

The girls were settling into St. Monica's Elementary School, and life continued full of school and sports activities, work and family fun time with friends. I now sat on the School Board of the Catholic Diocese of Dallas, governing 36 parochial schools with a myriad of policy issues, parent appeal hearings, complaints and compliance...and a growing rumor of sexual abuse of acolytes and students by priests. My intolerance for Catholic dogma and gender discrimination had been simmering for a few years, and I was eager for the Catholic Church to confront its troubling issues, especially concerning children.

Eventually, after six years of service, I resigned and began my quiet exit from a religious affiliation that no longer met my needs or brought any measure of peace. My path to peace was aligned with my lessons with Sissy Jean which contained much more compassion, understanding, inclusiveness and generosity of Spirit. My heart departed from Catholicism and entered a more practical Christian embrace of universal spirituality. That singular decision resulted in a sense of freedom and honesty that I had never experienced before. Authenticity was taking root, enabling a burst of growth and knowingness...and a belief that I could handle any illusion if I had enough wisdom to shift into higher consciousness and know Truth. My meditations became more frequent and more enlightening, as did my growing belief that I could make changes that were difficult, but necessary. I lived with those ideas until they became familiar and stable, but made no overt visible or tangible changes. Internally, I came to know where Spirit and I aligned, and that if I did not eventually confront and act on my truth that my soul would sicken and my personal power of life would die. I was going to have to put some decisions on the front burner and be a big girl, a mature woman, an honest child of God. The universe will nudge one to a healthy direction, usually by putting the illusions (that are unconsciously self-made) right in your face so that escape from truth is unavoidable.

Joe was distraught and sad. He had learned that his law partner, Don, had been diagnosed with Stage IV lung cancer and was probably going to die within months. The shock was evident for days, with gatherings between the two lawyers and their families trying to come to grips with the future and to comfort one another. Don was a hardened Vietnam veteran who had seen his share of shock, unfairness, death and trauma. As a result, he was stoic about his illness and impending death. Joe could not sleep, went into work late, stopped coaching the girls' teams and was sullen. It was obvious to me that he was depressed. When Don died, Joe found a lawyer to rent his unoccupied space. He seemed pleased to have another person back at the office, and used the insurance money paid out for loss-of-a-partner to buy a new car and make some improvements at home. Depression dissipated, work continued and the marriage stayed the same. Then Joe began to say that he couldn't hear as well as he used to and ordered amplifiers for phones and stereos. After seeing an otolaryngologist who performed surgery to replace the stapes in his ear, he experienced no improvement. He complained daily about his hearing difficulty. I felt such sympathy for him because I could only imagine the impact that it would have on me, my practice and my family if the same were to happen to me. I practiced patience, read articles about hearing loss, investigated hearing aid devices and shared all of this with my husband.

Six months later, Joe walked through the back door, put his briefcase down, took his suit coat off and announced he had sold his law firm. I stood still, unable to move, trying to make sense of what I had just heard.

"What did you say?" I gasped.

"I said I sold the law firm today. I sold it to Pat," he responded firmly.

"But, why?" I asked, still nailed in place and in shock.

"Because I hate the practice of law, I don't want to suck up to people to beg for business like Don did and I can't hear!" he screamed.

"How much did you sell it for?" I asked hesitantly.

"You won't like the answer. Fifteen thousand," he answered flippantly.

"Joe!!! No!!!," I screamed in response, knowing the firm's furniture, equipment, machines, law library and client list was worth probably ten to fifteen times that.

"Sorry. It's done," came the matter-of-fact answer.

"What are you going to do for a living?" I asked harshly.

"Well, I'll be a house-husband, do the books for your practice, manage the ten rent houses, mow the lawn, clean the garage, build things and have time to read," he said calmly.

"But that will put all the responsibility on me to support the family. I am already exhausted with my work schedule. I don't know how I can do more," I protested breathlessly.

As he shrugged his shoulders, I knew that a coin had dropped and a bell had rung. Most of all, my heart had lost its love. I no longer respected this man and his cavalier attitude and decisions. The growing narcissism, selfishness and dependency was suffocating and menacingly irritating.

I began to be able to compensate for the loss of his income by ramping up my practice and raising fees. I loved practicing and steadily focused on the best for my patients. The sacrifice of my health, my free-time and my feeling of security was the only safety net for food on the table, mortgage payments, private school tuition and a good life for our children. Long past visiting any ideas of victimization, I harbored silent anger at myself. Knowing that I enabled Joe daily with my willingness to accommodate his decision and its consequences, I was complicit.

> Guilt upon the conscience, like rust upon iron, both defies and consumes it, gnawing and creeping into it, and does that which at last eats out the very heart and substance of the metal.
>
> Robert South

I was so excited. Phil called and said he was moving to Texas. Good news! My brother and I would finally be in the same place, able to see each other, and he could be an uncle to his nieces. His daughter was now living in Tennessee near the Three Corners area, and he rarely got to see her. The bad news was that Phil and Dad were at extreme odds, and Phil could not abide one more day in Indiana working with him. I totally understood because Dad always saw disagreement as disloyalty. There was not a history of ever overcoming that trait. Phil had finally had enough to know that the situation would not change.

Unfortunately, Phil's quick, second marriage had failed. His second wife had told me that he would not let her in emotionally and not confide or be close to her. She thought he was so damaged from his first marriage experience that he was overly cautious and self-protective. I think she was insightful, but unable to convert his fear. Just two good people that didn't make it work.

Shortly after Phil arrived and was settled into his apartment in the mid-cities between Dallas and Ft. Worth, my dad called. He was screaming expletives on the phone and telling me that he was going to have Phil put in Leavenworth for stealing a piece of construction equipment and transporting it across state lines. I remembered that I had heard a similar threat the summer before my senior year in college. As I calmed him down him down by saying that I could not help him if he continued to scream, I began to understand that his threat was in earnest. We agreed that I would talk with my brother and call Dad back within twenty-four hours. My heart was palpitating when I hung up. Dad had a way of going from zero to a hundred so fast that I often experienced psychological whiplash. And I needed some time to think.

Phil's answering machine recorded my rather urgent message,

and he called back that evening. Recounting the message from Dad, I heard my brother sigh as he told me what was going on. Dad had promised him half of the company if he worked for him for ten years, receiving five percent ownership per year. Having endured five years so far and going crazy, Phil told Dad he couldn't take it anymore and was leaving. As payment for fulfilling the first five years of the promise, Phil rationalized that a piece of construction equipment was a minimal compensation for his partial fulfillment of the contract. Of course, the contract was only verbal. Dad held the aces, and he knew that. Phil was heartbroken because the equipment was vital to getting work in Texas. We agreed I would help him, and he would return the equipment. But he also said he never wanted to see the Old Man again. I understood.

Phil came back to life in Texas. He played sand volleyball at his apartment complex, met new friends, went Country-Western dancing on the week-ends and won trophies, dated a new woman each week, eked out a living and made sure to pay child support on time. He was happy, young -looking again and the clown I had always known. We spent each Christmas and the Fourth of July together with family. Being a wonderful and entertaining uncle, he was a favorite of our girls who squealed with delight at the sight of Uncle Phil who often showed up at our pool on the weekends. As he slowly introduced us to Anita, he was letting us know that she was someone special, someone he honored and cared a great deal for. Since he took such special care of her for months after her horrible auto accident, we knew that he had her in his heart. Everyone loved this small dynamo of intellect, wisdom, personality and kindness. Phil had found some measure of peace and trust with her. Accordingly, she had our vote.

Phil was true to his word. He did not speak with Dad, who, himself, seemed to have invented stubborn and passed it onto Phil in DNA! My brother reminisced about Mother frequently, but not a word about Dad. I knew it took some energy to always avoid any mention of him.

Once I confessed to him that I was not happy in my marriage, but he was silent with no response. A part of me believed that Fippy wanted my marriage to be a good one so that there was at least one place that was warm and safe and loving. He didn't want that illusion of stability to go away.

I learned that Joe had a disability income policy that I never knew existed. He was investigating filing a claim for long-term disability. He claimed that he was deaf and, therefore, could not practice law. This was of immense concern to me because I had begun to believe that a premeditated plot might be in motion. Occasionally, I would notice Joe answering questions when they were asked from his back and at a distance, or he would be on a phone without an amplifier having a long and detailed conversation. After cocktails, he almost always suffered no apparent impairment when hearing conversations that were happening simultaneously. With a tinge of guilt, I started to purposely take notice. What I found seemed to verify my suspicions. Fearful that fraud might be an issue, I made an appointment with the insurance agent. After explaining my concerns, I was assured that with the doctor's report, the surgery and the selling of the law firm that there was enough evidence to pay the substantial claim. Then, I REALLY felt guilty about questioning my husband's integrity. However, for several years before he sold the law firm I was uneasy with some of his behavior that appeared to push the line on the canon of ethics. Discussions on the subject were unpleasant and unproductive. He said I should trust him more...when I was beginning to trust him less.

One evening over cocktails on the back porch we became surprisingly honest. I stated that I thought we should consider going our separate ways and looking for a life that suited us better than our marriage. He agreed, with a caveat. He proposed that we continue living together, rearing our girls, participating in the community and our service projects and sleep in separate bedrooms until either the girls were out of high school or until we met someone we wanted to date openly. We were very civil about the discussion, agreed to think about it and return to the discussion at a later date.

This was my first step of freedom to be authentic about my desires and my future. To an outside world, this might not have seemed like much, but to a dedicated mom, a recovering Catholic and a therapist with a good reputation, this was life-changing. I was beginning to give myself permission to live my beliefs, but I still could not imagine inflicting pain upon the two human beings I loved the most: Eleanor and Emma

The next day after Mass (I still went with the girls, but did not partake in the sacraments) I delivered the daughters to homes of friends to spend the afternoon, and I went to my study to meditate. Sissy's help was essential in sorting out my feelings and moving forward in a healthy way.

"Loved one, it is pleasant to be with you in conversation. I am here to listen and teach. Tell me what sits in your heart space."

"Sissy, as much as I know that I should stay in holy awareness and high consciousness, I find myself feeling guilty for my thoughts and guilty for my expectations AND guilty for feeling guilty! I'm a mess!"

"Annie, you are not a mess. You are in a powerful struggle of Ego Mind persistently reminding you of all the church rules, the society rules, the daily living rules that keep Ego in business! You allow yourself to be drawn into thoughts of judgment, reprisal, sinfulness, hurtfulness and guilt. These, as you know are all contrived. Not one of them is real for a child of God who knows that you absolutely cannot lose what is holy. You cannot, in reality, lose anything. Everything you want is yours, but you cannot see it living in your daily illusion. You never need to lose, to sacrifice, to be guilty or to suffer. Ego demands those emotions and those behaviors. And life seems to honor those misconceptions and illusions because you do not take the time to shift your consciousness into holy awareness, where above the fray you see the nonsense, the conspiracies of Ego, the gaminess of everyday evolution toward chaos and untruth."

"Sissy, I understand what you teach. I believe it. I really do, but I find I cannot live the Truth well. I don't know how to walk around in high consciousness all the time, especially when I get tired or frustrated or am focused on others. I need to deal with guilt and what it does to me."

"That's a good start, dear one. Guilt is self-spanking. It is Ego Mind saying that one 'should' act or believe in a manner different from what you feel, and when you do not comply, Ego administers the punishment...the self-spanking. Ego whispers, incessantly, that you have misbehaved, broken the rule, hurt another or are just a bad person. None of that is ever true. There are no opposites in Spirit Mind. There is no good vs. bad, no win vs. lose, no well vs. sick, no happy vs. sad and no right vs. wrong. In high consciousness there is only this moment, this holy moment, this holy thought, this holy acceptance that you are perfect and whole, just the way you are.

Ego loves guilt because you self-accuse and condemn and judge, which is the very life-blood of illusion. In fact, Ego builds a cascade of emotions that delivers an allegiance to Earth-bound illusions and their exponential growth.

When you experience some bit of anxiety, a consequence of self judgment and fear of potential loss or hurt, you start to defend against the discomfort. That very discomfort cascades into anger, which is nothing more than the unresolved fear of loss and hurt that anxiety is still holding. Then, if you do not resolve the anger by shifting your consciousness, the cascade brings you to guilt, where you feel sad, hurt, unworthy and sacrificial. That illusion then further cascades into depression, which is all that unresolved anger and guilt directed inward where it begins to erase the memory of higher consciousness and drags you into a pit of despair that is Ego's dark den. For some unfortunate beings that believe in that darkness, the choice is to leave the pain and exit this plane. Ego has no conscience, no concern for your soul and holy existence. It profits from the illusion of the separation from the One, the separation from love and peace and eternal acceptance of self."

"That helps so much. I only hope that I can remember the Truth when the world seems to be climbing on my back."

"Dear Annie-girl…what you must remember is that the story you are hearing and repeating to yourself is NOT true, and there is NO jury, NO executioner, and if you continue to turn from the embrace of that reality, you will visit insanity, sadness, untruth and loss of self. We will do this together. I am always here, always with the tablets of Truth and always with the commuting of Love. You and I are one. WE are eternal together, as are all."

I sat for a while thinking about how to stay in high consciousness because it certainly was a lot easier explained than accomplished. Thought was at the core of the vibrational frequency of everything. It was thought that made us feel our emotions: "I think he is nice," so I feel warm towards him, or "I don't think he should act in that bigoted manner," so I feel unfavorable toward him. Thoughts like these were the mothers of the offspring feelings, and our feelings often dictated our reactive behavior. So I began to try to develop some sort of recipe for trying to stay in high consciousness. The absolute first step was to call myself on any judgment because judgment itself is a killer of anything spiritual, kind, loving or caring. I would make it a point to call myself on judgment when I recognized that my thoughts were going in that direction.

Secondly, I had to see Love in everyone. Holy Jesus, Mary and Joseph! That is just damn difficult when encountering many of the rascals of the world, the mean, cruel, premeditated villains that you want to slap some sense into. But, true to my promise to myself, I began to say a mantra: "Divine love in me salutes Divine Love in you." Sometimes, the mantra had to be said in my head many times. Other times, it helped immediately. Then, I confess, there were times I just walked away so as to not damage my consciousness further.

Unconsciousness was rampant on the planet. There were millions who were good people, wanted to do the right thing, wanted to help others…and were still unconscious without the profound joy of aligning in the peace of Spirit. When I reached moments of alignment, I felt total love. I wished it happened more often, but I, like so many, got wrapped up in the routines and demands of daily living. Ego Mind took the reins, and I would become frustrated and self-recriminatory. Try as I might, I was about as Ego-human as anyone, and that made it harder. I was not ignorant. I KNEW the Truth, but living it well was an enormous challenge. The one thing I always counted on was the knowingness that there was one spiritual being who never rejected me, never judged me or admonished me, always had faith in me and made me see where I needed to go, even if I had a hard time getting there. Sissy Jean helped me live better, think better and be better. I could not imagine how others who had not opened to the wisdom of their non-physical helper(s) could have such assurance and feeling of unqualified love. I began to pray for open eyes and open minds and that I would be able to find the discipline to keep being aware to shift consciousness and feel oneness. It was a big order, and as with all big orders, there were big challenges.

Phil and Anita took the girls skiing to Red River where everyone had a blast, and the daughters returned home asking for a promise to take them skiing. Early March, we went to Vail, and the girls and Joe skied. I read and walked and enjoyed multiple meditations on the quiet mountainside away from the ski slopes. It was there on one glorious sunny afternoon with the sun merging with the snow that I made a decision that was to turn my life upside down and bring joy, fear, sadness and change. I did not know it at the time, but the decision to do one thing for myself, to make the time to do it and actually dedicate myself to the task was exhilarating: I decided to take flying lessons. Remembering that flight with Dad years ago and the thrill of defying gravity was still intoxicating. I would go through the necessary steps to get my private pilot's license. It would be a gift to myself.

When I flipped through the Yellow Pages to Flying Schools, the first one listed was Airport Flying School at Addison Airport on the north edge of Dallas. It wasn't far from home or office. I showed up one Saturday morning in April and took a demo ride that served to underscore the commitment of my decision. Asking who the best instructor was, the owner gave me a name. He looked at the young man's schedule and informed me that the instructor had no openings. I took down the name and signed up for Ground School for eight weeks every Tuesday night.

When I showed up the third Tuesday night of the eight session school because I had been on vacation, I was told by the instructor that I could make up the first two sessions. However, I couldn't miss any more times or it would be too difficult to hire him for make-up lessons. The instructor was the same man that the owner had mentioned previously for in-flight training. Impressed that he knew his material, taught it well, tolerated no nonsense and still had a sense of humor, I vowed to wait to get on his flight schedule. He was a proven entity, and I had no time for experimentation with instructors.

Each Tuesday I checked the man's flight schedule. On the fifth week I found a cancellation and quickly filled in my name. When I showed up for the flight lesson, he was matter-of-fact, firm, slightly impatient and all business. I felt uneasy at altitude when he began turns, stalls and procedures that made my tummy roll. By God, I vowed not to throw up all over this smarty pants who I was sure was making things difficult on purpose. Swallowing hard and methodically, I survived the first flight, and my stomach soon acclimated. Once on the ground, I felt proud to have handled the difficulty and announced that I would see him next Saturday morning. He acknowledged me as he departed for a flight in his own aircraft, a Citabria, which is an aerobatic plane. It was obvious his stomach was made of something much superior to mine!

The Ground School class was composed of doctors, lawyers, an accountant, a re-possessor of all types of luxury cars, planes and racehorses, businessmen and me. It was the custom to show up at a local watering hole-in-the-wall after class for a beer or glass of wine and chat a while, then go on our way. When the fifth class was over, we all headed to the tavern. Bill, my instructor, and I showed up first. We ordered our drinks and chose a table big enough for the others who were to arrive soon.

The other class members never showed up. Bill and I talked

until two in the morning, just the two of us. Since I don't believe in coincidence, I am certain it was serendipitous. As a therapist, it is easy for me to get people talking, which is exactly what happened. This man was a Harley biker, a maverick who marched to his own drum, unabashedly transparent, unapologetically opinionated, a committed worker, self-sufficient, kind, but stoic. I found him extremely interesting because he had the adventurous behavior that only lived in my head, but not my choices. The universe spoke to me in so many ways that night. It re-introduced me to living dreams, to excitement that thrills but damages no one and to being an individual who knows his spirit and who listens to his Truth. He became a beacon of independence with a light that was shining on what I wanted in my own life, without ever knowing. I knew at two in the morning that I needed to speak with Joe about what I wanted to do, but I would think it through and not be impetuous. Bill, as a symbol of the freedom and life that I sought, was significant. However, as a person, he was just an interesting individual that represented my dreams to live more, love more and be more. He was not a focus or a reason for my urgent need to speak with my husband, but he was the slap on the backside that got me moving.

As we sat on the sofa in the den, I looked at Joe and said: "It's time." He sat for about ten seconds before he agreed and asked me to tell the children. Surely, a decision of this magnitude should be from both of us together. I was disappointed and upset that he left this daunting task to me. I did not do well. It was just too hard to watch their hurt and feelings of betrayal by their parents. I looked like the bad guy because I was the messenger. As long as I live, I will not forget that moment when my children were hurt, angry and forlorn. Nor will I forget the cowardice of Joe who had purposefully put me in this horrible situation. I had turned their world upside down without direction. I had much work to do to salvage the feeling of a loving family that I genuinely desired…just the three of us.

> If you are lucky enough to find a way of life you love, you have to find the courage to live it.
>
> John Irving

Joe found an apartment nearby and slowly began to move things from our home. I agreed that he could take anything he wanted with the exception of the girls' bedroom suites and Eleanor's grand piano. He was careful not to make the home look empty. He took his mother's antique bed from the guest room, all the art, china, silver, crystal and filing cabinets. I didn't actually discover that most of it was gone until I got ready to set the table for Thanksgiving! Most of the items were stored in the china cabinets, so I would never notice their disappearance. He also removed my life-long collection of antique dressing spoons. The filing cabinets held the all the rent house information, title policies, tax records for the family, my business and our investments. I asked for those files to be returned. He argued that since he was still doing the books for my business and tax filings for the other concerns that he should keep records at his place. I confess that I did not have a good feeling about this, but I avoided the argument and the major effort necessary to move them back. My intent was to cause as little disruption or change as possible.

The children were having a hard time, and there were multiple times I thought of reversing course, but I knew that I would be miserable, and they certainly did not need to be raised by a self-victimized, sacrificial mother with no authenticity. So we grew used to the new situation. Friends of the girls assured them that divorce wasn't that bad (since half of kids live in families of divorce), and their embarrassment began to wane slightly. The nuns at school gave me a harsh shaming on several occasions, and they determined that I was selfish and had lost my way. Actually, I was beginning to find my way. But the Sisters and I did not have that discussion.

I was progressing nicely with my flight instruction from Bill. I was thrilled with my ability to fly reasonably well, make my first solo flight and then fly several cross countries to evidence my ability to navigate, make flight plans, land at new airports, manage all radio communication and sing in the cockpit all by myself. The feeling of freedom from earth-bound noises and expectations was exhilarating. I bought a little two-seater Cessna 152 for ten grand and began to fly much more and rented it out for instructors to use, thereby, essentially, flying for free.

The year before Joe and I separated, we bought one side of a newly-constructed duplex and moved Dad and Ginny to Dallas. Dad had been borrowing money from me for some time. To save face, he signed some near-worthless vacant lots he owned in my hometown over to me in addition to some signed promissory notes that he prepared so that it was presented as a bona fide business deal. He was becoming forgetful, and the construction companies had been foreclosed on by his local bank. I had to make sure the monthly money I sent him went directly to his bank account so that Ginny didn't know. His pride was still in full bloom. I rationalized that the children could enjoy grandparents, and I could keep an eye on Dad's health. Practicing not being mad at him, I forgot that my new viewpoint would not change his behavior. Me! The shrink! I created a story that I thought would work. And I was well aware that it is much easier to see the psychopathology in others than in oneself!

Dad went to the airport with me a couple of times to see me take off and watch me land. I swear he was prouder of that than all the degrees, my hard work, my successful practice, being the mother of two wonderful daughters or anything else. Actually, it was the one thing we agreed upon together. Flying is the best form of physical freedom other than a democracy. It is addictive and harmless. He couldn't wait for me to get my license so I could take him flying as a passenger and a co-pilot.

One day, while visiting Dad and Ginny at the duplex, I noticed him drinking a whole bottle of apple juice, being irritable, speaking harshly to his wife and just being a pill. I got close to him and asked to smell his breath. It smelled like Juicy Fruit gum. I said, "Dad, I think you have diabetes. I am going to make an appointment for you at the doctor."

"The hell you say. You're not an M.D!" he bellowed.

"Dad, I diagnose suspected diabetes all the time. I see patients in therapy for depression, anxiety and oppositional behavior that have had rapid onset, and I send them immediately for a blood glucose test to rule out diabetes. Many times the test is positive, and the patient gets the help they need instead of spending thousands in therapy."

"Well, if you think so, make the appointment," he murmured. Ginny and I looked at each other in amazement. Dad had agreed without argument or refusal. Now we were both worried!

A former patient of mine, an internist, was the perfect match. I shared with the doctor that I would like for him to see my dad and explained why. I also explained that he was a difficult man and to be prepared. He laughed and said he would be happy to take Dad as a patient and even promised to give him a happy pill!

Two days later, Dad learned he had diabetes and had extremely high blood sugar. We bought all the test kits and made sure Ginny would monitor the consumption of Oreos and Canadian Club. At one visit after his diagnosis, Dad mentioned that all that Purdue education money had paid off. I swallowed hard and kept my mouth shut. The sadness I felt on the drive home was the realization that I was now becoming the parent, and Dad was receding into the child. That feeling sat hard on my heart and played havoc with my mind and memories. Everything in life was changing: my family, my family-of-origin, my belief system, my interests and my awareness.

Joe was slow to file the divorce papers, but I was in no hurry because life was settling into a new and comfortable routine. Word got back to me that he was dating which made me relax a bit more and believe that we would all find our way with new people and new goals. As flying lessons were winding down, Bill began to plan things for us to do. I saved the week-ends that the children were with Joe to spend time with Bill and to ride the motorcycle which I thoroughly loved to do. Dangerous as it might be, the feeling of freedom was so delightful. The rounding of a curve when one actually becomes the curvature itself is so satisfying and heart-pumping that I transformed into a covert biker woman, secretly loving putting on my leathers and do-rag and zoning out on the back seat, swaying with the bike. Bill introduced me to camping, hiking, and aerobatics (stomach issues still required methodical swallowing on most maneuvers). His old beater van ran like a charm due to his mechanical skills and ingenuity. I began to genuinely trust this man could handle any situation.

Bill was the oldest of nine children in a significantly dysfunctional family that operated through intimidation, screaming and violence. That signaled red flags for me all over the place, so I was careful, cautious and always observant. He had some deep-seated anger issues, some deficiencies in social graces and some worthiness issues.

However, none were so well defined that they couldn't be addressed. His character assets were honesty, superior work ethic, financial responsibility, spiritually grounded in metaphysical Christianity and practiced it daily, and fun...fun...fun. I looked forward to being with him, and he was safe for me. He told me up front that he would never marry. That statement gave me so much permission to enjoy our relationship without constant evaluation about where it might be headed.

He had had two five-year relationships. His first ended with the woman dying in an accident, and the second ended because of abusive alcoholism. He was set upon loving, but not upon committing. Those were his issues, and they relieved me of any psychological burdens which would normally accompany a developing relationship. I enjoyed my practice, my family, my extracurricular activities and my spiritual understanding.

Joe called to say he was coming to pick up the girls and would bring me the latest financials. I was upstairs in the master bedroom when I heard him knock on the doorframe, asking permission to enter.

"Hey, didn't know you were here already." I said as I looked toward the door.

"Yeah...say, can I talk with you a minute?" he asked.

"Sure," I said as I sat on the edge of my bed, and he took a seat in the chair close by.

"What's up?" I asked.

"Annalee, this is very serious. I love you, and I do not want a divorce. Let's try again." he pleaded.

"Oh, Joe, I'm sorry. I do not want to hurt you, but the separation has made me know that we made the right decision. It is hard on all of us, especially the children, but we are acclimating, and I am happier. We need to finalize the divorce and move on with our respective lives and find good times." I answered.

"Okay. Then let's sit down next weekend and come up with an equitable division of our assets. I will bring a list of everything," he offered.

The list was typed out, well organized and ready for division. Texas was (and is) a community property state, which means that everything is divided fifty-fifty with the exclusion of gifts, unmingled inheritance and separate property. Our division would be simple. He asked that I take all the rental property, the homestead and Treetops, my 401K, car and personal items. He knew my practice was worth nothing to him since I was its sole producer and the practice could not be sold. Joe would take all the cash in his bank account which included the very large insurance settlement, his car and personal items. The division was 54% to Joe and 46% to me. I was assuming nearly one million in debt on property mortgages, and I agreed to such a burdensome division because he had no job. If a rental property were vacant, and he did not make the mortgage payment, my credit would be ruined. It was clearly a situation where I had no choice if I wanted to protect my credit and my investments. Keeping the homestead where the girls lived with me and were comfortable was a bargaining chip Joe used, saying with some slight threat, that if I did not agree to the settlement, he would have to ask for the house to be sold. He knew I would do almost anything to not disrupt the lives of the girls. The last item was child support. He did not want to have court-mandated child support because he had no job. Was his large six figure cash settlement not for child support? I acquiesced, and he put everything down on a yellow tablet, instructed me to hire an attorney of my own to do all the paperwork, and we were divorced shortly thereafter.

He continued to do my office financials, billings, payments, investment tallies and lawn care. He introduced me to his girlfriend, and I told him I continued to date Bill, and all was well. Actually, Joe seemed jovial and in good spirits whenever I saw him. He was buying cars, furniture and vacations at a rapid rate. But we were divorced. I was not going to question any of his behavior as long as it did not affect me or the girls.

About a year post-divorce, with all going quite well, I came out of my office into the waiting room. Joe and the next patient were seated there. Asking the patient to please wait a few minutes, I invited Joe into my consultation room and asked why he was there. He explained that being the father of our children and wanting a proper place for them to stay on visitation that he wanted to move into the duplex where my dad and Ginny lived. Astonished, I said I couldn't do that. I could not put my dad on the street, and Joe had funds to buy a place if he wanted. Then, for the first time, I heard a bullying threat that took my breath away. He presented me with a letter that he said explained that in the divorce he got the duplex (untrue), that they would have to move, and that he was sorry. I still refused to sign, and I had not read the letter. It was at that moment that he said he would take me to court, accuse me of unethical activities and take the children. His demeanor was something I had never witnessed in nineteen years of knowing him. After catching my breath, I said that although his behavior was unbecoming, I would sign the letter. But I needed to talk with Dad first, so I asked him to please wait until I called after seeing Dad and made new arrangements for their living quarters, movers, etc. He agreed and said he would assume the mortgage on the duplex, not present the signed letter and wait for my call. I asked for the letter back since it was no longer needed. He refused and remarked it was insurance for him. He walked out of my consultation room with a smirk.

The threats were vacuous, without any truth, but Joe could be a troublemaker armed with a law degree and lots of free time. I had neither, and I had a family to support. Then, four days later, I got a letter in the mail from my dad that said I was a traitor, and he never wanted to lay eyes on me again. I had to calm myself down when I confronted Joe with Dad's letter and what it obviously meant. He chuckled and said my dad deserved whatever he got. I sank to the floor, leaning against the wall with the phone still in my hand. At this point, I hated my ex-husband! I tried not to. I called on help to not feel the hate, but it persisted. I kept asking myself how a person could be so heartless, rocking myself to a calmer state. Emma saw this and was scared, so I told her the truth, and she did what any child would do to help a grieving parent. She told me it would be all right. She meant well, but she didn't need to be party to this egregious event.

On one hand, I felt darkness invade my spirit and my well-being as the guilt of Dad being removed from his home began to overtake my thoughts. Not knowing where he was now and loathing the character of my ex-husband, coupled with enough self-blame about how could I have not seen these characteristics in Joe before, I felt like a fool...or worse. Mindful not to expand or dramatize the story, I stayed steady, dealt with life, and meditated. But I still felt overwhelming guilt at treating Dad so badly and in a manner reminiscent of his own.

And on the other hand, I was falling into fierce love once again. With Bill, I felt light, young, buoyant and revived. Knowing that I didn't have to concern myself with commitment decisions, I simply embraced the moment. After almost two years, I was surprised when he said he thought we should live together because we loved each other and were meant to be together. He was equally surprised when I replied that as long as I had children at home I would not live with anyone outside of marriage. Then…surprisingly, to my shock, he said he thought that we should get married! I laughed, said that any proper proposal would have to be on bended knee, beseeching my acceptance. All to which he said he would see what he could arrange. We left it at that. But we both knew that we were going to spend our lives together.

I often revisited my feelings of guilt about Dad and my involuntary abandonment of him. My stomach would not stop its intermittent churn every time I thought of him getting the letter I had signed without reading it. My imagination was rich with ugly scenarios, and I began to think I had created this illusion to live out my life-long angst with him. Then, just as we were beginning to have a pleasant relationship, he was put out of his home by a letter signed by the daughter he trusted. I searched for any subconscious meanness in me, any unknown harboring of resentment, any feeling of retribution and found myself unable to conclude that I wished to create this illusion. I don't do vengeance well…I simply can't hold on to the feeling long enough to activate any vengeful action. I can't recall a time that I was ever vengeful. There have been many times I wanted to take a bite of somebody, but I couldn't imagine liking myself afterward. My most guarded nasty characteristic is that I am silver-tongued in expressing myself in such a declarative way that there is no doubt left about where I stand or what I think. If I ever exceeded a proper limit, I apologized. The good news was that I rarely felt the need because it felt like a kissing cousin of judgment. Many friends have expressed their envy of my ability to say what I think without trepidation or getting tongue-tied. So many have said that they can always think later of what they could or should have said. Who knows which action is better? For me, I will speak truthfully when I feel it necessary.

Dr. Merle Bonney, my favorite graduate psychology professor, gave a lecture on guilt for an hour and a half one day. The remembrance of that lecture came to mind as I was wrestling with my feelings and Dad. Dr. Bonney, professor emeritus, small, hunchbacked and with his forefinger missing due to a lawnmower accident as a kid, gestured with his middle finger to make a point, and all us of would laugh because our sweet idol was always "giving us the finger!" He would then slap his forehead and continue with lectures that felt like recited poetry. He touched our humanity and demanded that we always be better than yesterday.

I drove an hour each way from home to the university. One day while driving the Interstate, I was behind a horrible accident of two cars in a head on collision. One car had passed over the median in a construction zone. After pulling off the highway, I ran to the nearest car. There were two children in the back seat of the smoking vehicle. And a newly-arrived Samaritan and I pulled them out and waved for cars to stop and help. My accomplice got the adults out, but it was evident they were dead. I thought of my two darling daughters at home, and wretched at the side of the road. The State Troopers arrived quickly, took my statement and told me to get back in my car and go on.

I had seen death before many times in North Africa, but never of children. Shaken to my core, I arrived late to Dr. Bonney's lecture on guilt. As I scooted through the back door into the classroom where my six male classmates sat, I tried to, unobtrusively, take my seat. Dr. Bonney pointed his middle finger at me and asked me to tell him something that I felt guilty about for a long time.

"Miss, did you hear me? Would you please tell me something that you have carried as guilt for some time. We are all friends here, and we will keep your confidence."

I was not at all worried about confidentiality because my guilt was not something that the media would relish. It was my own personal and very private hell. All these years, in spite of "knowing" better, in spite of the beautiful conversations with Sissy Jean, and, definitely, in spite of not being able to change things or go back and do it differently, I felt enormous guilt about not telling my mother that she was dying so that she could make decisions and say good-byes her way. I had kept that promise to Dad to stay quiet, even though I believed with all my heart that it was wrong. Just so wrong. I would not want to be treated that way. In my prayers, I had often asked for forgiveness for the promise I made to Dad, but guilt still visited.

"Well, Dr. Bonney, I feel very guilty that I agreed with my dad to not tell my mother that she was dying of cancer when I was a teenager. It was the wrong thing to promise, and it still haunts me."

"That was a very hard promise, and it must have been difficult to keep. I am sorry about your mother. Now, tell me, please, the three components necessary for authentic and necessary guilt."

I really respected this man, knew he had a great reputation, was of high moral character and was a favorite of hundreds, if not thousands, of students over the years. Nonetheless, at this moment, I thought he was being mean.

"The three necessary components of guilt are 1) premeditation, 2) malicious intent and 3) harm. All three must be present." I replied, knowing my lectures notes well.

"So, was there premeditation?" he asked matter-of-factly.

"Yes, sir. I made a promise to my father to not tell."

"I see. And do you believe that there was harm done by not telling your mom she was dying?" he asked, a bit more softly.

"Absolutely. She was denied choices and conversations that should and could have occurred. My brother and I needed to say proper and loving good-byes."

"Of course you did. And I join you in your regret, although I bet your mom knew how much you loved her," said the caring, empathic epitome of a true psychologist and human being.

"Now, tell me there was malicious intent!" he said with his face directly in front of mine, with eyes filled with tears. He took my head, held it to his eighty year old chest and sighed. Then he released me, asked me to stand and turn around. Thinking that it bordered on mean to ask me to do this since I had tears flowing silently, I did as he directed, only to find all of my male classmates tearful, too.

"Do you see your big, husky classmates with tears in their eyes? Those tears are not for your story, but for one of their own that now brings home the truth about guilt. It is almost always a manufactured emotion in good people. Unfortunately, the mentally ill or bad apples don't have enough of that emotion," said the professor that I loved as "THE" professor of all time.

On particularly rough days, when you're
sure you can't possibly endure anymore,
remind yourself that your track record for
getting through bad days so far is 100%

Unknown

23

Dad and Ginny were constantly on my mind. However, they had vanished! Even the post office and utility companies were unable to help. Nothing. I desperately wanted to apologize for the hurt I had caused. The only thing I could think of that might yield some information was a private detective. Within 48 hours I had an address and a phone number of a trailer park about two hours south of Dallas. Since a phone call would surely result in an ugly hang-up, I wrote a very true and heart-felt apology letter. After two weeks, I wrote another. Nothing. So I made it my custom to write a letter every two weeks with news of the family, the girls' activities, my plans for travel and anything I thought might be of interest. In each letter I reminded him of my sorrow at our separation and that I was eager to see him. I was very concerned about their financial security since I had been supplementing their social security for some time. Dad had changed banks, so I could no longer secretly fund their account. Dad, historically, got mad, raged, threatened, and then backed off... with me. Phil never had that waiver. So it was continually surprising that I did not hear a peep from him.

One night, I needed some sweet and fun memories to bolster my spirits, so I drifted into a history of my romance with Bill. I remembered being surprised when he asked me out since I thought he was married. He quickly assured me that he was definitely NOT married, had recently exited an unworkable relationship and thought I was interesting. Then he added he would like to hang out together. That got my attention. So I accepted a date to go to the miniature Grand Prix race track to race little cars. My hope was to beat this super-masculine driver at his game. He handed me his driver's license and a credit card and asked me to get our tickets while he visited the men's room. I suddenly gasped! His driver's license indicated he was ten years my junior! When he re-joined me a few minutes later, I told him what I had discovered and that I could not date someone a decade younger. "Nonsense," he said and took the tickets. We proceeded to have the time of our lives racing for an hour. Of course, I eventually won!!

I nicknamed him "Ace" because he was a perfectionist at everything he did: flying, driving, mechanics, cleaning, camping, closet arrangement, record-keeping, log books, car maintenance or anything. He was meticulous. I found little that he did not do well. Liking the nickname, it stuck. And for the last 36 years he has been known by our good friends as "Ace-Man" or just "Ace."

Although I found him to be lots of fun, a maverick, and a good-guy biker (all feathers in his courtship cap), his best qualities were being tender, patient, understanding, helpful and kind. They weighed even heavier in his favor. He was a quick learner, resilient, investigative, inventive...but never, ever boring. I was hooked for sure. My friends were protective and skeptical of my growing relationship. The exception was my business associate, Dr. Nancy Glass. She saw through the diamond-in-the-rough stuff, and witnessed my growing happiness and how good we were together. She never voiced one word of judgment or skepticism. My other good friends who cared deeply for my welfare and my decisions expressed concern. I had to trust myself.

One weekend we flew to Epcot Center, stayed on Lake Buena Vista and just relaxed. As we sat on a park bench we were fascinated with a sky-writing plane penning out a message. We each started saying the message out loud. It read "I...love...you." Ace informed me, tongue-in-cheek, that he had arranged the sky-writing, and he hoped I liked it. At just that moment the last word appeared... "Rosie." He laughed and proclaimed they misspelled my name. His sense of humor was so present, fun, quick and endearing. Henceforth, my nickname became "Rosie."

Another vacation when the girls were away, we flew to Honolulu after Christmas for a few days. It was a thrill to rent a small plane, and I flew as pilot-in-command from Honolulu to Kauai over open ocean and then the Waimea Canyon, (a box canyon where a pilot can fly in the mile-wide canyon and then must climb aggressively to exit upward at the end of the fourteen mile traverse). It was breathtakingly beautiful and I felt empowered, skilled and so glad that Ace was the co-pilot.

On New Year's Eve, while we stood on the balcony of the hotel across from Waikiki Beach, I heard bands playing. Coming down the boulevard was a huge New Year's Eve parade with bands, floats, fireworks, dancers and all manner of entertainment. I quickly called Ace to come see the parade I had arranged for his birthday which is New Year's Day. He was appropriately appreciative, went along with the joke and put it in the same category as the Rosie joke.

I not only immensely enjoyed his presence but also admired and envied his sense of freedom and individualism. We worked so well together.

For years I had loved poetry, mainly because so much can be said with so few words. While dating Ace, I began to write frequently. At our two year mark, he had six loose-leaf notebooks of my poems. Some silly, others profound, some risqué, but most were just loving declarations.

One of my favorites came to mind: <u>The Gifts</u>

Before I loved you,
My soul was not really empty;
It just had space to spare.
Quiet corners lay agape
Hoping for the magic that would
Let me trust more than just myself.
Before I listened to love,
I could only hear the echoes
Of my own questions;
And the answers volleyed between
Inviolate and doubt;
Questions gave birth to greater,
More strident inquiries.
I felt unanchored.
Sometimes afloat.
Life, death, love, God,
Where was the fit, snug with mitered edges?
When I accepted love,
The gifts appeared, freely served,
By your gentle offering.
I, who create trust in a world of others, now
Discover this elastic bond with you.
Surreptitiously, you weave it into my soul.

You give the intangible form and substance.
You make trust a hollowed word.
    Because you love so purely,
You speak of power for goodness,
Bequeathing me introductions to
White Light, Inner Circles, Great
Mysteries and beauties of the Other Side.
And always,
    Always,
It is your abiding love, my heart,
That wraps these gifts I now store
Forever vaulted safely inside me.
Love opens me...to fill you.
The gifts become a circle
Ringed with vibrations
That touch us both
At the same time.

In February, as a treat, we went to the Broadmoor Hotel in Colorado Springs. Ace would ski, and I would drink hot chocolate, read and enter good conversations with interesting people around a blazing fire pit at the bottom of the slope. I knew that we were in this special place because Ace would propose. While seated at the best table in the elegant, lake-side hotel restaurant, I just knew he would make good on his pre-Christmas question. Didn't happen!

After exiting the slope for the last time the next afternoon, he filled the largest claw-foot tub I had ever seen with hot water and poured in the bubble bath. We both got in, facing each other with bubbles up to our chins, and enjoyed the warmth of soothing water. Ace looked at me and said: "This bathtub has a ring." I was horrified, being the neatnik that I am. I could not abide the thought of an unclean tub. Then with a smirk, he brought his index finger up out of the bubbles and displayed a diamond engagement ring.

"You're supposed to be on bended knee, not your butt," I said laughing heartily.

"You know me; I have to do it my way. And I love you with all my heart, and I want to spend my life with you. Will you marry me?"

I was enjoying the moment, the sweetness of the proposal and feeling so much love that I took a moment. Then, Ace said: "You're not going to say No, are you?"

"Of course not! We will live happily ever after. Yes...Yes...Yes," I answered lovingly.

At spring break in March, we took the girls with us to L.A., were married by a beloved minister, went to Disneyland in the afternoon and flew to Maui the next morning. The four of us skied, para-sailed, beachcombed, sampled all sorts of international restaurant fare and spent a week just having fun. I had not announced the pending wedding to anyone but Nancy. Showers, dinner parties or lots of wedding talk were not at all interesting to me. Not telling my brother was a decision I would do differently if given the chance. But I feared he would secretly plan some sort of surprise celebration...which he was known for. He forgave me and liked my new husband.

Ace was never going to marry and never going to have children. After helping rear six of the other eight siblings in his family of origin, he had had enough of rearing kids. Now, he was married with two adolescent daughters who were normal, active, sometimes mouthy, but always caring, very busy girls. They were slightly embarrassed by his Harley until the boys at school were excited that their stepdad had a motorcycle and was a pilot. He upgraded the van to something that the whole family could use, took us all camping, floated the Guadalupe River with their school friends, had pool parties in the back yard and took friends on motorcycle rides and airplane rides. The new family situation took some getting used to, but the girls tried hard to make it work, as did Ace. It was a real problem when Ace and I came back from Treetops and found the garage full of garbage bags filled with beer bottles. We soon discovered the pool sweep was broken and some of my good jewelry was gone. Worst of all, Ace's custom-made hunting knife with a turquoise handle and his pistol were missing.

Emma confessed to inviting fifteen people over for a party (she was supposed to be staying with the superintendent of schools), and SIXTY teen-agers showed up. It was apparent that they had ransacked the house because the gun was well hidden. Ace soon discovered that his leather motorcycle jacket was missing as well as his rifle. As calmly as he could manage, he informed Emma to call all the friends she knew were in attendance, tell them that her stepdad said that we would wait three hours for the missing items to be put on the front porch with no questions asked. After that, he would call the police to start fingerprinting the closets. Everything was returned except the hunting knife and my diamond drop. Emma told us she knew she was grounded until the next Ice Age, and we confirmed her assessment of the situation. It was a big lesson for all of us. Missing weapons had us hyperventilating. We bought a gun safe soon thereafter.

As summer came, Emma went to camp in Santa Barbara, California, and Eleanor went to Spain for a month long immersion in the Spanish language. Ace was flying charter flights carrying sports teams, World Soccer teams from all over the world, singers, actors and musicians. Though he worked long hours and a difficult schedule, it was always fun to hear about whom he had met the past week. Being married to a pilot is being alone half the time, talking on the phone to his hotel room and waiting to see him again in a few days. I got a bit of a breather with the girls gone. Ace was working and summer office hours were always a little lighter. I found some time to read, cook, meditate and enjoy life.

I had neglected my sweet times with Sissy Jean. I was so happy, so busy and so into something new. Nevertheless, I missed her loving presence. Her insight and way of making me think always gently nudged me into higher awareness where consciousness is so healing and enlightening.

Again, as I sat on the swing on the back porch in the shade of a massive oak, I closed my eyes and went into deep meditation. Immediately, the loving voice of Sissy wafted close by upon my call.

"Sissy, I am so glad to be with you and tell you how happy I am. I never knew this kind of daily happiness existed. Can you tell?"

"*Of course, sweet one, I can tell. Your whole being vibrates differently. You now allow the free flow of energy within your body without resistance. When you were not happy, and when illusions dominated your life, you resisted and stopped the flow of energetic love that is a promised gift from Source. You lived many years unaware of the restriction on your being because you did not surrender to the holiness of non-resistance. You were unwilling to trust your inner self to enable the surrender. Now, you have let go of unwillingness and restriction and love has opened you to unlimited abundance and grace.*"

"Oh, Sissy, I wish I had done this so many years ago. Why did I not give myself permission to live with more joy in my heart?"

"My beloved, there was no mistake in the path you took at that time. The illusions you created with your former mate were what you needed to learn about the necessity of letting go, letting others find their way, believing you deserved daily, abundant joy, coming to know that the judgment of others is irrelevant and that you are always the total cause of anything that happens or doesn't happen in your life. When you finally understood that, your consciousness shifted into higher awareness and happier results."

"I so wish everyone knew what I know from talking with you. The planet would be so much more peaceful. Anger, rage, vengeance and violence would disappear."

"Yes, Annie, the world would change drastically. It could bathe in the essence of love and goodness. Fear, as we have discussed before, condemns so many to their self-imposed restrictions. The act of surrender is a very courageous event for low-vibrational humans, yet it yields so much reward."

"I love living without fear, without so much doubt or wonder and without rules that make no sense. Trusting myself to leave the rigors of religion, the unnecessary commitment to an unhappy relationship and to love my family unit without reservations is a freedom I give thanks for every moment."

"Stay focused in awareness, Annie-girl. Awareness has its constant reward of love, compassion and peace."

I fell peacefully asleep in the warmth of the summer air and with the slight movement of my meditation swing.

When I entered my office the next day, flowers, full of fragrance and color, were setting on the reception room table. The card read: "Congratulations on your new office space." We had recently leased and decorated new cornered and windowed offices near a very favorable location just off a major freeway. Nancy, a closet decorator, had made everything beautiful and inviting, so I was not surprised at the delivery of the bouquet. However, I was surprised that there was no signature. I just assumed it was from the building management.

The truth was to unfold the next day. As I was wrapping up my day with phone calls and patient progress notes, there was a knock on my consultation room door. The door opened slightly to reveal the smiling face of my ex-husband. He asked if he could have a moment of my time and if I liked the flowers? Taken aback for a second, I said thank you and that I didn't know they were from him. Smiling devilishly, he took a seat and asked me to join him.

"Joe, why are you here? Is something wrong or did you just want to see the new offices?" I asked.

"Your offices are elegant. And, yes, there is something wrong."

"Please tell me," I asked, my heart picking up speed, thinking immediately about the girls.

"Well, you know that when we got divorced that I was mentally ill, but I have now recovered. I agreed to an unfair division of the community property, and we should re-divide our assets in a more equitable way. So I would like to arrange a time when we can do that."

"Joe, we were both sad that our relationship did not work. We made the right decision to divorce. I am a psychotherapist, and I did not notice any mental illness. Sadness, yes. As you know, I took all the debt, all the responsibility, no child support and no cash from your sizeable account. You, actually, got a sweetheart deal," I said matter-of-factly, trying to hide the slow seething in my chest.

"I don't see it that way. I want you to reconsider. I'll be in touch," he said flatly. He departed without another word.

There was a sinister nature to his tone. Although unrecognizable to anyone else, I had been married to him for seventeen years. I knew that more was brewing, and I could not imagine that I was creating an illusion with Joe in it. I quieted the negative thoughts, went to get groceries but still had a slight churn in my mid-section. On my way home, I thought of his choice of the words "mental illness" and tried to discern his purpose.

Eleanor asked if Dad could use Treetops for spring break so he, his girlfriend and Eleanor's best friend could go on vacation. I agreed, knowing that Eleanor and her best friend would have a great time at the sea. However, while they were gone, I got a letter from Joe that was sent the day he left. It sounded so crazy and bizarre that I had to read it several times, talking out loud to myself about its contents. In psychology we often use the phrase "word salad" to refer to the speech of schizophrenics when they are in a bizarre, alternate reality. It read like that, but there was no possibility that Joe was schizophrenic, and that was provable. We had spent some time in marriage counseling with a recognized psychiatrist. When I asked him during a session about Joe, he professionally informed me that fear and laziness were more of what was active in Joe's personality.

Both the psychiatrist and I knew that Joe did not have any significant mental illness.

I called my divorce lawyer and reported the recent visit and letter from Joe and asked for his advice. He volunteered to write a cease and desist letter, and asked me to record everything I could remember, just in case the need arose.

My birthday party was in full swing in our living room with good friends, good music, good food and drinks and really good conversations. In the midst of all this joy, the doorbell rang, and I went to answer it thinking it was the arrival of a late guest. But when I opened the door, I was greeted by Kathy, Joe's girlfriend, stepping forward to hand me a letter. She turned to leave, and I shut the door. I felt the familiar tummy churn. The former ebullience that had buoyed my spirits so high was now gone.

All the guests were finally escorted to the front lawn, and we waved them goodbye. I returned to the kitchen where I had left the letter atop a cookbook. Upon opening it, I found a crazy collection of sentences supporting a re-opening of the community property settlement in light of his "severe mental illness" and a deadline for responding. The next morning I was going to have to call my lawyer again. Needless to say, I did not sleep well and spent most of the night wondering how in the heck I had manifested this illusion. What further lesson did I have to learn with Joe?

Emma came home from school hysterical, shaking uncontrollably and clinging to me so hard that breathing was becoming difficult. I calmed her by rubbing her back and patting her head and convinced her to sit and tell me the truth because we could solve anything. She blurted out that her dad had come to school to tell her that she would be getting a piece of paper from the sheriff that would make her go to court to talk, and if she didn't talk she would go to jail.

I became Mama Grizzley Bear. No one was going to frighten my sweet Emma or Eleanor...let alone threaten them to achieve his heartless initiative. As I explained what a subpoena was and that I would intervene on her behalf, Emma loosened her tight grip on my hand and said she would trust me. Frightened, bewildered, betrayed and threatened by her own father was shattering to my twelve year old daughter. Within twenty-four hours, I scheduled an appointment for her with a counselor. This situation was too much for me to handle, and she needed an objective person who she didn't need to protect.

Every few weeks the girls would receive articles on depression in envelopes addressed to them. Typical of teenagers, they paid little attention to reading long articles. At the end of the school year, Joe informed the girls he was going to Houston for help with a very serious illness, presumably cancer. As they relayed this information to me, my first thought was MD Anderson, the world-renown cancer research hospital. Both girls were crying and fearful that their dad was dying. Emma was afraid he had AIDS since it was all over the news, and she had written a paper on it recently.

It's darn difficult to assure your children that all is well when you don't know what the heck is going on! We all decided we would pray for his recovery, and expect good news. Then…Emma took a phone call from a pilot friend of ours that was in the Bahamas. He reported that someone had broken into our home there, and she should tell her mom and stepdad. When the news was relayed to me, I knew immediately that Joe was at Treetops without permission. Calling a friend on the island, my suspicion was confirmed. The girls were in the den with me when I made the call. They were furious. We had been praying, hoping and wishing him well, while he had been lying to his daughters about being in Houston for medical treatment. He was actually illegally in residence at our vacation home. My fists clenched and my heart raced.

When Joe returned home two weeks later, he called the girls and reported that he was out of the hospital. They angrily confronted his lies and said they did not want to see him. Ace went into protective mode by changing all the locks and codes at our home, and then hired a locksmith to put Medico locks on all the doors at Treetops. It would take a diamond tip drill hours to remove the high-dollar Medicos. Additionally, we hired a caretaker to check on the house each week and to report on intruders or any other issues.

I was dealing with the disbelief of all this, daughters who were hurt and venting their anger on me (because it was safe to do so), navigating a new marriage, racking up legal and security bills weekly, managing a full practice and, unwittingly, sort of holding my breath. My intuition has always served me well. So when I saw the man in an old suit sitting in my waiting room with the next patient, I knew. He asked me to identify myself, handed me the envelope and announced, politely, that I had been served. My patient asked if that happened often; I laughed, and said: "All the time," jokingly.

Tragedy in life normally comes with betrayal and compromise, and trading on your integrity and not having dignity in life. That's really where failure comes.

Ted Cochrane

24

I fearfully retreated to my bedroom to be alone. When I opened the envelope with the lawsuit inside, I saw who the lawyer for the claimant was--the son of the man to whom Joe had sold his law firm. I was totally exhausted by Joe's crazy letters, having to involve my divorce lawyer to handle some cease and desist issues, and, frankly, wanted to be rid of the man who had lied to me and wounded my children. I simply sat there and let myself cry.

On the surface, I wanted to be able to be nasty, mean, vengeful and irresponsible and not concern myself with the illusions that kept producing such ugliness. That feeling was something I could not hold on to nor embrace nor put into practice. I would like to imagine that I could return in kind the morally reprehensible, hideous accusations that were now spelled out in the lawsuit. I wished for all it was worth that I did not have the conscience I had lived with all my life. Why couldn't I just put it aside for a while and fight like a warrior? I simply was no good at meeting Joe on his turf of deceit, cruelty and cunning scenarios. On the one hand, I felt gratitude that I was not a match for Joe. On the other, I wanted to battle, get down and dirty and win. The absolute truth was: I was damn mad…and for good reason. Even with ALL the financial responsibility for our children, investments, and going to work every day, I tried to be a good wife in a new marriage. Must I also handle the growing nuisance of an ex-husband who had vacated all responsibility? In spite of all my "knowingness," I sank into feelings of retribution, self-pity, angst and anger. Even though I knew better, I did it anyway.

The lawsuit was something I had never heard of called an Equitable Bill of Review. It claimed that I had unduly influenced my ex-husband in the agreement of the original division of the community property. He petitioned the court to review the original division, determine it was not equitable and issue an order to re-divide the community property. While more than mad, I logically found some humor in the assertion that I had unduly influenced Joe. If I had that kind of power, he would not be suing me. Lately, lots of things were not making sense.

Joe could have served my attorney as my agent. However, he made sure I was served at my office late on Friday afternoon so I would have to stew all weekend. He was right, of course, because I became more indignant and madder with each passing hour. I called my attorney and heard his answering machine. I left a message, knowing it would be Monday before I would hear from him.

Surely, Monday would bring some relief. My lawyer would tell me what to do and lay out a course of action that I could wrap my head around. However, when I picked up his message, he informed me that a Bill of Review was above his pay grade, and that I needed to hire a lawyer that could better handle this suit. He wished me luck. Well, damn!

The lawyer that my divorce lawyer had recommended was available for an afternoon appointment two days later. I rescheduled my patients and showed up with my lawsuit papers in hand. I was eager to know how to proceed and have a plan that would be simple and fast. Little did I know that the law works slower than a Galapagos tortoise.

As I walked into the lawyer's waiting room and looked around, I felt a myriad of emotions. The lawyers in this office handled family law cases only. The three women sitting in the reception room were obviously there for divorce and child custody reasons. One looked like a deer in the head lights, and one was trying to support her friend who was crying, softly saying she couldn't live if "he" got custody of the children. For a moment, I felt some guilt that I didn't have to worry about a custody battle. But, at the same time, I was grateful that custody of the children was not the issue. The two receptionists were ready with Kleenex boxes and words of sympathy and support, being very caring and good at their jobs.

A lovely lady with amazingly good energy approached me, introduced herself as Jean LaMont. She was the legal assistant to my new lawyer, Steve Hulme. In my research of him, I had found nothing but compliments, praise and good recommendations. The comments found in my investigation said he was bright, down-to-earth, focused, possessed a great sense of humor and was forthright and quite clever. After meeting him, I had to agree.

He informed me he would respond to the lawsuit with a general denial, and we would go from there. Steve was easy to talk to, gave me a feeling of assurance and confidence and didn't seem overly concerned. The degrees on the wall confirmed a law degree from the University of Texas, a school that had a reputation for just being accepted as an honor. I left feeling I was in good hands. Jean walked me to the door and assured me that I was not to worry. If I had questions or concerns, I was to call her. She also gave me her number. She was the agent of my relief.

My next meeting with Steve was an explanation of what was being alleged and what the lawsuit meant. He carefully and exquisitely explained that a Bill of Review was rare, but it was an option under the law to correct a wrong. There were three prongs to the bill: a party had been unduly influenced (like putting a gun to the head) unmixed with negligence on the part of the complaining party, misconduct of the court (judge or jury being paid off or something like that) and fraud (misrepresenting the assets of the marriage). Joe was claiming that he was unduly influenced by me for two reasons: he was severely depressed, and I used my skills as a psychotherapist to persuade him to sign the agreement. Neither one of these allegations was even close to the truth, but I had to show that he was wrong. Steve informed me that this was not a criminal trial where I was presumed innocent until proven guilty. This trial would determine the rightness or wrongness of people's actions, and then decide the financial consequences. Being very insistent on what was alleged was NOT the truth, Steve smiled and informed me that it was his job to prove that.

Depositions followed at a slow pace. I was deposed on video for hours. My friends were subpoenaed and deposed. Hearings on procedure and subpoenas for financial information, taxes, my office records, bank records, investment properties, etc were conducted. Monthly legal bills were exceeding my ability to keep up. The court had decided to bifurcate the trial, splitting it into two parts: the first trial would determine if a second trial was needed. If so, the next trial would decide about the division of the assets. However, before the first trial ever began, there were massive issues. Steve and I showed up seven times for hearings, only to be sent home four of those times due to scheduling issues of the other side, illness of a party, appearances in other cases, etc. The rescheduling was nothing but a blatant attempt to make me cancel a day of patients. This purposeful ruse by Joe was designed to not only inconvenience me but also cost me dearly. I knew Joe knew how to manage the courthouse inner workings, and Steve would only look like a whiner if he brought it up to the court. We suffered through it, went for a drink at happy hour with Jean, laughed and gave ourselves permission to vent joyfully.

Then…at one of the hearings, we learned that Joe had written to my major investment holding and informed them that there was an ongoing lawsuit about the ownership of that asset. As a result, they sent a sizeable dividend check to the court. The judge then divided it between Joe and me without a decision about the Bill of Review or any determination about the facts in the case! Steve and I were incredulous. The court should have held the funds in escrow, but it distributed them prematurely. Telling Steve something was amiss, I then learned that the judge and his wife played bridge every week with the parents of Joe's attorney. It was obvious that the distribution was not for Joe, but for his attorney's fees. So much for a fair legal system. The judge knew we would not insult him or confront him before a scheduled trial.

As I was recovering from that little trickery, my husband took some time off to go to Treetops to do some painting and cistern repairs. Ace was a typical pilot personality: focused, calm and informational. However, his voice on the other end of the phone was so pitched, so angry and distraught that I had trouble understanding what he was saying. Finally, he was able to report that he had found Treetops vandalized, obviously by Joe. All the doors were off their hinges, making the Medico locks useless. The house had standing water from roof leaks because it had been tampered with so that water could penetrate. All the tools were missing!

The emotional distress with actions such as these was overwhelming. The reality of getting workers there to fix the problem, shipping materials from West Palm Beach on a freighter and getting them up the hills to our property, replacing tools that we had brought in our suitcases over the years was an enormous and expensive task. We were dead in the water unless help arrived. And besides that, Treetops was in a foreign country outside the criminal jurisdiction of Joe's destruction of property as evidence in our ongoing lawsuit. The confirmation that Joe was the culprit was that the police had all the Medico locks, given to them by Joe, who informed them that his ex-wife had violated HIS property. The caretaker apologized that he had not been able to prevent the destruction due to being off the island for a week in Nassau for a family funeral.

Ace and a longtime friend, Ron, from Florida, ordered the materials, began the demolition of the old roof, fixed the doors, put on new pedestrian locks, hired Haitian migrants to carry lumber from the dock up the steep hill to the house and began construction of a pitched roof. The old roof was a butterfly basin, with a pipe in the middle that caught the rainwater and drained into a cistern. The new roof was constructed with proper pitch to drain into a gutter system that connected to the underground cistern. Within two weeks of the arrival of materials, Ron and Ace had the roof done and connected to the cistern. The checkbook was screaming for breath, but the two hard-working men had, essentially, salvaged the beloved house.

Finally, a year after being served, deposed and twisted into an emotional pretzel, the trial started. I can attest to the fact that there is nothing like looking at a room full of potential jurors and knowing that they hold your finances and the welfare of your family in their hands. As voir dire (examination of a prospective juror) continued, I heard testimony from people who were reasonably objective. There were religious zealots who thought divorce was immoral, housewives who thought a woman should not work outside the home, an attorney who was indifferent, as well as many others.

I thought of my children who should never have to know this consequence of a divorce. Thankfully they were sheltered from this uncomfortable, and, at times, absurd proceeding. I thought of the interrupted lives of these potential jurors who had been compelled to come to court and be interviewed for a conspicuously artificial show of ingenuity. Then there was the expense of the civil court system for a delusional whim of an unethical man who was unwilling to accept his life or responsibility for his actions. I felt consumed by the surrealism and absurdity of the event. I squelched an understandable scream and continued the charade. My only saving grace was that Steve bought Jean, Ace and me burgers and beer until we found the ability to laugh at life for an hour or so late in the day.

The jury was seated, instructed and focused. As the trial began, I asked for divine guidance for all of us in this newly-oiled mahogany room of intended and promised justice, and hoped for clarity and wisdom to prevail. I meant well. I believed my prayer, but I soon was swept into the delusional testimony of the man I had lived with for seventeen years, put through law school, and was the father of our children. Surrealism reigned.

Joe was the first to take the witness chair. The court asked for his name and address. Joe stated his name, then refused to give his address saying he wanted to protect himself. The very first statement out of his mouth got the immediate attention of the jury. The court did not ask for an explanation, but it became evident that his claim of fear pertained to me and my husband, the two people in the world who wanted nothing to do with him. Since the children would no longer see him, we actually did not know his address. Joe began to explain how depressed he had been, how much he was unable to function and how much under my psychological control he was, but didn't recognize it until post divorce. His behavior was absurd, rehearsed, and totally untruthful. He spent long minutes in vituperative railings that astonished all present in the courtroom. Then I heard the question and answer that put me over the edge. His attorney asked if he was now practicing law, and Joe answered that he was unable to do so. When asked where he went to law school and how he paid for it, Joe answered in great detail about how he worked nights and weekends to put himself through school, pay for law books, etc. I leaned forward, ready to yell, but caught myself. The flashbacks of working five days and four nights a week, studying with him all weekend while cooking and doing chores and almost a week in the hospital for exhaustion were memories that exploded in every part of my being. I sat, trying to settle my feeling of dizziness, my churning stomach and the rage that pulsed through every corpuscle of my body. My insides were out of control, and I shook as I held onto the chair arms to steady myself.

I barely remember the rest of the testimony that day. I saw his arms flailing in the air as he described something, cementing his Hollywood performance of "mental illness" in the minds of the jury...and me. The character on the witness stand looked and acted crazy as hell. I had never, ever seen this behavior before! Knowing Joe's history with fooling the insurance company and doctor about his feigned deafness, I began to suspect that he was building a case even more sinister for presentation to the jury. At one point, I heard him say that I had lifted him in the air and hurled him down a set of stairs. The jury chuckled, looking over at my five foot three frame. The plan was so clever and seemed to be working. He knew the jury was now convinced he was lying, but also were convinced that he, indeed, was mentally ill, and, therefore, it was reasonable to think that I had taken advantage of this poor man.

When I dragged myself home and looked for the girls, I found Emma in pain on her bed. Rocking back and forth, holding her head, she managed to tell me that her head felt like it was cracking open and she was blind in one eye. Ace and I got her into the car, drove to the emergency room and waited for the results of the MRI. The doctors would not give her anything for pain until they knew more about a possible diagnosis. Hours later we were informed that she had optic neuritis, an inflammation of the optic nerve. Indeed, it was extremely painful. At home, I tucked this teenager into her bed, watched her breathing as it became more rhythmic when the pain medication took effect but still felt the rage of the day's proceedings.

Needless to say, I showed up at court the next morning still mad and very sleep-deprived. Steve told me just to be myself as I was invited to take the witness stand, but the "self" that walked across the court room to the witness chair was not the "self" that I lived with most days. I had been drawn into the illusion of a trial that was foreign to reality, was a staged performance, was void of truth, dignity or decorum. It was, in truth, a farce. I thought of Sissy for a moment, but could not rise above the spectacle to sit in the peace of higher consciousness. Besides, the court room is no place to start a fight about illusions. Joe already appeared delusional and theatrical.

Suffice to say, I was a horrible witness for my case. Tired and angry, I came across as a shrew. In the minds of the jurors I could probably be fully capable of doing whatever I was accused of. The title of Doctor, which Joe's attorney used to a nauseating degree, made me sound like I was rolling in dough, insensitive to the plight of my ex-husband and shameful. The ten thousand dollar Cessna 152 was made to appear as a Lear Jet, with me flitting around the skies having fun while poor Joe could hardly take care of himself.

A local psychiatrist who had interviewed Joe for four hours only, testified that Joe suffered from histrionic personality disorder. As a therapist, I was well aware of the characteristics of that disorder... and then I KNEW. HPD, as was depression, is one of the disorders that can be easily faked. Joe had done his homework. All ten types of personality disorders are incurable, but HPD specifically notes that the patient is "easily suggestible, easily influenced by others or circumstances." The patient is also flamboyant, boisterous and attention grabbing. It was the perfect diagnosis for what Joe was claiming. All the components were easy to pretend. The irony of Joe's choice of playing "the histrionic" was that he had always been an introvert, as all his friends could have testified. I spent seventeen years dealing with his introversion. His Dallas psychiatrist spent only four hours with the patient and was easily duped. The travesty was just one more part of the circus playing out in the courtroom.

A second psychiatrist, whom we had seen ten years before for marriage counseling, testified that Joe might have had depression, but he had such an introverted personality that it was hard to tell. He remembered that Joe did not like social events or any attention focused on him and did not like the practice of law.

How could the two psychiatrists testify to very different and opposite disorders without an explanation?

I did my best to explain to the jury that I have never witnessed any of the bizarre behavior that was being displayed in the court room. I talked about our children and Joe's saying he had cancer when he was actually at Treetops destroying my vacation home. Nonetheless, I could see contempt in the jurors' eyes that I had a home in the Bahamas. Ironically, I understood their perspective.

Finally, the trial focused on the financial division of the property which was 54% in favor of Joe. Steve was able to show that Joe had done all the books for my practice after the divorce until I remarried, prepared the tax returns, done the accounting for the investments, managed the rent houses, coached the girls' soccer teams and made multiple trips to the Bahamas. It was discovered that Joe had bought cars, taken trips and day-traded on the stock market with disastrous results and was out of money. Hence, the lawsuit. Steve was able to get the point across that I had always taken care of this man who was now out of money and wanted to come back to the well via the courtroom. Additionally, I learned for the first time that Joe had filed the lawsuit only hours before the statute of limitations expired.

I sat in the chair next to my lawyer and felt naïve, stupid, duped, used, manipulated and embarrassed. My caring attitude and doubt about handling a divorce that hurt the children, as well as my standing in the community, were all used against me by a man I had trusted and lived with for seventeen years. I was numb...just numb.

The verdict came. The two attorneys and the judge went into chambers. In a civil trial the jurors are asked to answer questions. They had decided, but not unanimously, that I had influenced Joe in the division of property. They also found that Joe was negligent in his behavior and in making decisions. It had been shown that he was able to handle so much of the business issues of the family before and after the divorce. The jury decision meant that Joe did not meet his obligation to the first prong of the Bill of Review. The court should have ruled for the respondent (me) but, instead, the judge said he thought the parties should have a second trial and look to see if the finances were divided fairly. Steve and I were astounded.

If a man knows not to
which port he sails,
no wind is favorable.

Seneca

About twice an hour, one phrase kept running through my mind: "You are one hundred percent responsible for everything that happens in your life." The sentence poked at me like a sticker caught in your skin that you could not get out. It wasn't just an annoyance. It was a demanding invitation to do something to take care of myself and find relief from the tension that affected every muscle of my body--the result being angst and continuing anger. Courtrooms are cauldrons that brew exhaustion, impatience and bewilderment, and I had been sitting in one for too long in the first go-around with Joe.

With the children at the homes of friends and Ace flying, I had the afternoon to myself, so I naturally headed for the shaded swing on the back porch. Touching the toe of my shoe lightly against the floor, I kept the swing in a gentle rocking motion until the rhythm matched my breathing and gave myself permission to go to the space that immediately aligns with Spirit. Here my heart filled with unspeakable, unexplainable love that soothed all illusions and dissolved me into deep meditation.

"Sissy, I am a mess. I have totally abandoned all my knowingness and have been snared by ugly illusions and destructive thoughts. Worse yet, I am embracing fear and great sadness, coupled with gnawing anger that sits in my throat. I know better, but I don't know how to combat the lies and betrayal that Joe has heaped upon me and with which he happily entertains a jury! Help!

"*Annalee, for the moment you have forgotten who you are. You are a child of God, holy in your very existence with a divine spark that guarantees that in God's plan there is no sacrifice, no loss, no betrayal. Everything is the same. In your courtroom, the illusions that you were experiencing were those that say you are the righteous, the condemned, the judge, the jury, the complainant, the defender, the observer and the disinterested. Your story is not real, and the proper response to everything is love.*"

"Sissy, the lies are horrible. Am I just to sit, listen, sing songs in my head while he babbles on about absurd scenarios for his own entertainment? Am I not to defend the ludicrous history he recounts to the jury? Am I to be a silly lamb with no response?

"No, sweet one. That is not at all what I am saying to you. You are in the illusion of a courtroom, and you are called upon to enter the illusion, be truthful and forthright...and trust. You cannot lose anything. Money, reputation, time and your innocence cannot be lost. The illusion may say they are lost. The Ego mind of others may determine that the illusions have different meanings. I promise you that nothing...do you hear me...nothing can be taken from you that matters unless Ego Mind determines it is part of your definition. What has gone on and will continue to play out in your courtroom is NOT who you are. The courtroom is a schoolroom. Let's look at what you are learning, and what you can learn in the next trial."

"Will you sit with me while I try to figure out the purpose of this illusion?" I asked, hopefully.

"Of course, and, as you know, I am always with you. Let's begin."

"I think this trial has been manifested by the both of us, Joe and me, to finally find some ending to a relationship that was never satisfying to either one of us. I have been able to let go, move on, find love, continue parenting and be responsible. Joe has not been able to do that. He is angry, dependent and hurt that someone else benefits from my love and sharing nature. He is using the tools he knows work best for him and that frighten me. He has a law degree as part of his arsenal for combat against my perceived abandonment of him."

"Yes, Annie, that is the illusion that both of you are engaged in with enormous help from Ego Mind plus an adversarial court system. Lawyers are willing to participate and friends encourage or support the illusionary stage. Many props and actors support the belief that there is goodness in judgment. THAT is the greatest untruth."

"Money is the biggest illusion. In court, one side wants the money of the other, and one side doesn't want to let go of what they have. Lives are played out inside this illusion as torment, hurt and destruction rain havoc on all the players. You will continue to feel anger and betrayal if you do not step back, see that it is a game that feels real, but is not. You will not feel better until you re-align with Source and confirm that NOTHING can hurt or destroy you. You must find a way to relinquish your acceptance of the legal illusions you find yourself involved in. You must replace fear with love, anger with forgiveness, anguish with tolerance and despair with knowingness. Your internal spiritual compass is always available to you."

"Sissy, you taught me that if I recognize and judge something in someone else, that actually is a mirror of myself. The illusion plays out to make the point. Joe is deceitful, a liar, a thief, a disingenuous actor and fake. Am I that, and I just don't see it?"

"Annie-girl, you are all of those things, if you choose to be. Joe stands as a reminder to stay in higher consciousness and not shift downward into Ego world. He is a fearful man, unequipped at this point to shift into any higher paradigm. Your duty is to see the holiness that exists in him and not judge him. Forgive him and bless him and his journey. Let him go and give him back to God."

"So, my job is to trust, bless and love. If I lose money, Treetops, health, reputation and time, I have to accept that it is all illusion, and that I will survive. I will find and give love and realize that I have lost nothing. I will try."

"Annalee Grace, your life, as is anyone's, is a trial by illusion. As you know, all is illusion with purpose. We are on the planet to put ourselves through the trial of all our illusions. You have chosen to do the double illusion: that is to experience a trial within a trial, a formidable task with rewarding discoveries. Your ultimate discovery, in spite of all the machinations and stage plays offered by Ego Mind, will be that nothing is more important than love... and no court can destroy that except by the fear hosted by Ego."

"So, Sissy Jean, my final lesson in knowingness will be that I release my brothers from the slavery of their illusions by forgiving them for the illusions I perceive in them."

"Yes, yes, yes! You blessed your soul with that thought, and I invite you to share it with all humanity."

"Sissy, I know the love you always speak of. I feel it so naturally when I am with you, but I find it difficult to put into words. Can you help me with that, please?"

"It would be my greatest joy in this moment. Spiritual love is our shared inheritance that awareness of Truth provides. When we are fully without judgment, fully forgiving, fully living our lives in harmony and, most of all, fully surrendering without any defiance, we are broadcasting love, teaching that it is the medicinal healer and the destroyer of Ego...and we feel a constancy of good will and gratitude. Spiritual love has none of the ego qualities of illusionary love. And it is surrender that brings the blessings of peace."

"I know that humans will not live in a perpetual state of spiritual love and harmony. It is important that one knows what it is and that it can be experienced, accessed, shared and taught. The hope is that your human race will begin to recognize and acknowledge that ego activity does not lead to

anything useful, kind, loving, aware and harmonious. Since you know and have experienced moments and minutes of spiritual love, you are a teacher, a guide, a resource for discovery and, at times, an example."

"Sissy-girl, that's heavy!" I sighed.

"No, Annie-girl, that's heavenly!" She giggled.

For the second time in my life, I shared the story of Sissy Jean. I knew I could trust Ace to understand and be accepting of my relationship with her. To my surprise, he told me about Roger, his non–physical being that he had discovered in his twenties. He had not shared the story before with anyone. We were beside ourselves that we both were open to communication from the Other Side and could share so much of that holy experience together. We soon found out that Sissy and Roger had been in cahoots with many things, including our meeting each other. The astonishment was exhilarating and empowering in that we both had a connection on two sides of the spiritual spectrum. Ace was more open, more accepting and more grateful; he taught me to trust more, seek more insight, live more with the concept of surrender (and sometimes with the concept of reckless abandon)! and to never, ever give in to fear. He was fearless. I was more cautious, but willing to stretch to limits not reached before. I was absolutely with the right partner…and not by accident!

The second trial was going to be scheduled. The preparations for this one were purely financial. Spending hours collating invoices, bills, checks and check registers, expenditures for the girls, their tuition, school uniforms, camps, trips, clothes, medical visits was a dizzying task. Pure presentation of the facts, coupled with the belief that I would survive anything the court decided, I felt less fearful and anxious. I was not thwarted by Ego Mind. I felt the difference in my physical body. I walked and talked with confidence and certainty of purpose. This time I was going to bring blessings and feelings of my internal harmony to the courtroom.

While I sat at my desk, returning patient calls, an idea came to me in a calm and declarative manner. Steve and I needed something that would get the judge's attention and remind him of his mandated impartiality. I called Steve to ask if he knew a retired appellate judge that we could hire to sit in on some of our days at trial. For an hour or two the court would know that an appeal was a viable option for us. Steve replied that he knew the perfect person: Judge Countiss, a former appellate judge. Judges dislike being overturned on appeal. Judge Countiss' presence would certainly be a gentle warning for the court to be mindful of all rulings.

Joe still had not contacted our daughters. Both daughters were healthy teenagers, hanging out in groups and more interested in social events than any court case that involved their parents. Eleanor was at an all-girl Catholic school with Ursuline nuns, and Emma was at a co-ed Catholic school on the other side of Dallas. Since neither daughter had a driver's license, Ace and I were constantly driving to pick up or deliver one or both at varying locations. All parents of busy and involved teenagers know the drill. We prayed for the day Eleanor could drive. Since she skipped a grade, she was the last one in her class to get a license. Eleanor excelled at everything: academics, activities, popularity and school government. Emma excelled at socialization. School was simply the place all her friends were everyday. She was bright, but not at all interested in academics. She probably distinguished herself from her older sibling, as is normal.

The second trial began with just the judge and no jury. It was evident that Joe's lawyer expected the court to re-divide the community property and set aside the original agreement. Steve made it clear to the court that our intent was to look closely at the division to see if it was indeed fair. Specifically, he intended to show that it was more than fair to Joe and should not be changed. Judge Countiss, our second chair at our counsel table, smiled as he took notes.

As Joe's attorney called witnesses, accountants, actuary and insurance agents, I let my mind wonder a bit. Looking at Joe, I felt some pathos, some sorrow mixed with my disgust at his changed personality and immorality. As I distanced myself from the actual proceedings and his further charades, I saw a lonely, rapacious, lost and pathetic man who knew how to bamboozle others. Although bright, Joe had no idea of who he was and what direction to take to make his life meaningful. I vividly saw suffering. From my hours with Sissy Jean, I knew suffering is created through the narratives we weave to see ourselves as pitiful, used, abused and misunderstood in the mayhem of our Ego minds. For a few minutes, I was abiding in higher consciousness, but the courtroom illusion soon refocused me to the task at hand.

That evening, resting all curled up in my favorite chair, I opened a letter from a mortgage company that I had been negotiating with for several months. Soon after the first trial, the mortgage company for the duplex that Joe had taken from my dad and Ginny informed me they were going to foreclose. No payment had been made in eleven months. It was then I learned that my name had never been removed from the mortgage as Joe had promised. He also had changed the address of the mortgagee to HIS address. As a result, I had no idea that he was one year delinquent, and that thousands of dollars were owed. My only recourse was to pay the amount due plus interest and penalties. Then, I began to demand that they restore my credit since they did not communicate with me to verify change of address.

I had spent my life making sure I had a credit score in the 800's. Now, thanks to Joe, a mortgage company was going to ruin it for the next seven years. The company finally relented and restored my credit score with the reporting agency. I was now just learning of their decision in the letter I held. It was not a big sigh of relief because there were so many other factors that had accompanied this fiasco. Evicting Joe was a long, legal process. When I finally was able to enter the house, I saw all the wires cut, paint splattered on walls, the fireplace painted bright orange and carpet and drapes destroyed. Ace took pictures and then worked for weeks between flying and taking care of rental properties to restore the duplex and rent it. I got up from my sanctuary chair and gathered the pictures of the destruction to take to court with me to show the judge the behavior of the complaining party. Actually, I had a lot more to complain about, but that was not going to serve me well.

At an appropriate point in the trial, Steve asked for a minute to search his case boxes behind the counsel table. The court waited patiently. Finally Steve approached the bench to place the pictures of the vandalized duplex into evidence. When the judge asked Joe if he was responsible for the destruction evident in the photos, he shrugged his shoulders without an utterance.

I began to feel a shift in the attitude of the court. It had not gone unnoticed by the judge that I had gone to work every day, was supporting my children without child support, was having to spend thousands in legal fees, was forced to be absent from my practice for trials and hearings, had to repair the vandalism to Treetops and the Dallas duplex and was parenting two children who would not see their father due to his unconscionable behavior. I don't know if I had just lost respect for the whole justice system, or I really was in a state of awareness that put me outside the tentacles of Ego's intrusions. I knew I was okay, no matter what the outcome. That feeling went a long way towards underpinning my sanity.

The boring trial which consisted of hours of recitation of numbers, reasons for expenditures and countless explanations of every check in the register was finally over. The judge would write his opinion and deliver it to the parties in the foggy future. TS Eliot again came to mind: "It ended not with a bang, but a whimper." We packed all the boxes of evidence, loaded them onto the dolly, then into Steve's Suburban. As we shuffled out of the courthouse, we were thankful that this chapter was closed.

Several long months later, Steve walked into my office between patients. With a face which offered no clue to what he would say, he volunteered that the judge had delivered his written opinion and verdict. I have to confess that in spite of all my beliefs and preparations for bad news and knowing I would be just fine no matter what, I still did not want to lose such an unfair and unnecessary proceeding. Steve read the verdict to me, as I shook my head in disbelief.

"We won?" I asked, needing verification.

"We sure did." Steve said, smiling.

"The original community property settlement stands?" I asked, still needing assurance.

"That's what it means," Steve stated firmly.

"What happens now?" I asked with a hint of trepidation.

"Well, they can appeal, but I don't think that the court committed any reversible error," my attorney said, offering his best legal opinion.

He left the papers on my desk and exited my consultation room. I welcomed my next patient. It was only later in the day that I would enjoy the relief of this two-year long fiasco finally ending. The conclusion of several years of legal wrangling, two trials, multiple hearings, many days of missed work, repairs of two vandalized properties, a year's worth of overdue mortgage payments and legal fees had ended up exactly where we started. A couple hundred thousand dollars spent for nothing but the illusion of a poor, lost, tortured soul seemed to be a hard lesson.

Nothing real can be threatened;
Nothing unreal exists.

A Course in Miracles

At long last the trauma of the ever-so-protracted courtroom drama was over. I was suddenly exhausted and felt the need for a change of scenery that might afford me time to recuperate.

I eagerly hopped onto the back of the Harley with Ace, and we were off to Colorado! Ace was gracious enough to allot me one half of a saddle bag--barely enough for underwear, a T-shirt, some toiletries and a notebook. This Spartan lifestyle was well worth the privilege of occupying the "Queen seat" behind my beloved Ace.

There is absolutely nothing more spiritual to me than cruising through the mountains of Colorado with the wind in my face and the ever-present comfort of Sissy Jean. The majesty of the Black Canyon, the resplendent beauty of the descent from Slumgullion Pass down into Lake City and the painted rock boulders on the highway from Grand Junction to the southern border were the best of illusions. I was in constant vigilance and a state of high consciousness as I began to feel alive again. I felt the reciprocal love of my husband and ached to do more with my daughters. A state of gratitude prevailed as I developed a to-do list for self-improvement and spiritual connectivity. My intentions were uplifting, and I returned to the pleasure of reviewing my known absolutes as I leaned with the bike as it magically hugged the curves and shifted gears climbing and descending the narrow highways carved from the breathing granite edges of God-given mountains.

I delighted while mentally clicking off my beliefs of what I knew for certain, enjoying the convictions: 1) We are all one, 2) The One, Source, God is Love, 3) Higher consciousness changes the world, 4) We live in a schoolroom experiment, 5)There is no death, 6) The only proper response to everything is Love, 7) Life is hard due to Ego, 8) Love is easy due to Spirit, 9) Emotions are direction signals to return to Love, 10) Life on Earth is an illusion that makes us grow if we want to and 11) only true forgiveness gets us Home.

Eleven certainties were enough for one ride. From nowhere, the back of the bike began to fishtail, and I held on tightly. Remarkably, I felt no fear. Ace slowed the bike by shifting down the gears as we safely descended the steep, canyon road. My body weight on the back of the bike was helping steady the machine with a flat back tire. As with all bikers, we had encountered some hairy situations before. But we were stranded in the mountains and had not passed another soul for over an hour.

After Cool Hand Ace handily brought the motorcycle to a stop, I got off. He said that he hoped someone would come along soon because we would need to trailer the bike to change the tire and hoped we could find a bike shop with the right size tire. Since I knew there are no accidents or coincidences in life, I thought that the universe would find a way to provide. For a moment, I visited the idea of why we manifested a bike breakdown on a mountainside. There had to be a reason, since all is illusion. When one asks the universe a question, an answer generally appears.

An old, old jalopy from the era of long cars with vinyl roofs approached. The curled vinyl and the fading paint that might have once been blue described this vehicle that was slowly coming to a stop. The car may have been something to look past, but the occupants were notable. They were tattooed on every visible skin part, partially toothless and lacking in recent hygiene. A husband and wife walked over to our bike, shook our hands, identified themselves as Harley riders, volunteered they knew a good bike shop and offered to help. Kindness comes in varied packages! This was a good lesson not to judge at first glance! The guys chatted while his wife and I sat in the front seat of their car which appeared to also serve as their residence. On the console between us lay a loaded nine millimeter handgun with the clip showing. I began a conversation about where she was born, about their bike and their travels. She was forthcoming, gentle and honest. Her initial scariness quickly melted into gratitude, and we had a fine interaction. The guys informed us of the plan. The new biker friend would take his car to town and bring back a trailer from the bike shop where his buddy worked. Then the two guys would securely load the bike, take it to the shop and the mechanics would stay late to change the tire. Ace would stay with us girls so no harm would come to us. The guy asked if we had "heat", and Ace said we did. Little did I know that "heat" meant a weapon. He just wanted to make sure we would all be safe while he was gone. After eating some peanut butter crackers from our tour pack, we saw the jalopy (now thought of more like a rescue Cadillac) coming toward us with trailer attached and a helper in the passenger seat.

Several hours later, we had a newly installed rear tire and had become friends with our rescuers and the mechanics. We showed our sincere gratitude by inviting them to dinner anywhere in town. Their choice was a real dive, but the burgers were great and the beer was ice cold. Ace and I enjoyed ourselves with such authenticity and appreciation for gentle, kind angels in costumes that would have brought my judgment in another time or place. We learned a great lesson that day...well, at least I did. Ace already knew! He had been a biker since he was twelve and knew a brother when he saw one. He would have done the same for those guys. They lived to ride the wind.

My self-imposed prescription of mountain air and beauty designed by the imagination and generosity of Source was the healing medicine I needed to cure the devastation wrought by courtroom illusions. My aching heart was weighted down by witnessing such bizarre behavior and the deterioration of a human being that I once cared for and desired. I often asked myself whether he was delusional now or was I delusional for years of co-existing with him....or both. It seemed impossible to fathom that the kind man I had married had become cruel, vindictive and loathsome. I sighed and handed many of my mental musings back to the Universe because the trials were behind me. Order, peace, and comfort could be reinstated back into my life. I mentally devised a plan to pay off every debt incurred by the lawsuit and restart my annual contributions to my 401K that have been foregone for five years due to legal expenses. With the pure joy of being free from any judge or jury deciding my future or my finances, I felt fortified with the strength to move forward. I would put the past into a "need-to-forgive-self-and-others" category when I had time to give forgiveness proper attention.

It felt good to be back at the office doing therapy with willing and interesting patients. I was no longer on high alert about the next phone call from Steve on my messaging service reporting some new wrinkle in an ongoing drama spelled out in legalese. At times, I still wondered how I had managed to manifest all this now-resolved legal drama. Then, with no warning, Steve's voice on the message informed me of a pending appeal! A guttural scream of "Noooooo!"

echoed around the consultation room as I hung my head and affirmed I could do anything if necessary. And…I had to! Luckily, we had our second chair, Judge Countiss, the retired appellate judge, who would respond with the necessary brief.

Learning that we had to order transcripts of the trials, pay the court reporter to type them and give Judge Countiss and Steve a retainer deposit for doing all necessary work prior to the appellate proceeding, I laughed out loud about my carefully planned financial recovery program.

A focused internal program of spiritual and physical recovery was necessary, so I asked Sissy to help me.

"Sissy, I want your help to guide my thoughts and behaviors to a place where I no longer manifest the drama I have recently experienced. Most of my life I have focused on survival and caring for others. Now, I know I must give more attention to my well-being if I want to continue teaching and guiding patients to healthier lives. I feel scattered, and I want to feel whole."

"*Dear one, you are already in possession of one of the most necessary qualities for spiritual growth and happiness. You have a passion for life, and that passion is what now speaks to the desire to grow and thrive in a loving way. You embrace adventure, debate, new ideas, innovation and change. This openness is the door on the path to transcendence. You also have never lost hope in the face of all your struggles. You have certainly experienced moments of hopelessness, but they were transitory and not definitional. Hope allows one to always find a path to survival.*"

"*As you know, your personality is an enthusiastic one which gives birth to the happiness that is possible for every human soul. Your curiosity to understand so many things in your illusions has led you to prepare yourself with knowledge gleaned from formal and informal studies. You now have the maturity to begin to manifest the love you have felt at times of heightened awareness. Awareness is the key. Nothing of what you wish to experience and know for sure will ever happen without awareness. Otherwise, you may live a good life, but not an enlightened and whole one. Just remember that there is always time to learn, now or in another life cycle. Give yourself the gift of patience alongside your gift of commitment and endurance.*"

"Sissy, patience with others is not difficult for me, but patience with myself has not been my long suit. If I can imagine and define the goal, I want to be there as soon as possible. And I have been known to physically collapse from fatigue when my pursuit of the goal was relentless or falsely deemed more necessary than my well-being."

"Yes, child, I know. You know, also, but have refused to use enough energy for yourself to continue your pursuits in a healthy manner. That may be your most needed focus for change. A tired or sick soul will be in low vibrational energy and not of much use to its goal. Grant yourself the gifts of travel, adventure, scheduled vacations, family time and times of total relaxation. You love Treetops, the woods, the sea and open spaces. Seek out these things and satisfy your natural hunger for beauty and times of meditation when the mind is empty and the soul is full."

Not long after my visit with Sissy, all the patient calls had been returned at the end of a long work day of counseling. As I was gathering my purse and papers ready to go home, I just plopped back down in my desk chair and said out loud: "Take a minute to do an inventory of your life right now, and focus on the good stuff."

With forced patience, I leaned back, took a cleansing breath and began to tick off the events for which I felt gratitude:

Eleanor had graduated from high school with honors, was at a fine university and had joined a sorority with a sister-family at school. She was also a National Merit Scholar which financed her four years of undergraduate study. It also helped ease the financial strain from the lawsuits. I suspect her kind and loving heart chose a university that offered her a full ride to help her family.

Joe had left Dallas and moved to his small Indiana hometown where his mother still lived. I secretly cheered the news of his move because he would no longer be driving by the house and leaving gifts I had given him during our marriage on our front porch or dropping off hate mail. And, I must confess, I hoped his focus would transfer to something or someone else, and he might recover his senses and sensibility.

Ace was flying and happy to be in a cockpit carrying passengers to different places. He was always steadfast in his help and care of our home, Treetops and our family.

The Reagan Administration had eliminated the tax benefits of owning the rental properties, so I would begin to sell them as soon as the appellate process ended. It had become quite burdensome to keep up with the properties as they aged.

Emma disliked academics more each year. Our focus was that she reach high school graduation. So far, we were on course, with only a few bumps here and there. She was fun-loving, obsessed with immediate gratification and ADD. Emma not only kept us on our toes, but also filled us with laughter with to her unwitting transparency.

My practice was so full I had a waiting list. I relished going to work each day, watching people grow and enjoying that every hour was different and interesting. To continue being a responsible contributor to our family's comfort was not only fulfilling, but also enjoyable.

My spiritual work was growing in importance and satisfaction. I joined a meditation group with a quirky and talented teacher and advanced my meditative ability which allowed me to enjoy Sissy even more.

At long last, I allowed myself to think of Phil and Dad. My brother was happy and doing well. He was still in a committed relationship with sweet Anita and the center of a great group of friends in business, and he sang in the church choir. He was finally grounded. We spent times together on holidays and summer weekends at the pool. My "twin" was never far away, which gave me great pleasure.

A friend of my family-of-origin knew the situation with Dad. She had reached out to try to broker a meeting of some sort, but she was promptly and rudely rebuffed by Dad and Ginny. I thanked her and accepted the situation for the time being.

A few months later, the girls received a letter from their dad with pictures of him and his new wife, saying that he was now "safe" and happy. I was overjoyed!! The prayer for refocus had been answered, and maybe, just maybe, he would find his grounding ability and things would change for the better. I even let myself entertain thoughts of joint holidays and creating a friendship with his new wife. But we needed to get past the appeal first and have some healing time. I was, naively, excited about that family-oriented illusion because I had experienced many couples in my practice that hated each other and spent hundreds of thousands of dollars on the divorce, only to see newly constructed families jointly enjoying each other and finding new peace a few years later.

The appellate hearing was quite a different experience. Sitting in the courtroom of the of the Court of Appeals of the Fifth District of Texas with all three judges high above on raised dais and both lawyers at lower level counsel tables was a TV drama scene. As we waited for the appellate judges to appear, Joe and his new wife entered the courtroom to take their seats. I caught my breath as I saw them and felt embarrassed for his wife as she caught my eye. We could have been sisters. She had my same body shape, weight, smile and personality, but with brown eyes, not blue. The similarity was unmistakable and spoke volumes. I looked away and did not reengage eye contact for the remainder of the hearing. The attorneys argued legal points. The judges interrupted with questions. Thankfully, the proceeding was much quicker than I expected. No drama whatsoever!!

It would be a year before the appellate court ruled.

We can easily forgive a child who is
afraid of the dark; the real tragedy of
life is when men are afraid of the light.

Plato

27

Life seemed to gravitate toward normality with the trials over. The antagonist was in another state, and the appeal was somewhere in the background making no noise or interruptions. I began to trust that the illusions were manageable, and I could relax into a routine of family and professional life without cherry bombs, intermittently, being dropped in my lap.

A family friend from my hometown who also knew Joe called one evening to laugh, support and gossip a little. Joanie always had the latest skinny on everything! Sissy Jean had emphasized that gossip was pre-meditated character assassination, but it was hard to redirect Joanie when she was on a roll. Her latest tidbit was that Joe had convinced his mother to sign a universal power of attorney for medical and financial decisions. Then he promptly put her in a nursing home, bought himself a home and was sitting on several boards and managing a trust for a wealthy family. So much for being deaf and mentally ill!! My honest reaction was simply that I was grateful that I was not the target du jour. A feeling of some gratitude that he may have established a workable relationship and workday life for himself occurred. New wife, new work, new home, new vision.

I also received a call from Joe's brother, Bob, who was an honest, stand-up guy and mayor of a medium sized Indiana city. He was mad, bewildered and in disbelief. Joe had taken all their mother's monies, deposited her in a mid-level nursing home and was buying a property for himself. He asked me what was going on. I reported the facts, succinctly and rapidly, not really wanting to invite his family into the chaos. He was a gentleman, thanked me and said he would be in touch. I hoped not.

Almost eight months after the call from Joe's brother, I was sitting on the back porch ready to start a meditation when the outside phone rang.

"Hello, this is Annalee."

"Annalee, this is Donna, Joe's wife. Please don't hang up. I filed for divorce from Joe today. I would like to ask you some questions."

"Donna, first, please tell me why you are getting a divorce."

"He threw a beer in my face. He drinks too much, doesn't tell the truth, has wild-ass stories about you that I believed for a while, refuses to really work or get a job and is unkind to my children. We live off my earnings, although he tells everyone he is a lawyer. Big deal. He doesn't practice law, although he passed the Indiana bar."

"What are your questions?" I asked.

"Does he work or does he expect someone else to take care of him?" She prodded.

"My experience is of the latter," I answered emotionless.

"Is he moral?" she asked more forcefully.

"You will have to answer that for yourself," I answered.

"Was he violent with you?" she asked with a hint of a whimper.

"Only at the last of the marriage and during the court proceedings. I never saw that part of him until he was forced to consider being on his own without a support system. I am sorry this is happening to you." I offered.

Her gratitude was genuine, and I could tell that she felt a semi-sisterhood bond talking to another woman who had experienced the betrayal and theatrics of this husband/con man.

It was not long after that Steve called with news. The appellate court had confirmed the lower court with a vote of 3-0. We had won unanimously! I was more relieved than I ever thought I would be. Maybe this was the end. Maybe we could live our lives without a court decision hanging over us for months or years. Or until he appealed to the Supreme Court of Texas!

Judge Countiss notified me that Joe's appellate attorney had informed him verbally that he was to take the case to the Supreme Court of Texas. The judge was almost apologetic, and I assured him I had no real concern. He laughed, telling me those were the consoling words he was supposed to be telling me! Joe made it known via his lawyer that all he really wanted now was Treetops, and he would leave me alone.

I paid no attention to the Treetops issue until our original Bill of Review judge notified us that Treetops was out of his jurisdiction. What a cop out!! It was listed in the community property settlement and was acceptable. Now that it was an issue, he punted to "lack of jurisdiction." Joe was ecstatic! I knew I would soon be served with a lawsuit filed in Nassau, but I already had a relationship with a very fine Bahamian attorney who had helped transfer the deed to Treetops solely into my name. I had taken care of this legality immediately after the divorce. The divorce papers had to be certified by the original court, the customs and immigration people and the Supreme Court of the Bahamas. Suffice to say, all was in order.

Almost three months to the day after the Texas Appellate Court ruling, I was served with the expected Bahamian lawsuit. I called Luther McDonald, my lawyer in Nassau, who asked for the court case number and said he would be in touch.

When Luther called a week later, he informed me that a civil suit in the Bahamas is different than in the US. The plaintiff must ask the court for an estimate of attorney's fees and deposit in escrow the amount ordered by the judge before any trial can be scheduled. The judge had ordered Joe to deposit twenty-five thousand dollars. About a month had passed when Luther called again and said the legal action had been withdrawn. The Commonwealth of the Bahamas has no tolerance for frivolous lawsuits.

Secondly, the elevation of the Bill of Review original lawsuit to the Supreme Court of Texas apparently did not happen due to non-payment of attorney fees. I believed the final bell had rung.

A notable transformation had taken place within my being. I no longer lived with fear or apprehension. I felt myself living in higher consciousness much more often. Love was easier and being loved came with more comfort. Friends were more easily embraced, and fun was always one idea away. Life was good. Ace was so helpful, the kids were doing well, and I loved going to my practice every day. My spiritual life was designed by me and lived every day in my own knowingness of the Truth. I wanted a retreat, however. A time of solitude to contemplate, organize, feel, plan and just be and do some needed forgiveness work. I made a plane reservation for the Bahamas.

All by myself, I had time to sit on the beach where I did not encounter another soul. A spot I named Four Palms because of the four palm trees that were all by themselves right next to an inviting small mound of sand was perfect for meditation. Sissy and I had been there many times before.

"Sissy, I have learned so much and still feel naïve. I feel a need to enumerate the lessons so as to not forget. Then I need to do major forgiveness work, starting with me."

"*Yes, Annalee. What you propose will serve you well and help keep you in awareness, higher consciousness and guided toward spiritual healing.*"

"First, I have to feel the gratitude for Steve, Jean, Nancy and my family. Their support never waivered and always came accompanied with good humor and positive thinking. There were times I felt the weight was too heavy. They were a balm for my weariness and underpinned the facts with logic and love. Their gifts were enormous. These feelings will last a lifetime, as they should."

"*Annalee. Earthly illusions teach many things. Your courtroom illusions brought to the foreground those parts of you that needed healing. I know you have already become aware of your excessive caretaking of others. Your ex-husband expected you to meet his needs life-long, regardless of your marital state. You had never really announced to him that he had to take care of himself…and that he was able. You thought that marriage was so sacred that you had no other choice. Please know that a marriage that is not filled with love, support, truth and joy in bountiful supply is not a marriage. Instead, it becomes a prison that Ego Mind has built. Know that you experiment with a relationship to learn. Maybe you just rent each other until consciousness brings some light that guides a way in or out. Living authentically is high vibrational activity that results in a path toward Love. As you know, Love cannot be defined by Ego Mind, only by Spirit Mind. Forgive yourself this very moment, here on the sand under the palms you love, for having lived for so long in self-imposed misery. Know that it is no longer an option.*"

"Sissy, I want to forgive myself and others. I totally believe that we are not free until we forgive. I know there is not a path to Love and Peace until we declare forgiveness of everyone for everything."

"*Dear one, forgiveness is turning from the idea of sin to the Truth that your practice of higher consciousness brings to your awareness. Forgiveness has absolutely nothing to do with making the wrong a right. It is freeing the mind from the shadow of guilt that lingers after a disabling thought or act. Forgiveness allows you to decide to give up the wrong. It allows you the freedom to feel the peace that naturally comes when you no longer carry a hurt or resentment. You simply decide not to repeat the Ego act that might be ugly or hurtful to self or others. In doing so, you are healed.*"

"So, in forgiving Joe, I give up judgment of his behavior. It will allow him to have his path forward. And I will forego repetition of my previous co-dependent behavior?" I asked.

"*Annie, you have been reading* The Course in Miracles, *which says: "Nothing real can be threatened; nothing unreal exists." Remember that phrase at all times. Truth is indestructible. Ego can lure you away from your vision of Truth by believing in the illusions. Forgiveness is turning from the power of the illusion to the power of Truth which is your personal, deep knowingness. Pain will come into our lives no matter how hard we work at avoiding it. Suffering is believing the pain is real. You embrace it and make the illusion real. That needs your forgiveness. Forgive yourself for the moments you bought into the illusion of suffering. Always forgive others for presenting the illusion.*"

"Sissy, I have come to know that the proof of forgiveness is when the offense no longer sits in your heart, relentlessly gnawing at your peace. I am going to inventory my heart space and see what still sits there."

As I sat in that peaceful place, soaking up sun in the sweet island breeze, my inventory revealed a forgiveness for all of my shortcomings and for all of Joe's antics...save one. My heart simply could not truthfully forgive his abandonment of his precious children, the daughters given to us by Source and two women whose hearts wanted the best of love and circumstances for their girls. I wanted to forgive him. I tried to forgive him. I prayed I could find a way to forgive him. I just couldn't. I even thought that not forgiving him for such a hurtful act was a way I could protect my beloved children. It was an illusion of absurdity, but it lived in my heart.

Sissy and I continued our conversations for several more days, always loving and having fun with one another. During our years of her caring love, I had never, ever heard a word of judgment or reprimand. She was my dearest source for Truth.

I gave a great deal of thought to why I married Joe in the first place. My conclusion was that I wanted someone who appeared to by the polar opposite of my dad. Kindness, patience, appreciation and a family-oriented attitude were paramount characteristics. Joe displayed all those when we dated, and I found him comfortable and safe.

My excessive willingness to do everything possible to help him through law school, even to the point of my exhaustion, had unwittingly taught him that I could be counted on no matter what. When the practice of law became unsavory after the death of his partner, he knew if he sold the firm without consulting me that

I would pick up the slack. I was pathologically responsible. I set no boundaries that might break up the family. He knew, without question, that I would protect and provide for the children. Therefore, I would do the same for him, especially if I were convinced he was disabled due to partial deafness. He was right. What he did not count on was the fact that I might some day want something in return. I longed for shared responsibility, physical and emotional intimacy, fun adventures and similar spiritual beliefs. Thank God I knew my limit when I thought my soul was dying. That happened on my fortieth birthday when I did a vision quest revealing the truth: I had to leave. It took me two years, but I did it within the illusions I perceived at the time.

The hardest part was coming to know that I was not selfish. Rather, I was in a process of healing and growing, and I could honor my children better with authenticity than with giving in to expected social norms. Additionally, I found it interesting that I had married a man so like my dad in many ways while thinking he was just the opposite. Many of my patients also thought they were mating with the opposite of their offensive parent. However, I had seen that they, much like me, had unwittingly been drawn to the familiar with poor results.

The trial had its lessons, too! Courtrooms are as stuffed with many acts of illusions as any place else. American justice has a noble mission. However, I now know that judges and juries who are compelled to make decisions about my life are also illusions with which I have to live. They do not define me or my purpose!

Money was the elephant in the room. Joe wanted more money from me because he had squandered his. I was always the provider, so he came back to where he thought there was a possibility. After building a clever scenario, it was possible he could be awarded some funds, once again, without working or contributing. He even considered the possibility that I would take pity on him and share my part of the community property division. My reputation for being charitable was an invitation to him for some possible gain. Nevertheless, I was staying in consciousness and holding to my boundaries. Sticking to my decisions was costly. This was not about money. I could always make more money, if needed. I needed to prove to myself that I had courage, was a woman of my word, was principled and had an identity with which I was comfortable. It was not so much about beating Joe in court; it was about living with myself. It was time.

Steve also warned me that if I gave in, it would be an act of enablement inviting Joe to keep filing frivolous lawsuits for any myriad of reasons. We needed to put a stop to this fiasco. Steve was doing what lawyers are paid to do--protect me. I was desperately trying to protect myself from further self-damage and resentment. We had the same goal for totally different reasons.

I was back in Dallas, catching up at the office, getting news from Eleanor at college, learning that Emma was still going to classes and hearing Ace's voice on the phone from a hotel room on his route. I could now settle back into the life I enjoyed, fortified from rest, meditation and sunshine. Several evenings later after dishes and laundry, the phone rang around eight o'clock. A baritone voice identified himself as a sergeant with the Indiana State Troopers and an investigator for the governor's office. After verifying that I was Joe's ex-wife, he said he had some questions. I informed him that I would call him back because I needed to make sure he was who he said he was.

It took almost half an hour to get the Indiana State Trooper Post in Indianapolis and trace down my sergeant. I thanked him for waiting and asked him what his purpose was. He answered that the governor of Indiana had selected Joe to fill a state judge vacancy and that it was his job to vet Joe.

He asked lots of the usual history questions, verifying degrees, addresses, former employers, work history, arrest record and much more. He sort of sounded like Joe Friday on TV's DRAGNET. Then I heard: "And he owns a home in the Bahamas?" I informed the officer that I owned a home there, but I was not aware that Joe did. He gave me the address of Treetops, and I said that Joe claiming ownership was in error. He said I should be careful with my answers because lying to a law enforcement officer carried a penalty. I offered to send him a copy of the deed. He was grateful and accepted.

The conversation became more friendly as he continued with questions. Child abuse? Alcoholic? Street drugs? Bar room fights? I was sounding like a broken record with a string of "no" answers when he asked: "Any diagnosis of mental illness?" My affirmative answer stopped him short.

"Do you have proof of that and the doctor's name?"

"Yes. I have the court transcript from our trial. The doctor's name, address and diagnosis are all sworn to in court."

"Will you please fax me those documents also?" he asked.

"Sergeant, I have been through two trials and many other issues with this man. I really don't want to be involved any more than the law requires. And does he need to know you have talked to me?"

"Miss, I will not involve you. But let me tell you a story. I started my investigation in his hometown with nothing but glowing results. In fact, it was a high school friend that now works closely with the governor that nominated him for the post. Everything was leading to a good vetting until I talked to the president of the bank he used in Huntington. Joe owed the bank a little under $50,000 and was not making payments on the credit account. When they pursued the matter to recover the funds, he wrote the bank a letter saying he would kill himself in the same manner his father had done years before. Further, he would leave a note naming the bank as the harassing culprit. His brother was mayor of the city and a decent man, so they closed the account and forgave the debt. The banker showed me the letter of which I now have a copy. Does this sound like the man you know?"

"It is not the man I married, but it is the man I divorced. May I ask a question? When you interviewed him, was he hard of hearing?"

"Not that I was aware of," answered the officer.

The court vacancy was filled by someone else, although Joe did become the municipal judge for traffic violations for his home town for a short time.

Emma was soon to graduate high school, but she had absolutely no interest in college. When asked if she would try one semester at the local community college, she told me not to waste my money. Another day of school was the last thing she wanted. I asked what she really wanted to do. She offered that the only thing she wanted was to be a mother and raise a baby. I laughed and assured her it was a noble goal. Continuing, Emma explained that she did not want a husband, just the baby.

We talked at length about the maternal, financial, educational and spiritual responsibilities of rearing a child alone. She was not deterred in the slightest. She had a goal and was willing to make it happen. If it did, she wanted me to support and embrace her decision. I had been very direct with the girls in their young adulthood that they own the responsibility to choose their paths, experiment with what worked for them, be mindful and considerate of others, have a good work ethic and an attitude of gratitude, evidenced by charitable works. I had no doubt I would be a grandmother within two years!

Eleanor had one year left at the university, a serious boyfriend and was an exceptional student and the student activities chairperson for the institution. She managed a million dollar budget at age twenty. The daughters were totally different, and both totally lovely and totally loved.

I relaxed into believing that all was pretty much in order and moving peacefully along. Since I wanted to put the house that Joe and I owned together behind me after the girls were on their own, I let myself muse about a different homestead with a very different energetic vibe. I called a realtor.

28

We had been in our new house for almost a year. Emma had graduated and was pregnant. Eleanor had graduated from college with the highest award given and was now at her new job in Houston. This gave Ace and me time and energy to entertain on weekends.

Phil and Anita were included in any fun group activity and were always at our home for Christmas. Anita's son, wife and grandson were included. The sweetness of the family gatherings gave me enormous joy. Phil and I had managed to create a real family, a sense of trust, fun times and lots of love and hugs. We took pride in changing the paradigm from the unsuitable family-of-origin model.

A surprise call from Ginny informed me that Dad was in the final stages of Alzheimers and in a nursing home. I made the four hour round trip every two weeks so I could have as much time alone with him as possible. My letters for years had gone unanswered. Now, when Dad could not walk and rarely spoke, I had been notified of his condition and his location. I spent about five minutes of anger, centered myself, gave thanks I could see him and moved forward.

I visited him several times and massaged his body while listening to his intermittent rants of World War II battles. In one of his deliriums he proposed to me. Of course, I said "yes." It soon became very evident that the most loving thing I could do for him was to pray for his departure. I was grateful to have had the opportunity to give some comfort, say my good-bye and openly bless his exit. It gave me peace to remember my Grandma saying: "there's a lot of getting in the giving."

I was between patients and retrieving phone messages when I heard her voice: "Annalee, this is Ginny. I'm calling to tell you that your dad died about an hour ago. Here is my number if you want to call."

Quickly, I said a prayer of gratitude. I knew Dad finally was back to perfection, was in the Light, free of pain or regret and, thankfully, was released from his disabled and non-functional body. Both of my parents were together which gave me reason to smile. I called Phil, who thanked me, and said he would not let me go to the funeral alone. After some discussion, we agreed to go to Indiana without our partners and to say the eulogy at the funeral home chapel. Ginny was delighted.

When it was time, Phil whispered: "You're up, Sis." We stood together in front of the small gathering of relatives, fellow war veterans and some townspeople as Phil punted to me to speak. I happily recounted our father's war record, his military and track and field medals, his professional career as an engineer, his two marriages to good women, his community volunteerism and his booming voice. I also balanced the short speech with some honesty in mentioning that he was known to be a difficult man, opinionated and stubborn. That brought some hee-haws from the military men in the audience. I thanked the people who came to say good-bye and managed to give the entire talk without mentioning his fatherhood. After thanking Ginny for her care of him at the end of his life, we sat down.

Ginny had chosen an open casket funeral which I disliked because it focused on the body, not the transition. But Phil and I did not have a vote. As was customary, the funeral director guided the mourners, row by row, to file past the casket for their final respects. When just Ginny, Phil and I were left, Ginny whispered that she was going to her car and that she would leave us alone with our dad for a final good-bye. She would see us at the cemetery.

Phil took my hand and we walked to the casket. His grip became so tight I thought he might break the small bones in my hand. I didn't move. Then...my brother began to shake. It became an uncontrollable shake as he held me tighter. We were two orphaned children with full realization of the finality of our relationship with our parent. After another minute or so, which felt like an hour, Phil got his breath and practiced trying to control his body. Finally, the wailing and shaking stopped. After more time had passed, my sweet, sweet brother uttered his words: "Well, at least, now, I can stop hoping."

I knew exactly what those words meant. Phil had spent a lifetime waiting to be loved and accepted, praised and held in respect and esteem. Death of hope is a tragedy of immeasurable proportion. I closed the casket lid in a deeply symbolic gesture. Now we could go on with our lives of purpose and Truth. Dad now was in the Light where perfect Truth abides.

As we arrived at the cemetery, we were ready for the military rifle shots, the hugs from everyone there, and our offering of an invitation to lunch for all at Dad's favorite café. That was the last time we ever saw Ginny.

I chose a window seat, wanting to look at the clouds while I inventoried my thoughts. Phil buried himself in SPORTS ILLUSTRATED, and I gave myself permission to think about what could-have-been. Dad could have embraced his kids after Mother died, found support and solace with us and given some back. We could have been a solid threesome until we found our footing. Instead, he wanted a new partner as quickly as possible to mitigate the pain he never processed. He was so courageous in war, as evidenced by his medals, but so fearful of emotions in civilian life that he abandon his kids...and grandkids.

Phil deserved to be supported for his talents that were so different from what Dad expected. Inherently, my brother had the creative vision and naturally sweet personality of our mother. Dad favored me for many reasons. I was the science-oriented mathematician and focused student. I envied the carefree life of my sibling, but it never was appreciated by the task master Father. A part of me wanted to yell at the body in the casket that it would have taken so little on his part to love his son. They both could have found joy and camaraderie in simply loving one another. Love didn't have to be earned, proven, begged for or bartered. It was a gift given from the Divine in each of us to one another, whether we could detect their divinity or not. Dad had worked so hard, but had not found peace. He would have another chance, as we all do, until Truth is our definition.

All is illusion. We choose our parents and circumstances to learn particular lessons. I could forgive my father, but the illusion that resulted in damage to the heart and confidence of my brother was a very difficult one to witness. I asked Phil if he wanted to talk. His answer, without looking up, was a simple "nope." He was resigned. And...maybe, relieved.

Upon returning home, I immediately began the preparations for Eleanor's wedding. She was to wed her college sweetheart. Both

Ace and I adored him and were comforted in knowing our daughter was marrying a good man. It was a sweet, simple wedding near Four Palms on the Bahamian beach with only the parents watching as they recited their vows. Later, they returned home to a grand reception and celebration in a Dallas ballroom with college and family friends.

With Emma, we had become the stereotypical grandparents. We were convinced that our grandchild, Matthew, was the cutest, the smartest, the boldest and most affectionate child ever! Emma was certainly experiencing motherhood. She was growing more loving, protective and subjective every day…and tired.

1994 had truly been a year of endings and beginnings. Dad had transitioned and Ginny disavowed any relationship with us. That chapter was closed. Eleanor was committed to her marriage, and Emma was fully invested with her new son.

Ace and I began to travel more. We took motorcycle trips to the Blue Ridge Parkway, the Natchez Trace, California Highway One and repeated expeditions to Colorado. Last but not least, Phil and Anita were wed in Las Vegas in the Elvis chapel. This was so typical of the humor Phil had about serious events. His married and very pregnant daughter stood up for him as Anita's son did for her. The family celebration there was exhilarating, tiring, and unique. Limos were crowded with guests who had flown in from all over the country. They all laughed because Phil had 13 as his lucky number, and he was getting married thirteen years, thirteen months and thirteen days after their first date. That took some planning!! Another wonderful beginning.

The final "ending" event was one I could not have anticipated. Joe always had perfect timing. Just prior to the Christmas holidays, I received a call from my state licensing board. They informed me that a complaint had been filed against me. My mind immediately raced. Certainly no patient I had treated would have reason for a complaint. Then, the board representative told me it was filed by my ex-husband. The sigh I uttered was audible on the phone. The complaint sounded very familiar to the court rants and detailed all my alleged shortcomings and grievous, unprofessional acts. Finally, the board representative informed me that, after investigation and consideration, they were dismissing the claim.

I thanked him, and I asked if I needed to see a copy of the complaint. He chuckled and informed me that the fatal paragraph of the complaint stated that Joe was taken advantage of by me because he was bi-polar (a third self-diagnosis) but was now cured. I smiled inside, told him I understood, and we said our good-byes. The licensing board, made up of psychology professionals, was well aware that bi-polar disorder is not curable. It blew all Joe's credibility, thank God! Although I did not know it at the time, I was never to hear from Joe again. He had run out of accusations and statutes of limitations. At long last, it was finally over.

Sissy intruded on my gratitude, and I knew the reason. If I had finally learned a lesson, we would debrief and chuckle with the experience.

"Dear Annie, why do you think the harassment of your ex-husband has ended?"

"I'm pretty sure the reason is that I no longer need the illusion that calls me to defend myself or take care of another that is capable of taking care of himself. I have given up my need to pathologically caregive, and I have stuck by my boundaries. And, of course, I feel so much like I walk in integrity by virtue of forgiveness…save one thing."

"My Annalee, you are so right. And the day will come when your heart, knowing the Truth, will forgive Joe his abandonment of his children. There will be a tipping point where it will be very clear to you. Be patient and honest. It will come."

Now it was time to clean up the left over complications from the lawsuits and Joe's subsequent actions. We would never see him or hear his voice again, but we had to have Steve help us lift every *lis pendens* Joe had filed on all the rental property as well as our personal residence. That legal maneuver kept us from selling any property. After weeks of work with title companies, we were told that the same legal procedure had to be done when each property sold…for the next ten years!

Ten years after our divorce, I learned Joe had filed bankruptcy and used MY social security number. That is a federal offense. It was corrected with no small amount of time and energy. Courts and credit agencies work slowly. Joe evaded any federal charges somehow. I had learned to keep all drama to a minimum and surrender all that I could to the universe. Illusions were still being created by Joe, but I saw them as just that. I handled what involved me and moved on. Illusions are impotent when Ego is not included.

Phil and I learned three months after Dad's passing that we were named in his will to receive one dollar each. We were aware that such a provision was the legal way to disinherit us so we could not contest the will. Since I had supplemented their social security until they moved, I suspected there were not many, if any, assets in his estate. His last Will and Testament was his final testament of his rejection of his own children. Neither Phil nor I thought much of it because we were well aware of his feelings. Ginny was now eighty and had moved back to our Indiana hometown. Each time Phil and I saw each other we would teasingly ask: "Did you get your dollar yet?" The other would always reply: "Still waiting, how about you?"

Yet another lawyer letter arrived saying he represented Ginny and wanted the deeds to the properties that Dad had signed over to me "for safe keeping." These were properties of little value that I had bought from Dad when he needed money. I signed quit claim deeds to her without reservation. I thought she could use whatever funds they might yield to her.

The next letter from her lawyer wanted the deed to Treetops. After buying it from Dad with all the necessary legal work in the US and the Bahamas, repairing it from two hurricanes and investing heart and money in what was the only family home left, I forwarded the copies of the deeds proving ownership. I never heard from the lawyer again. Sadly, I was unable to keep Treetops after Hurricane Floyd because I could no longer secure hurricane insurance. Most of the insurance companies had gone bankrupt after paying claims on such a devastating storm. A wonderful Bahamian businessman from Nassau who had a vacation home next to ours which had burned bought Treetops. The transaction was easy. He kindly offered the home for our use anytime he wasn't there! We went back once, but it was not the same. We blessed it and said our final good-bye. That ending broke my heart. Treetops didn't feel like an illusion. It felt like Paradise.

We returned to the island several times, rented homes on the beach and enjoyed old friends. Hurricane Floyd took Four Palms and all the houses on the ocean. I had to find a new meeting place for Sissy Jean and me. I found a new little hump of shaded sand that was perfect.

A smooth sea never makes a skillful sailor.

Unknown

When the opportunity came to go to India, Nepal and Tibet, I was all in. The seventeen of us, mostly friends already, were on one travel visa, meaning we better all stick together or be in a heck of a mess. All of us agreed to fly any route we chose, but were to meet up in Katmandu, a city with which I had already become enchanted. Mount Everest stood guard over this colorful land full of smiling people, great poverty, big Buddhas everywhere, bright-colored spices in sacks of one to two hundred pounds, prayer flags strung between buildings, always waving, and streets so crowded I squeezed between folks for blocks to get to the hotel.

Having traveled in third world countries before, I was accustomed to no bathrooms, no toilet paper, only bottled water (always making sure the cap was sealed), food that didn't resemble any I had ever seen before and the dismissive attitudes toward females. Learning to take all this in stride had always been preferable to getting upset, complaining or arguing. Just get with the program and enjoy the difference!

Our Nepalese guide was an affable man, budding entrepreneur and altogether wonderful. The female assistant decorated us with stick-on third-eye decorations, delighting herself with our giggles and squeals, while answering every question with humility and good will. Her beauty was intoxicating, her intellect sharp and her international relationship-building equal to any ambassador.

Never having done any street drugs, I did not notice that the plants growing along the highway in Nepal were, actually, marijuana plants. It was easy to tell the potheads on the bus because they were all yelling for joy and screaming for everyone of us to look at the height of the plants. I later learned that there was an entire colony of Americans in Katmandu that have been there since the sixties!

Leaving the beauty of Katmandu and boarding China Air for the flight to Llasa, Tibet, I was seated with Jaine, a colleague and good friend. As we began to pass Mt. Everest, the summit now visible as we were above the clouds, we were all in awe and silenced by the magnificence. We were so close at one point that we could see the trekkers and the sherpas climbing the mountainside. Jaine and I conversed for some time until I began to notice that we were traveling due east when our destination was westward. Expressing my puzzlement to Jaine, I reached for the seatback to retrieve the universally-known map of the routes of the airline. I plotted every course available to the east considering that we were probably not at full fuel capacity, and all I could find for a possible major city airport was a place called Chengdu in deep central China. Such a discovery gave my heart a bit of a startled moment. This was late 1990's when China was not open to the West. We were interlopers with a group visa, the first known to be granted such a visa to enter China via Katmandu, not through Beijing. As Americans, we were accustomed to freedom and the trusting protocol of our government, so it was difficult to imagine anything nefarious. We were well-intentioned tourists, so we innocently expected welcoming hosts. I, in particular, became hyper vigilant, watching the flight attendant talking in a jovial, animated manner with all the military personnel in first class and with the Chinese passengers in coach. Nothing was abnormal, but as she did not speak English, I had to take any cue from the reactions of her passenger conversations. Actually, all seemed normal and without any emotional disturbance. I began to doubt myself and my abilities as a pilot. Then, after quick consultation with Sissy, I knew I was to be quiet and obey. She knew of no imminent danger.

Upon landing at the suspected Chengdu airport, all the other passengers deplaned and then the flight attendant escorted us to the front stairway where we descended in a group to meet our Chinese military escort, complete with an AK-47 resting on his left shoulder. We soon entered a room with no chairs, so we stood dutifully in a huddled group waiting for some instruction of what was expected of us. We had plenty of time to wait, which did not help the anxiety of the group. Finally, a woman with no facial expression whatsoever signaled that we were to surrender our passports and visa. The feeling of being naked without documents that allow international notifications with embassies is one that grabs at your chest and feels ominous. We complied, kept our purses, cameras and money, but not our luggage. The next hand signal indicated we were to follow her, which we did as little robots and encountered a decent passenger bus waiting for us. It didn't take another hand signal to know that we were to board the bus. We were then being driven somewhere while passing the biggest marble statue of Lenin that must exist on the planet--and many of Mao. We were finally offloaded at a rat-infested, condemned hotel (former nursing home) to spend the night, we supposed. Hoping it was not our new quarters for an extended period, we trudged into the lobby. The guard in olive green, Mandarin-collared, rough cotton uniform with the AK-47 over his left shoulder made us feel the expected Communist country welcome. Ascending up the stairs with some trepidation, we were all assigned rooms and were told by sign language, again, to keep the door open.

My roommate had "turista" and was hogging all the bathroom privileges, was vomiting in the wastebasket, using the toilet that didn't work and sitting next to the bathtub with at least two inches of dead roaches in the bottom. There were no sheets on the thin mattresses, no pillowcases on the equally-thin pillows, and the light bulb that hung from a cord in the middle of the room was dim. I opened the windows for some air circulation, and put my purse on the bureau (of sorts) and tried to help my roomie who, understandably, wanted to be left alone. I toured the rest of the rooms only to discover that my room was the worst, by far. That was probably best since some of the group were beginning to show signs of emotional fatigue, stress and breakdown. Jaine and I were the shrinks. We had to keep it together to help with the mounting anxiety of some of the others.

In the middle of the night, I heard noises. Little, scratching noises. There were shadows of small animals at the window. I sat up, then stood up in the middle of the bed, pulled the chain on the ceiling light bulb and saw the rats (size of cats) running along the wainscoting railing!! I reached over to the bureau, grabbed my purse that contained a box of crackers in an aluminum foil package, threw it in the corner of the room and screamed: "I don't do f.....g rats!" to which I heard several "Amens" from the hallway. The man with the AK-47 said something in Mandarin. I shut up. The rats munched away, eating through cardboard and aluminum packaging, for which I was grateful. My roommate was still in the bathroom, missing all the excitement of a horror movie.

The next morning, after no water and no breakfast, we were rousted from our beds by a hard tap on the open door with the butt of the guard's rifle, escorted down the stairs and once again put on a comfortable bus. By this time, there were tour members that had entered different stages of panic attacks and unabashed terror. Once on the bus, we began to recall the route from the day before and were fairly certain that we were being returned to the airport. At the terminal again, we were perplexed. We wondered around the terminal, never straying far from one another. Some of the group were able to use Nepalese money to buy popsicle-looking things which would provide some water. We all followed suit. Then, all of a sudden, a nice Chinese lady waved to our party to follow her. It occurred to me that we do the most outlandish things when we don't know the language, the customs or the order of things. Like obedient sheep, we followed. This gesture led up to another Boeing 757 with a stairway entrance to the aircraft. We happily followed along, boarded, strapped ourselves in and assumed we were going to Llasa, once again. We still were absent our passports and group visa. There was a moment when it crossed my mind that my family may never know what happened to me. We weren't exactly hijacked, but we were in custody and without State Department identification. On the other hand, we had no guarantee of where we were going and what our day would hold.

Once seat-belted in, I started to chart the course to Llasa. As we climbed to altitude and leveled off, we were somewhat flying in the direction of Llasa, but I couldn't be sure. More than two and a half hours later we landed at a remote airport in a prairie meadow deep in the Himalayas. After entering the small shack that served as a terminal, I found an English speaker. Actually, he was there with a bus ready to take passengers to Llasa, a two hour drive away. Having trouble breathing in the high altitude, I needed to conserve energy and regulate emotions. Waiting for our luggage on the single, ancient conveyor belt, I wondered if any luggage really accompanied us on this return trip to our original destination. After an interminable wait, I heard the familiar sound of the retching conveyor belt, and luggage began to appear. As I was waiting for my lone suitcase to appear, I noticed all of our passports wrapped together with a large rubber band coming down the conveyer with the visa wrapped on the outside of the bundle. I quietly picked it up, passed out the little blue books, gathered my suitcase and scurried to the bus, while being decorated with a white prayer scarf by the bus driver. I thought:

"Well, one can always use prayers of good will, so I will wear this scarf all day!"

Once in Llasa, I knew I was in trouble trying to breathe. I had been diagnosed with a lung disorder several months before, but didn't know how severely it would affect me at high altitudes. The Dallas doctor had originally diagnosed me with adult cystic fibrosis, had said to get my affairs in order and that I probably had two years, at most. I didn't believe him. I considered that, maybe, I was in denial, but my "knowingness" knew he was wrong. After more testing at my insistence, the diagnosis was not good, but not fatal. I had inhaled an African fungus from a large cloud transported trans-Atlantic to a stationary position over Texas. Many thousands had this fungus in their lungs, but I was the rare bird that had an extreme allergy to it, so it caused all sorts of problems...but manageable problems, worsening with age.

The next morning the group set out to see the Potula, the palace of the exiled head of Tibetan Buddhism, the Dali Lama. Having respect for the teachings of Buddha, as well as other masters, I truly wanted to see the building, but was unable to walk or think straight. The group left me in my hotel bed with plenty of hot tea, as is the custom in every room. Mid-morning I felt faint, dizzy and disoriented. Within a few minutes, a Tibetan maid entered my room, poured a cup of tea, took a tiny envelope out of her pocket, poured it into the tea and mixed it thoroughly. Then, she came to my bedside, lifted my head gently, and brought the cup to my lips. Slowly, over a period of ten minutes or so, she poured drops into my mouth for me to swallow. I remember telling her "thank you" in English and falling asleep. About an hour and a half later, I awoke, got up, walked around my room and was feeling fine when the rest of the group returned from their tour of the Potula. Still taking it easy, I found myself feeling rather comfortable and talkative.

The next morning I asked the concierge to help me identify the maid who had been so helpful and gracious to me the day before, describing her as Tibetan (since all Tibetan women wear a full body apron of many colors) and about five feet one and working on my hotel floor. The concierge was indignant, informing me that they did not hire Tibetans, only Han Chinese in their hotel. I said he had to be mistaken because I could identify her if I saw her again. He was insistent that the high altitude had affected my experience.

I knew I had not imagined the encounter with the maid or the consequence of her hot tea potion. I sat down immediately to ask Sissy Jean if I was all right, and did she know of the Tibetan maid. All Sissy said was that there are times the nonphysical come into form for situations of help or protection. She said I should trust my experience and accept it. It didn't matter whether others believed it or not. From that point forward I said nothing more about it, but I offered up thanks to my benefactor.

In a remote region outside Llasa, we were privileged to enter an underground monastery of Buddhist monks for a meditation sung in chants. I was mesmerized, hypnotized and transformed with the beauty, the elegance of feeling and the potent connection to Source. There are many ways to awakening to the Truth, but my experience with the Buddhist chants affirmed that their hypnotic trance-like chants offer one such opening to the connection we all desire. Prayer often offers the same connection, but the music of the chant that day cracked open a space that could never again close. I felt blessed, whole and good.

On the bus ride back to the hotel I thought of the four thousand monasteries that had been destroyed and all their monks massacred by the Chinese Communists. We were fortunate to be able to meet with one of the four hundred surviving monasteries. My heart knew that all the slaughtered souls were safe and perfect on the Other Side, but the hearts of those who slaughter live in darkness and fear. When one is good, knows the Truth and loves his neighbor, there would be no need for heinous acts. Only fear invites such ideas and behaviors. Ego Mind and fear always destroy. Still, in the final analysis, this is all illusion to present a lesson. My lesson was to affirm an open heart and expand my powers of forgiveness to the killers. It took me some time, but I got there.

Returning to India, I felt suffocated by the number of people, the rancid air, the poverty and even some of the customs. As accepting a person as I knew myself to be, void of much judgment, I found myself irritated that the Indian government was testing their nuclear weapons while I was witnessing starving, begging emaciated children in front of my luxury hotel, complete with marble floors and exquisite oriental rugs that roaming sacred cattle were allowed to poop on! The dissonance between religion and human needs and government priorities was deafening. On the street, I bought oranges, filling my skirt lap with them for children who came running. My friends did the same, until we were out of money, save our travelers cheques. By the time I left India, I had spent all my money on food for children, left all my clothes, save the ones on my back, for the hotel maids and wondered how they all survived. One morning, before leaving New Delhi, I could not sleep. My circadian rhythm was all screwed up. Getting up, I stood on the balcony of my hotel room, facing the back streets to see the city at night. I uneasily watched an ox-driven cart load the dead bodies that had been placed at the side of the street. The wood for a funeral pyre was expensive to an abject poor family member, so the city collected the corpses for a collective pyre later in the day. Seeing corpses was not pleasant, but seeing the bodies of small children always made me cry. I knew full well that the body was useless, and these souls had stepped over, forcibly, but still had made the one step journey to peace and eternal love. For some reason, I wanted them to have the choice.

Thinking of my own children back home, I wanted to protect, educate, enlighten and wrap them in a bubble of universal good, free from the ugliness of poverty, ignorance, archaic customs that discounted their dignity and any kind of intentional hurt. I felt my motherhood at a heightened level, energized by an abhorrence of the egomaniacal politic of the world. They so deserved the beauty and comfort of a loving society that fought for the uplifting of character and service, and honored their presence in the world. At that moment, I re-dedicated my voice to speak for love, dignity, tolerance, compassion, inclusion and honoring all beings. The divine in me saluted the divine in all. Period.

As I continued to stand on the balcony I remained focused on the idea of tolerance. It is, really, one of the easiest characteristics of personality to embrace. If one likes something, tolerance is a breeze. If one finds an issue with difference, the unknown, the misunderstood, the judged and the maligned, it is much easier to forgive than to escalate tensions born of ignorance, prejudice or fear. Actually, I thought, fear, so pumped by Ego Mind, was humanity's most insidious weapon, used to manipulate or control when we cannot allow ourselves to be accepting, loving, forgiving and peaceful. Standing on that balcony in India, my nostrils filled with filth and pungent odors, I still knew that what I was feeling was life-changing, planet- changing, universe-changing…at least for me.

World travel stretched my tolerance, enhanced my awareness, helped me embrace the unknown and investigate emotions of the people I met, rather than collect data with questions and facts. As humans, we are emotional bodies, honest and authentic, bombarded by rules, customs, laws, histories and judgments which are all transported through our thought system, mostly controlled by Ego. It is not a workable, viable or productive manner of living day to day, and for that reason, most individuals find life much more difficult than need be.

It was at that moment that I pledged to not judge without thinking the issue through, using Father Uribe's formula to see as many sides of an issue as possible, and then decide…not judge. The best example I could think of was when I was teaching midwifery to Peace Corps volunteers back in the sixties. The young women volunteers were making slight fun of Chilean women in the mountains, squatting to birth their babies, pulling them out and biting the cord in two and wrapping the umbilical with a strong reed. Most of the volunteers were expressing gratitude for modern hospitals for their future birthing experience. So, I said: "Do you think that gravity while squatting might be an easier delivery than lying on your back with your legs elevated for the convenience of the doctor?" Sometimes, what is different and archaic makes more sense. Put judgment aside, and wait on awareness and consciousness to provide the natural conclusion. It is so much more peaceful and accepting. And it feels good.

Then I heard her soft voice:

"What feels good at the time and also in retrospect is a good signal that you are in high consciousness. Loving gestures cannot feel like anything but heaven…a true alignment with The One. Ugly gestures may feel powerful, but never good. As long as Ego Mind keeps you in the illusion of dog-eat-dog, us versus them, attack and conquer, compete and destroy, cheat and win, lie and deceive, judge and belittle, no human will advance. He will return again and again through many lifetimes until one day he will begin to want light rather than darkness. Karma is a teaching method: karma means balance… not retribution. All humans are born good, with great ability to feel the love that may be gifted them by parents, relatives and others. If love is lacking, darkness creeps into the emotional body which so craves the loving memory of the Other Side. It hurts to not be in the presence of Love, so the hurt turns to anger which keeps one imprisoned in low vibratory energy, seeking out

reinforcement from other low energy sources. That's how gangs, dictatorships, cults and gossip groups emerge and thrive. You are standing on a balcony overlooking a city of millions who all want love, comfort, assurance, personal power and enlightenment. Wherever you are in your world, the soul next to you wants to awake, know the Truth…and know his part in it. Left alone, every soul would seek the Light. Left in the middle of human chaos, the journey is much more difficult, but the end point is always peace. It is ironic that humans fight so hard, so long and so dedicatedly and self-righteously to attain what is already theirs. Awakening is the gift."

"When I am home again, I want a long conversation with you about Divine Mind. I am ready."

"That conversation is easily had in this moment, dear one. Forgiveness is the key to the access of Oneness. As you forgive, you enter into peace. As you enter into peace, you align with love…the Love of Source, which is a peacefulness without description in human language. It is a penetrating energy that strengthens and honors the Creative Source. Forgiveness is the conduit to all awakening, all aligning, and all oneness."

"Your consciousness is ever-evolving, so each new situation invites a new awareness, a greater openness, a broader acceptance of all awakened possibilities and options for connectedness to everyone, no matter the differences. The idea of Oneness becomes real rather than imagined and illusions transform into spiritual realities. Hunger finds Love."

"Sissy, I need to get better at tuning out the static no matter where I am. With my patients, when I am focused on them, I am mostly successful at tuning out all the environment and am at one with them. But in the public, the daily places that our illusions take us like to like grocery stores, malls and gyms, I lower my high vibrational energy and just try to keep up with awareness of man-made chaos. Remembering to love gets really challenging in crowds and with harried souls just trying to navigate the illusions that they believe will bring long-wished-for relief. When we are back home, we will enter that lesson."

At Agra, I saw the Taj Mahal and was as impressed as are the millions of others that see that incredible edifice. But seeing it in one hundred twenty two degrees of Indian July heat was not pleasant, and was made worse by the wafting smell of the sewage trench that ran behind the Taj. Admitting that my temperament was definitely low vibrational, I returned to the Agra hotel to shower and center myself. Afterwards, I stepped outside where I encountered a beggar who spoke to me in English. Surprised, I opened a conversation with him, asking how he knew English so well. He explained that he enjoyed studying many things, without explaining more. Interested, I asked why he was a beggar when he obviously had talents to earn a living. He responded with a sentence I will never forget: "Madam, you misunderstand my purpose."

I stood transfixed. His energy was so high vibrational, I knew he was an enlightened soul. Being a beggar had a divine purpose for this man, and I felt it. I smiled. He smiled, and then he put his hands together and bowed to me. I have often thought it was my most powerful lesson promoting non-judgment, taught by a spectacular teacher.

I left India, ready to travel to many other parts of the world. That conversation was on my agenda with Ace as soon as we were in the same location again. He had been helping a new airline get up and running while I was in Asia. From then on, I would travel with him as much as possible when going to foreign lands, and we would have these spiritual discoveries together...because Sissy and Roger would help, as always.

> There's no bad consequence to
> loving fully, with all your heart.
> You always gain by giving love.
>
> Reese Witherspoon

30

The Swiss Air flight from Delhi to Zurich was luxurious as I was upgraded to first class for some wonderfully unknown reason. As eager as I was to get home, I still seized this opportunity to think, feel, absorb and plan. Although knowing all is illusion, existing on this planet compels one to navigate life's daily feelings and complex worldly circumstances. Suddenly, however, I felt the desire to contemplate love…all sorts of love.

Anticipating seeing my husband, I wrapped myself in the memory of so many adventures that made us laugh, be extemporaneous, overcome legal and family obstacles and share our spiritual knowingness together. I reveled in our joy of service together, our ability to detach from the material when needed, the courage to engage when something looked fun…or even when it was obvious that help was needed. We were a good team with compatible visions. I often told patients in marriage counseling that there were three things that every couple must have to be successful in a relationship. The first was love…maybe not even "in love," but some sort of loving, caring feeling for the other. The second was a need to have mutual respect for one another. But most of all, they needed a compatible value system. Without that, there would likely be a fatal domino effect. Without compatible values, one would begin to lose respect for the other. Loss of respect results in an erosion of love. Couples might continue together, but it wouldn't be a healthy relationship.

The idea of looking at all the places I felt love in my life was an inviting inventory worthy of marching through in the silence of the plane, somewhere over Afghanistan. It filled me with a light-headed moment of joy to start recounting the blessings of love in my life.

Mother communicated love through her unfettered interest in making sure we had competency with life tools. I learned courage through many 4-H contests, resilience at losses and humility in wins. I felt assurance of her protection as a buffer against the harshness of my dad and the softness of her voice when she explained life lessons. She was not a warm or affectionate woman, but her love was palpable in her caring behavior. If we hugged her, she willingly hugged back. Most of all, when we came home from school we were always greeted with a smile…not a big, flashy one, but a sweet, welcoming one. I missed her now every time I spoke of love. I had to forgive myself for not showing her, in my youth, more of the love I felt for her guaranteed attention to our care and her kind, slightly introverted manner. She was surely the most gentle and observant of the four of us. Hers was the sweet, safe and guaranteed kind of love that gave permission to explore, fail, get patched up and know you could always "go home."

As I thought of my brother, I shook my head and almost giggled aloud. He was a clown, a man of quiet brilliance and talent, a pathological giver, a guarded taker, an exquisite flag-bearer of all-things-family, the biggest tease and as good a person as I've known. His love never had to be said in words or hugs (much like our mother) or any kind of proclamation. It was magical and ever-present. Many times it was near impossible to get him to be serious, but when he finally agreed to focus his attention to any situation, he provided his skill in spades. Being a hard man to thank, he shrugged off all attempts at gratitude and made sure he eluded the praise and did something for the other guy first. This was his signature posture. If one were his friend, you received daily attention. I feel certain he had no enemies. If someone didn't like him, he was okay with that, moved on, slapped the fella on the back the next time he saw him and said: "Life's too short for you not to like me!" accompanied with a great belly laugh and an invitation to friendship. He was as near to irresistible as anyone I have known. What a lucky sister I was!!

Father Uribe's love was a channel from pure Source. He lived to show love. Finding many ways to impart love, he made me feel so competent, so precious, so loved as a child of God, so needed in the world and so humble to be a party to his abiding and ever-present love so freely given. That priest, without propagating or proselytizing, changed my life and its trajectory. He, above all others, made me want to be a good person, not because I should, but because it felt so energizing and whole. In my meditations, I often imagine a connection with him, hoping that he might be in the non-physical and approachable. I imagine he gave me what I needed, and his focus would be on others needing equal guidance from the Other Side.

Nevertheless, he has a sacred place in my memoirs of caregivers and near-sainted teachers. God bless Father Uribe. He knew his path, did not deviate, spread goodness wherever his energy resided and loved purely. What an enormous accomplishment to do what Source would have you do, even though free will was available at all times to do differently. His spiritual energy was so highly vibrational that I felt certain many others would underscore my feelings about him and report similar experiences.

My sweet grandparents, who took part of their meager life savings to help Phil and me when we didn't know where to turn, were saviors at a most needed time. Fippy and I had to have a touchstone that we could count on so that we knew life could be lived without daily fear for survival. I know we did not thank them enough, but I am certain they knew our hearts. They were saints that eliminated the fears of two souls they loved. We counted on that. They were love in action. And the siblings of my mother were consulted through all of our grandparents' decisions and always supported what was good for Fippy and me, knowing that it was possible that such actions could reduce their inheritance. My aunts and uncles were just down-home good people who believed in doing "the right thing." Any one of them would have taken us in. Knowing that safety was readily available was the survival ointment needed for the wounds we were trying to cover over and heal.

Sissy had taught me on this plane how we learn about love via our relationships. While thirty-five thousand feet above Iraq and enjoying the champagne and Swiss chocolates provided in first class, I smiled at the blessings of sister-friends. Those are girlfriends that always have your back, know all your secrets, know when to call and when to give you space and know you'll make the call when needed. They simply love you, warts and all. One feels so privileged to return the love. I had three sister-friends who were long term, and I would put them and their love up against anyone else worldwide!

Nancy was my colleague in the practice. We had met on the recommendation of my major professor who was also mentoring her through her doctorate. She was a couple years behind me. Invited by my professor to observe her through a one way glass as she did play therapy with cute kids, I was in awe of her easy connection with them, her versatile therapeutic interventions and how loving she was with everyone. She seemed like a magical pixie spreading fairy dust on those she was helping. Deciding to add a play therapist to my practice, I invited her to luncheon conversations several times to get to know her better. A practice partner is like a marriage, and I needed to feel comfortable, safe and trusting of the other. After deciding we were a fortuitous match, we joined our practices and worked together for over thirty five years.

We became intimate friends while going through adoptions, divorces and life's struggles together. We cried and laughed, trusted the shared confidences and advise of the other, and were always present in our discussions. Our metaphysical journeys, discoveries and awakenings have tracked parallel to each other, making the newness of awakenings so much richer and impactful. I continue to be amazed that I have yet to hear a judgmental statement from her. I wish I could claim the same for myself!

Nancy was the surrogate mom to my daughters. Every child needs someone they can complain to about their parents and trust to keep a secret and render sage advice. She helped them get out of poor decisions and confess to their parents. Quite often Dr. Nancy paved the way for a mother/daughter moment that was exquisite as versus catastrophic. To this day, the entire family still refers to her as "Aunt Nancy." I refer to her as "St. Nancy!"

Jaine, probably the brightest gal I have ever met, is a very different treasure on the spectrum. She knows exceptional kindness, generosity of time, money and empathy, is able to see to the heart of the matter in record time, works like a Trojan and is over-qualified at almost all she does. A master chef, decorator, art collector, reader of many genres, extensive world-traveler and premier jury consultant and psychologist, she has never failed to entertain, respond, embrace and confront in the most appropriate ways. I have counted on her blunt insight, her masterful manner of presenting an unsavory truth and her generous sharing of her dad and brother with me. I loved her late father, always owning my envy. She has honored me as a trustee of her wealth, a surrogate, at times, with her only son and a confidante with all major life events. Our love is so mutual, we can almost read the other's thoughts at times. What a wonderfully exquisite relationship.

I love walking into Jaine's house and meandering through the rooms. Each piece of furniture is meticulously placed but made to look like it could be easily moved to join a group setting at a coffee clutch. Every piece of art demands a conversation with extremes of opinion, while Jaine simply utters a non-valenced "umm."

Her generosity is legendary among her friends. Jaine is the one that insists we contribute at least 50-100 percent tip, saying: "So, do you want their job?" On her world travels, she is always eager to know the life goals of her guides who are obviously smart and hard-working, and she loves to give a leg-up to deserving individuals. Her only child, a son, chided her on one international trip by mimicking her, saying: "Hello, my name is Jaine. May I buy you an education?" He wasn't kidding! She would say that was nonsense. However, good friends know that, as difficult as some may see her as she surgically dissects and interprets situations, she is magnanimous and surreptitiously provides for the underprivileged and needy. Her style of love is undeniably efficient and wholesome.

Then, I relaxed into my feelings for Jean somewhere near the Swiss Alps. Jean had been that wonderful kind of soul that is always appropriate, unbelievably intuitive, tells the truth or stays silent if that be the better choice, finds a way to turn fear into laughter, chaos into an organized event and receives a "thank you" with a "nothing-to-it" response and a dismissive wave of the hand. She appeared when I needed an angel the most: the day I walked into Steve's law office, frightened, disoriented and needing an anchor. Sissy Jean and Jean have a lot in common, just on different sides of the planes. They both have an impeccable sense of humor, a secreted flamboyance and a humanity that is enviable and cherished by those they touch. When my life needs to be washed clean of nastiness that can penetrate without notice, I can count on Jean to always find the cleanser that reveals the silliness of the concern, accompanied with laughter. A "hell, girl, you've been through worse" is a soothing balm delivered with humor and love. What a gift!

One time we were reminiscing about our long-ago divorces from impossible marriages. I learned, by chance, that she still owned the house her late ex-husband and his second wife had lived in for years. Absent-mindedly, I asked what happened after her ex-husband died. She said: "Well, the poor thing needed some place to live, for goodness sake, so I won't sell it until she's gone." Charity is a natural element of Jean. It's not like she thinks about it; she just does what "feels" right. God, what a natural talent to carry with you all your life!

All love is born of trust and grows with nurture, reciprocity and appreciation. It has been my fervent prayer that we all could learn to spread it on the planet like a sweet icing that covers the delectable discovery underneath--precious brotherhood and the acceptance that we are all one.

Ace met me at DFW airport and took me home to continue our chaotic, yet rewarding journey together. I was eager to plan new adventures that would hold new discoveries. Loving the sea from childhood, we embarked on a plan to cruise to the many destinations on our list. We came to love cruising for its convenience of unpacking once, never having to make restaurant or hotel reservations, tours already planned to the best sights (a chance to create our own if desired) and meeting the most delightful people with whom we might form life-long relationships. We have the addresses with invitations of places all over the world! That, in itself, created an affirmation to universal brotherhood. Some of those addresses were in remote regions, Muslim strongholds, hostile territories and exquisite mansions. We might be greeted in saris, evening gowns, Maasai red wraps, Maori tribal wear, Buddhist saffron robes, Scottish kilts or naked Amazonian non–attire.

Being back at the office, seeing patients, returning calls, filing patients' progress notes and feeling the pressure once again of the hectic professional world, I took some time gifted to me by an undisciplined patient who had forgotten her appointment for the umpteenth time. I focused once again on love. In that free hour, I focused on patients.

I had to give gratitude for my love for the practice of psychotherapy and the many patients of a thriving practice. I relished going to work every day. Every hour was different and every hour graced me with a new story, precious feelings, miserable family histories and enormous damage to the psyche and heart all caused by the lack of love. My many years of training enabled me to diagnose and treat, but that was the minimal foundational necessity. My patients and my world needed love. They needed an acceptance that they could believe, partake in and trust. I became that willing conduit.

I possessed training in an outstanding doctoral program and internship, coupled with hundreds of hours in continuing education classes and mentorship with great professional colleagues. However, my intuition knew that these courageous souls that walked through my doors were looking for one missing piece...Love.

As a therapist, I knew that I could not coddle my patients and succeed in helping them. I developed a form of kind confrontation and slow and safe journeys through sad and sometimes excruciating histories. The result was moments of brilliant insight and often belly-busting laughter. I felt a spiritual mandate to walk these precious and courageous souls through the labyrinth of ego chaos to a place where they could hold onto a "knowingness" of their own making. My hope was to produce a belief system of their own creation that would offer relief and psychological salvation and healing. My mission was to make certain that the most egregious patient felt loved. I knew that Love is the cure, and it would have been unethical to do otherwise.

Then, there is the love that transcends all sense, all data and all logic. Loving my daughters is the privilege of my life. A Mother's love for her children excuses all wrongs, all deviations, all transgressions and all blips of immaturity. We are not in denial; we are mothers. We somehow find the circuitous path to love and forgiveness and acceptance. It is our fervent prayer that our children forgive us our ignorant messages, our misguided allegiances and our immature or inexperienced choices. Every day we give thanks for the existence of these children and for the granted privilege of rearing them. We love them to pieces and must be big enough to finally let them go when it is time. I was the most fortunate of women, having been gifted by birth mothers with the honor of rearing these girls to navigate a complex world with ethics, a sense of service and brotherly love. There is not a known method of translating my appreciative love to two women I love but do not know and may never know. I have to confess that I cannot imagine my life without the inclusion of these two precious, different, interesting, polarized and creative souls. Blessings have names: Eleanor and Emma!

Finally, as I was thinking of all the wonders and inclusions of love, I, cautiously, examined my world: the world of the Vietnam war, the world of government lies, the world of fear of communism and McCarthyism, the world of sexual revolution and birth control, the world of experimentation with mind-altering agents and the world of voices of division and of calls for the cure of injustices. It seemed overwhelming, never-ending and insurmountable. But, true to Spirit, Love is available, curative, universal and the only path to

Oneness. I, the friend of Sissy Jean, the ever-eager seeker of Truth, the soul willing to risk disapproval and rejection, am a loving pioneer of awakening and am humbled by the experience.

The next time I talked with Sissy, I asked:

"How can I teach love, explain love, guide others to love, but by example? I am a behavioral scientist, and I find no way to prove or describe love in a measureable way."

"There is no way to prove emotions. You know you have them, you will state you feel love, hate, anger, jealousy, envy and others, yet everyone takes what you report to them of your emotional feelings on faith only. When you feel love, you are in alignment with Source, with all Oneness; when you feel a negative emotion, you feel separated from joy, adrift with emotions that have no proof and no sense of worthiness," she giggled.

"You entered, at birth, into a world of matter and material. You were soon taught to acknowledge the teachings and rules of family, church, school and society and were slowly, often unwittingly, manipulated and trained to not think for yourself, not access the 'knowingness' that so freely resides in your Spirit connection. Your strivings sought to achieve approval, praise, acceptance and popularity. Fear and terror, retribution and punishment have been the Ego Mind motivators to acceptance of what is the majority view. There have actually been times in your history that thinking, investigating and acknowledging the direct connection to Spirit Mind and Source have been punishable offenses."

"My child, whatever you believe in will be. If you believe in love, you will find that you experience love. If you believe in evil, evil will present itself. You manifest from your thoughts. You create and are co-creators with Source. But Source will not participate in the creation of anything not born of love. Source is love, and all love is born of forgiveness. There is no other way."

"Then, soon, we must once again visit the topic of forgiveness. My head and my soul need its balm," I offered.

31

Life is an adventure.
It's not a package tour.

Eckhart Tolle

Since I had come from a fractured family, I wanted to create a workable and loving unit of four people who loved and trusted each other and would always feel the support they needed. A feeling of safety is near the top of the hierarchy of human needs. Food, clothing and shelter don't offer the relief from fear like safety does. A small child runs to a parent when scared because the parent represents safety.

Eleanor had wed a wonderful man at our home in the Bahamas, and Emma was the mother of our first grandson. We were quite eager to see their progress with life decisions and enjoy the wonder of our expanded family. Uncle Phil (the beloved!) was such an additive element to our family. His nieces were precious to him. He demonstrated that by not only teasing them but by attending their many ceremonies and events that focused the success of their young lives. He loved on them every Christmas Eve at our house with embarrassing stories of their youth, which our daughters saw as pure love.

Eleanor and her husband gifted us with a grandson and granddaughter. Phil and Anita and her family all joined for the family love fest on Christmas Eve, Fourth of July and Thanksgiving. It finally felt like a healthy, normal and loving family. We felt we had accomplished our goal by creating family love, family fun and family unity.

Emma, our younger daughter, was now a mother with a bushel of questions about how anyone could give up a child. The result was a search for her birth mother. Having always told the girls that I would support and actively help in finding their birth parents, with the caveat that we not disrupt or cause harm to their lives, I joined in the effort. What a mess! The social worker had told me that Emma's mother died not long after she gave birth. We could find no proof of that even though I was in possession of her name. When Emma was released to our care from the NICU, she still wore her hospital bracelet. Her mother's name and Emma's date of birth were imprinted on it. Even after hiring investigators and doing much research, Emma was not successful in finding any more information. I suspect the social worker was telling the truth about the birth mother being deceased since she had multiple addictions and severe diabetes.

Next, Emma set upon a path of confronting her adoptive father (my ex-husband) who had abandoned her. She informed us she was taking her son to meet her dad in Indiana. Further, she would live there for a while so they could get to know each other again. That began the second grand mess of her quest.

Upon arriving in Indiana, she appeared at his doorway, introduced herself and her son and informed her dad that he owed her an apology. Surprisingly, he offered her what she requested and invited her in to chat. However, he did not invite her to stay with him in his three bedroom house! With almost no funds, she found a room in a boarding house, got a job at a restaurant, found child care and began to work and visit her dad. After six months, she called Ace, her stepdad, and asked if he would come get her and her belongings. She told Ace that he was much more of a dad than the man she had sought. Ace, of course, obliged, and Emma was back in Texas once again with a new appreciation for committed family. Needless to say, my quest for forgiveness of Joe and his behavior was still ongoing. Every time I got close to true forgiveness in my heart, he committed a new egregious offense. This was obviously part of my path to confront my ability to forgive, regardless of the person or circumstance. I simply was too invested in the hurt Joe had caused the children to advance beyond my ego limitations and engage in spiritual clarity.

Upon returning home, Emma announced that she wished Bill (Ace) would adopt her. I told my husband this one evening, and he responded that it would be his great honor. We left it at that.

After several years we were able to go on the trip of a lifetime--a safari with the indisputable premier guide in all of Sub-Saharan Africa. We were finally packing our khakis, cameras and binoculars. Francesco Pierre Nina of the Tanzania Safari Company had a place for us. He accepted only eight people at a time to live in the bush in tents with twin beds. We were provided a bladder shower with sun-warmed water, a European potty chair with a three foot hole underneath and a bucket with sand and shovel at its side. The porters made us comfortable each time camp was disassembled and moved to a new location. This was not a fenced game preserve with permanent cabin/tents...oh, no siree! This was definitely in the wild with food cooked in the ground and served in a dining tent with linens. Cocktail hour was on the side of a hill with a nice fire. There we enjoyed storytelling and the comfort of too much adult beverage as we relaxed from our day.

After many inoculations for African diseases, we were to take our anti-malaria medication, Larium. I refused and warned Ace to risk malaria rather than the insane side effects of the medication that I had experienced in India. The memories of a hole in my tongue, mood swings, nausea, sweats and other deplorable and mysterious effects were enough to swear off. Instead we used Deet on our wrists and ankles at sunrise and sunset when one is most susceptible to mosquitoes.

After a twenty-two hour flight on KLM with a night in Amsterdam, we landed in Arusha. Here we were met by Francesco, who quickly loaded our gear and raced at extremely high speed to the city to avoid night bandits. It was the beginning of putting my life in someone else's hands for the next sixteen days. Indeed, the sensation of knowing you are free, but totally at the mercy of someone unknown to you, is a heart-catching realization. Acclimating to this new condition was fast and necessary since we didn't know the language, the territory, the customs or any regulations. After being deposited at a luxury hotel, we hurried to bathe and jump inside the mosquito netting on our king-size bed and pass out for nine hours.

The next morning introductions to the fellow travelers were made as we enjoyed breakfast together. Soon after, we boarded an eight passenger aircraft which would deliver us to the Serengeti. I was as eager as I could ever remember. Since childhood, I had read about the eco-system and yearned to see animals in their native environments. We came to a jungle- looking forest beneath us and the plane descended for landing. Eventually, I spotted the grass airstrip as we were on final approach. Curiously, the plane buzzed the airfield, climbed, returned to the approach pattern, then landed on the second descent. Later, I learned the first approach was to clear the airstrip of giraffes!

It is a heady moment to deplane and see giraffe, dik-dik, zebra and gazelle at the edge of the runway. The air, thick with the sounds of the residents, carried the smell of vegetation, the brightest colored birds imaginable, history, intrigue and danger, all existing together. As we climbed aboard two Land Cruisers with open roofs (so we could literally stand up through the roof to view and photograph), we simply could not absorb our visual discoveries fast enough. The casual meanderings of various animals for which I had yet to attach names were intoxicating. With all gear loaded, we began our trek to the campsite, chosen by Francesco from twelve thousand square miles. The Serengeti boasts swamps, kopjes, grasslands and woodlands which provide over seventy different types of large mammals and 500 bird species. Our eyes were always on overload.

Sometimes, the universe just blesses you beyond any product your own imagination could create. As we were en route to camp, we encountered a three-generation elephant family reunion. HUNDREDS of gorgeous elephants. There were grandmothers, mothers and daughters all around us. Bull elephants were relegated to the outer perimeters of the herd. We quickly learned that the king of the jungle actually is the female elephant. As we passed through the herd, we witnessed the birth of a baby elephant, somewhat harshly dropped from its squatted mama, but still a long way from the ground for an infant. The drop is nature's way of getting the infant awake as it moved and struggled to stand. I can attest that a newborn elephant is substantial! Francesco was quick to inform us how exceedingly rare it was to witness a generational reunion of elephants. We were blessed even before we reached camp.

I have rarely been any place where absolutely everything was a new experience. Safari was a guarantee of moment-to-moment introduction to not only newness, but also uniqueness. After we zipped ourselves into our tents the first night, I had to quiet my heart. Sounds of lion and hyena running through the campsite...and elephants scratching their butts on our tent poles kept my undivided attention. That will rock your tent for a minute of heart-stopping excitement!

Before retiring the first night we were warned never to leave our tent during darkness lest we be attacked by prowling, nocturnal animals. Indeed, safari members with other guides had suffered or even disappeared for not heeding these admonitions. We had porters who stood guard and watched from their own tents to guarantee compliance. The only exception was when we asked permission to unzip the tent one evening to observe the Southern Cross in the black sky. This view may only be experienced from the Southern Hemisphere.

We chose to rise early and go out to watch the cheetah hunt for prey, which happens immediately after sunrise. I don't know how professional videographers do it. My camera and I could not keep up with the speed of the cheetah on her chase. However, watching three cubs eagerly awaiting to feast on the jackrabbit, gifted by their mama a minute later, was akin to watching any loving mama tenderly attending to her brood. The savannah easily hides the cheetah, but we grew accustomed to spotting the tips of the ears through our binoculars. A chase would likely soon ensue. The beauty of this exquisite African cat will linger in my memory forever. It begs one to support the preservation of all wildlife and its natural habitat. Ace and I found we could not drink in enough of the beauty at one time. Surrounded by spectacular, multi-colored flora, wildlife, exotic birds and fowl and impending danger, we felt intoxicated and cautious all at the same time.

We were in the middle of the migration, an assembly on the move in the grasslands of one and one half million wildebeest and one million zebra. Everything moved with the rains that nourished the needed wild grass. As we were entrenched in the middle of this enormous herd, we found ourselves in the "maternity ward" of the wildebeests where they were protected somewhat from the immediate onslaught of the hyena, jackal or any other waiting predator. We witnessed the birth of numerous young. They had only seven to ten seconds to get up and run before, possibly, becoming lunch. The mother and other females ate the placenta quickly to give the newborn a fighting chance to survive. The herd females, instinctively, protect the young of each another. It will be their turn in the future. As I watched nature and survival at work, I remembered Darwin and his theory of the survival of the fittest. I learned in the Galapagos a couple of years later that it is really the survival of the most able to adapt.

The predators of the Serengeti are a lesson unto themselves. Coming upon a dead zebra, we watched the hierarchy of vultures as they came to feast. The "opening vultures," the ones who expose the entrails to the others, are the first to arrive. Then, they leave because only one vulture may eat at a time since their long necks dig deep into the prey's cavity, thereby their heads become prey to another bird if multiples feed at the same time. The major players, the giant and voracious vultures with seventeen foot wing spans, descend, one at a time. They devour until they are satiated and leave the rest to the vulture pecking order.

Each new safari day imprinted the acceptance that each creature is potential food for some other creature, depending on weight, strength, agility, age and speed. A healthy adult elephant is the exception. Inborn talents are incredibly displayed as hunts take on a form of wild ballet with heart-pumping jumps, turns, strikes and misses. My favorite cat is the cheetah. Unfortunately, its survival rate is only 25-30 percent. Most cubs are somebody's lunch. When you see it happen, you turn your head and know that it is what it is. We came upon a group of three hungry and scared cheetah cubs huddled under a tree. There was no mama in sight. We begged to rescue them. However, we were admonished, and the rule was repeated. Visitors could not interfere with the rule of the Serengeti by order of the Tanzanian and Kenyan governments. No one was allowed to take anything from the open preserve, carry weapons or interfere with the natural cause and effect of its habitat. Francesco guessed that the mama probably had been a meal for the local leopard.

One evening we saw a lioness lying asleep in a low tree branch, but high enough for us to drive under. We approached in our open-roofed Land Cruiser. The lioness did not move a muscle, but we were close enough to see the many battle scars covering her body. Francesco asked if we wanted to take it to the next level...and drive right underneath her. Who would say "no" to such an adventure? We parked directly under her where Ace could actually stand up and touch her, which he did not do. Francesco saw the full belly, bulging from a recent kill and knew we were safe. Still, it was thrilling.

However, some thrills were not so wonderful. We found a snake in our "bathroom." Another time army ants who can eat you alive marched towards our tent in a straight line. They were readily burned with oil lit aflame.

It would be exceedingly difficult for anyone sharing space with these wild creatures (their sounds, customs and hunts) not to have some spiritual experience even if it were not so named. This entirely NATURAL environment had no escape, but we did not want one either. I found I felt more of the ease of higher consciousness than anywhere I had ever been, save my secret woods in younger years. I lay in my bush bed at night, with eyes closed and a background symphony of animal songs, and graciously met with Sissy Jean, my constant companion and teacher.

"Sissy, I am so happy you are here with me in this animal world. I feel excitement each day on safari as I watch an environment that has not been manipulated or changed by the outside world of ego, profit, status or judgment. Yet, ironically, in its own way, the animal kingdom has set up a hierarchy of rules and regulations, so to speak, that are enforced with violence and death. So, knowing that all of this, too, is illusion, there exists a fascination of the comparison with humans and the teachings of Truth. Is this just a game?"

"Actually, my love, all illusion is a game until we enter the reality of the Truth. These beautiful and exotic creatures are also part of Ego Mind. Its creation and battles invite you to forget consciousness and enter the breath-taking illusions that simply represent a different view of Ego. These beautiful animals in their seductive environment provide a hypnotic illusion that entertains, involves, alarms and invites empathy. Please enjoy it for entertainment, but never lose touch with awareness of the Truth. You, my child, are awareness, as are all humans and any creature with intelligence."

"Do these animals survive death the way we do?" I asked.

"Dear one, all living creatures survive death because, as you know, we are not our body, nor is the elephant or the antelope."

"So, in essence, we are all temporary visitors to the planet with no other purpose that to experience what we encounter?"

"Exactly, my love. You separated from the Oneness, who is the awareness of pure Love and Truth, and came to this plane--in this case a planet named Earth, to experience what being outside of knowingness and love feels like. You gather your experiences, then spend a time (or lifetimes) learning how to return to Love and Unity. That is the end of separation and the acceptance of the reward of atonement."

"All the animals, too?"

"Yes, my sweet, but on a lower vibrational level."

One memorable night at dinner the guys fashioned bow ties out of black scraps and the ladies wore their blouses backwards with the sleeves tucked in and our bare shoulders showing. We pretended to have on lovely ball gowns to attend the Academy Award dinner for one of our group. This talented man had actually won the coveted award for some genius electronic discovery used by the film industry, and he chose to go on safari rather than attend the Hollywood ceremony. We fashioned a statue covered in aluminum foil and presented it to him with the appropriate accolades!

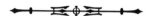

As we approached the Maasai camp, a young warrior was painted in the traditional white chalk for an initiation. He was excluded from the group we visited until his rite of passage was finished. We gave the women lipstick which enchanted them, and Ace, an amateur juggler, picked up three stones and entertained the children until his arms could not provide more. He was kind in trying to teach the little ones how to juggle. I bet they are still practicing.

Their primitive huts made of dung and straw were artistic, yet foreboding. Francesco and the chief had been friends for a long time, thus giving us access to the camp. It was on that day that we learned that besides English, French, German, Spanish and Swahili that Francesco also spoke Maasai.

One day we came upon a huge pond filled with hippos of all sizes cohabitating with crocodiles bigger than I had ever seen. As I approached the edge of the pond on an outcropping of rock, Francesco yelled, and I turned to see him wavering me back. When I stood next him on my return, he whispered that not long before, a young woman was standing on the outcropping, and a crocodile shot up from the pond, snatched and devoured her. Nice warning!

One of my favorite spots, because of its captivating beauty, was the Ngorongoro Crater. A volcano had erupted and collapsed on itself, becoming the largest unbroken caldera (fourteen miles wide) in the world and home to the highest density of lions anywhere. The three and one half million years old footprints of man have also been found there. No wonder…since we also visited the site thought to be the birthplace of man where the Leakeys did their extensive research at Olduvai Gorge. It seemed reasonably certain that evolution had begun in Central Africa. It felt beyond awesome to be standing in the birthplace of humankind (or the illusion of such an event)!

Leaving the beauty and fascination of the Serengeti was not easy, but our sendoff was unforgettable. As we were waiting for the morning fog to lift so our plane could land on the grass strip once more, we sat in our two vehicles and watched a herd of elephants walk towards us through the mist. As each one exited the mist, coming into view, we were blessed with their "good-bye" trumpets and slow march past us, disappearing into the mist behind us. No one said a word. It doesn't get any more memorable than a farewell by a parade of the queens of the jungle.

Since we loved our vacation journeys to interesting or far-away places, we joined three other couples two years later for a trip to Quito, Ecuador and the Galapagos Islands where Darwin did much of his research. Here we found humongous tortoises who average well over a hundred years old and five hundred pounds…and many blue-footed boobies. The story goes that Darwin tried many times to ride on the back of a giant tortoise, but fell off every time. It's hard to believe since these creatures move at glacial speed!

I knew I was having difficulty breathing normally in Quito at an elevation over nine thousand feet. The air was thin, and my blood became thick…not exactly recommended for anyone with major lung issues. Knowing we would be in Quito only two days going and one day on the return, I talked myself into believing that I could handle the short time at altitude. NOT!

After the 600 mile flight to get to the Galapagos Islands, we boarded a small ship to cruise around the islands. I was certain I would feel better. However, the first night on board, while eating a lovely dinner on deck, I became suddenly and overwhelming ill. Not recalling how I made it to our cabin, I woke up on the cold, bathroom floor, nauseous and vomiting. Somewhere in the fog of incapacitating illness, I knew vomiting uncontrollably and lung issues were not in the same category. I passed out again. My husband found me, helpless, and managed to get me to the twin bed which was to become home for the next four days. Recalling very little of the events of those days, I do remember the ship-board doctor being concerned that I was extremely dehydrated and needed an IV, but he had no such equipment on board. As he tried to give me one teaspoon of water, he jumped at the projectile vomiting it created.

My husband sat by my side, not knowing what to do. He felt helpless and worried. As I went in and out of consciousness, I tried to focus and evaluate my condition and my options. I knew a good deal about medicine, but I was not a physician. Finally, on day three I could think well enough to talk with Sissy.

In a feeble attempt, I called to her. She was immediate in her response.

"Sissy Jean, am I dying?"

"That is your choice. You are in a position to step over with grace or stay to work through major illusions in your life. This is entirely your call, as always."

"I want to learn all I can. If I survive this malady, I will re-dedicate myself to learning all I can to receive and transmit love, forgive everyone, everything and rejoice in the experience. If you have advice, please spit it out now!"

"Annalee, this is entirely your decision. Your essence is welcome here, but you also have much to teach and learn on your plane now that you know Truth. I think you will choose to stay to finish your work and your ministry. I know you better than anyone, and you are not finished with this cycle."

On day four I was able to stand and my tummy took two teaspoons of broth. I drank broth, sip by sip for the next twenty-four hours. It began to heal my body and spirit.

At the end of the seven day voyage, we all flew home. My clothes were loose due to the eleven pound weight loss in four days!! God only knows what bug or opportunity for enlightenment I had! I know whatever it was, I, somehow, meticulously designed the illusion for a purpose.

The good life is a process, not a state of being. It's a direction, not a destination.

Carl Rogers

Each April, Ace and I loved to tour the Texas Hill Country on his motorcycle to see the bluebonnets, Indian paintbrush, sombreritos, buttercups and a varied palette of many other beautiful wildflowers. Lady Bird Johnson was largely responsible for decorating the highway medians and fields with miles of gorgeous vistas provided by these springtime flowers. The LBJ Ranch on the Pedernales River is just west of Johnson City and also exhibits a plethora of wild-growing flora which is equally breath-taking each spring.

This year, however, we discovered that the Good Friday, three-day adventure was under a forecast of heavy rain. So, true to our nature, we switched plans and drove the pick-up south to the Hill Country and hoped for sunshine.

Months earlier, Ace had read about a high-fenced, thousand acre ranch development in the Hill Country near Blanco with twenty-five acre lots and a 3400' paved airstrip. It was 50 miles west of Austin and 50 miles north of San Antonio and was in the country with miles and miles of ranchland, cedar scrub and rivers. I suggested we change our flower-adoration plan and visit the ranch with the runway.

As we approached Austin, the rain stopped. Blanco was a quaint settlement of about twelve hundred people, one restaurant, two gas stations and thirteen antique shops. The area was populated with pick-ups sporting rifle racks in the back windows and NRA stickers on the bumpers. I thought my philosophy of universal love might have the potential for a few hiccups. Having grown up in a small town, I knew it was fertile ground for gossip but equally fertile territory for love and neighborly support. Neighbors in small towns bicker, argue, love and laugh. But when push comes to shove, there is support from all angles. It felt like it was home!

Eric, our salesman, wore starched jeans and a Stetson. He was easy-going and patient as we toured the many lots available. All but two of the lots on the runway were already sold. Thank God! The last thing I wanted was to live on the runway with a hangar attached to my house. The hangar would have been primary, with the house as an afterthought. I have never focused on the size of my home, but I am certainly concerned about comfort, whatever that looks like! My thought was that a retirement home should be most of what I wanted since it's probably the last home I would live in...before the nursing home.

Ace and Eric finally got with the program and asked what I might like. Casually, I said I preferred a lot at least a mile in from the highway and from the airstrip toward the back. Also, it should be bordered by the high fence with lots of topography, water and trees. Eric stood up, thought for a minute and said that he had just the lot. My thought was: "Yeah, what else would a realtor say!" Shame on me! Eric was good for his word. He drove us through the undergrowth to the top of a hill with the most glorious view. The building site was located in the middle of the lot, surrounded by lots and lots of magnificent oaks of all ages and had a perfect spot for a large pond down the hill. The watershed was just right for the proposed pond we wanted. Eric had certainly delivered. We were speechless as we stood and looked three hundred and sixty degrees at rock ledges and oaks, some over a hundred years old. Spiritual feelings of connecting to the land itself were abundant. It would provide the privacy we desired and neighbors just twenty five acres away. Ace and I stood at the top of the hill, looked around and uttered the most vulnerable words that can be said in front of a realtor: "This is it!" We signed the papers within the hour. We could not believe ourselves...the ones who prided themselves on exhaustive research and measured decisions. Our non-physicals were undoubtedly nudging us because our quick decision surprised even us! We never rethought our commitment. We knew we were both several years away from retirement but our retirement location was now decided. Ace could think of nothing else than the three thousand square foot hangar he would build at the edge of the runway on land specifically designated for hangars of owners not living adjacent to the strip. And it was only a mile from the house site. We were high on excitement on the five hour drive home.

Both of us went to work on Monday morning unable to think of anything but the Hill Country. He was busy flying for a commercial airline and did not get to his hotel until after ten in the evening. When I got home from doing rounds, I grabbed some crackers and cheese and headed to the computer. Googling "one story, rear view mountain home," I found ninety-nine floor plans. The first was almost perfect and had windows all across the back, but the rooms needed enlarging. Of course, I looked for hours at the other ninety-eight and then ordered a set of plans for the first one.

When Ace called, as he did every evening, I told him what I had been doing. He laughed and said he had also thought about building the house in the Hill Country. He suggested he could commute from there to work, and asked if I would cut my practice to four days a week so that I could fly to the ranch on Thursday nights and return Sunday evenings to Dallas. I said: "Consider it done!"

The search for a builder began. Like most people, we visited the Parade of Homes, looked at houses that appealed to us in neighborhoods close by and perused stacks and stacks of magazines. Soon we found a builder whose creative abilities were vast and interesting. We hired him to expand the plans on his CAD and bid the job. Hiring him and signing the agreement, getting the construction loan and getting a road built through the trees to the building site was my job. I was reared in construction and had so much experience in office work, estimation and contract review, thanks to my dad. Bill was sooo grateful not to have the assignment! He's a mechanical genius, but hates paperwork. I had all the I's dotted and T's crossed. I had memorized the floor plans, the roof elevations and the ceilings heights, (varied in almost every room). A big foyer where friends could gather and a huge kitchen island where family could sit and chat as meals were prepared were two must-haves. Oh, and a BIG back porch overlooking the valley and the next hill with breathtaking views for miles beyond. I went to sleep looking at color charts and awoke to thoughts of furniture placement. I was well aware that my life was not just about building a house. But it was the first one we had built from scratch, and I was beyond obsessed with all the details. It felt like fun and an extension of my self-definition as well as an opportunity to create and find beauty. There was obviously more than a good portion of ego involved. I was busy creating my nirvana. This all became altered when the builder was served with divorce papers, and, like most of us, he had spaghetti for a brain and his emotions were incapacitating him. I counseled and offered the best therapeutic suggestions known to man. I listened for hours, but he was so devastated that the process was going to take time.

The bank didn't care about his divorce nor the time needed for recovery. What could go wrong did go wrong. Materials weren't ordered, invoices weren't paid, subs refused to show up without gas money being fronted them for the drive from San Antonio or Austin to the country. One Friday we arrived at the build site and found migrant workers living in our woods and cooking over campfires during one of the worst droughts recorded in the Hill Country. Burn Ban notices were posted everywhere. Our Mexican brethren could have burned the whole ranch down! Eventually, I had no choice but to fire the builder. I was abysmal at this task, but committed to it under the circumstances. Ace and I took over as general contractors. We divided up the duties which made us semi-crazy. We simply could not do our full time-jobs, travel to the ranch every week-end, control the pace of work of the sub-contractors, keep up with the accounting and have a personal life. We were losing ourselves. The best parts of our relationship and our good mental and spiritual health were being destroyed. Letting the screwed up illusions about our dream home overtake our good sense and our knowingness was not good. All marriages have their ups and downs and spin-a-rounds. This was certainly ours! Thanks to God, Sissy and Roger, we came to our senses and began to observe the illusion instead of being the illusion. Nevertheless, it took a while.

Poor decisions or poor execution of good decisions have consequences. I was becoming weaker, more tired and lacked energy. After two hospitalizations for pneumonia, my pulmonologist and my husband declared: "enough is enough." Retire. Retire. Retire. I knew they were right. I desperately needed the rest that retirement would bring. Loving what you do can be so intoxicating and rewarding that it becomes almost impossible to think of saying good-bye. I envied my husband's government-mandated retirement at sixty-five. He knew his retirement date for years in advance. Commercial airline pilots, regardless of competency, dedication or willingness to continue, are forbidden by law to fly for an airline past their sixty-fifth birthday. I, however, had no such mandate, except for my declining health. I retired and committed myself to recovery and a vibrant daily life. (Sissy let me know that it was about time)!

I called all my patients, gave them three good referrals, lovingly blessed their lives, notified my licensing boards of my retirement and the diplomas and licenses were stored in the attic. I woke up with no specific agenda. Dear God!! I did, however, accept two board positions that I thought would require minimal time. This would keep my finger in development and progress of humanitarian issues. News flash! I had been on five boards previously and knew they ALWAYS took more time than told by the recruiter. Three years later my terms were over. I promised my husband that I would not accept another board position. I have turned down some juicy offers, but a promise is a promise.

Steve, our favorite family lawyer, came to the ranch, equipped with all the necessary legal documents for the adult adoption of our daughters by a father who loved them dearly. Ace adopted the girls in a sweet ceremony at the quaint, historic courthouse. The kids, grandkids, in-laws and parents were present for one of the happiest occasions that can occur in a courtroom. I have never witnessed a moment than contained more pride for my husband. Our darling granddaughter brought levity to the emotional situation as only a six-year old could by saying: "Gee, Mommy, you sure do get adopted a lot!" We were so grateful for Steve who led the judge through the procedure. We later learned that the court had never presided over an adult adoption. It truly is an emotional and loving legal procedure. It felt so good.

Ace ordered a kit to build a helicopter in the hangar. It was not a small remote-controlled hobby kit, but a full-size, two seat, enclosed cabin Rotorway Talon. This was an exquisite homebuilt helicopter that would take almost six years for my perfectionist husband to build. It was clear that this was a hobby that would cost more than could ever be recovered in re-sale. But, as with many things we love in life, the sacrifice is worth the monetary loss. To his credit, not only did he build a superb machine, it has been my favorite joy of all his toys. (The motorcycle was a close second). I thought I would get my rotorcraft license when he started construction, but I opted out after discovering it takes exquisite co-ordination of both arms, both legs, both eyes and great reflexes. This is Ace's forte as he has always been a superb pilot-in-command.

We have been amused by the comments of friends and family with their reactions to a homebuilt helicopter. Many begged for rides, some lectured us on the statistics of helicopter crashes, others could not begin to fathom that Ace could build such a complicated machine, and then there were those who were absolutely terrified at the thought of flying in it. Most said that it was Ace they trusted and would take their chances for the thrill they anticipated. All were rewarded with some degree of joyous adventure and pride in themselves for pushing their courage boundary to include a helicopter ride in an experimental aircraft. There are two former astronauts that live in our gated community, and experimental aircraft is a no-brainer to these two neighbors! One was the former civilian boss of the Shuttle program, and we were honored when he invited us to a launch that was executed perfectly. It is a different kind of thrill to see that rocket launch with Old Glory on her side, headed to the Space Station.

We have taken many an afternoon to buzz around the Hill Country in the chopper, dipping down to fly in canyons and pulling up to clear what seemed like small mountains. Law enforcement has called several times asking for help to search for victims drowned in a near-by lake. The most emotional search was after the Memorial Day Flood of 2015 where a whole family was swept down our local river. We were unsuccessful in finding any bodies, and none have since been recovered. Ace was a federal flight deck officer (federally trained and certified to carry a weapon in the cockpit post 9/11) when he was an airline captain. Therefore, he was grateful to be able to continue helping local law enforcement when asked. Our small police force knows we're the local go-to helicopter.

In celebration of our twenty-fifth wedding anniversary we decided to take a trip on Azamara Cruise Lines to Southeast Asia. The ship was small, intimate and friendly with the renowned Captain Smith from the Isle of Man. He was reputed to be delightful and approachable. All of the reviews lauded the trip with five stars from previous cruisers. Our three week tour included Hong Kong, Vietnam, Cambodia, Thailand, various islands and Singapore, before flying to Tokyo en route home.

We arrived in Hong Kong on the eve of the Chinese New Year. This meant boisterous celebrations with fireworks and parades all night long. My husband is like a silly kid when it comes to fireworks. He loves them, but we were beyond tired after twenty-two hours of flying in coach.

We were quite enchanted with Hong Kong Harbor. It is an artist's dream with colorful sampans everywhere. However, those sampans made it difficult to maneuver on tours. These boats are home to thousands where three generations might live on one small skiff. Cooking is done in the open air on the stern which made for an interesting and odiferous experience. There were times when I felt minimally apologetic for intruding on someone's dinner or outdoor space.

As I walked on China Beach in Da Nang, I tried to visualize the numerous American troops that had been stationed there. Sadly, I noticed the abandon Quonset hut hangers across the road. These were ominous reminders of the Vietnam War. What remained was only decaying rumble left for someone else to clean up.

Captain Smith, our champion, maneuvered our small ship up the Mekong River into Saigon (Ho Chi Minh City) with the necessary expertise. There were moments when the ship was tipped to such an angle that passengers had to grab the handrail to steady themselves as Captain Smith did what he called "The Mekong Slalom" maneuver to navigate the river. Once on land, everyone competed for space with over one million motorbikes. They were typically loaded with a father driving, a child on his lap, a wife behind with another child on her lap and another child strapped on her back. Both hands of the wife held plastic bags of groceries. No cars were allowed except for those of dignitaries, yet small trucks were intermingled with the never-ending sea of motorbikes.

Ace wanted to see the remnants of the war zones. I, of course, wanted to talk to Vietnamese people--at least with those who spoke English, which were many. We went to nearby fields on the outskirts of Da Nang where we witnessed the remains of huge, and I do mean HUGE, craters left by the bombs dropped by B-52 bombers. There were left-over bamboo spear pits built by the farmers whose land was being ravished and many underground tunnels built by the Viet Cong and local farmers. Ace, slight and muscular, wiggled down into the tunnels. He walked bent over to observe dormitories, hospitals, military headquarters, kitchens, etc. He was underground so long I became concerned that he had become lost. He told me later I was right. He should have dropped crumbs on his way! Not many Americans can traverse the tunnels that are still intact, but Mr. Adventure-whenever-possible was not going to pass up this opportunity. Of all the things we witnessed in Saigon, the propaganda films of the Vietnamese detailing how to combat the Americans with homemade weapons of bamboo were the most eerie. Ace and I had lost friends in the war. The films brought home the stark realization that every family, Vietnamese or American, was fighting for the lives or their country. All were patriots.

On three different occasions, I had the blessed privilege to speak for a bit with Vietnamese people who lived through the war with America. I must admit that I was expecting some lingering anger and some resentment resultant of our invasion of their homeland, or at least some hint of revenge for what they had endured. However, on all three occasions, these individuals were full of forgiveness and understanding. Individually, they expressed their sadness at the horrors of war and the atrocities that war brought. Remarkably, all three said that forgiveness was the only path forward. Without forgiveness one would live in the hellish memory of what was past. Each expressed the belief that what was past was past, and the present moment is all that is meaningful. It had taken me fifty years to know this and believe in it. These treasured souls had learned it via war and peace, rehabilitation and reconciliation...but, predominantly, through forgiveness and faith. Sometimes, you meet the Buddha on the park bench!!

Sitting on the balcony of our ship in Saigon Harbor after a day traveling up the Mekong River in a skull boat (one oar at the stern), I felt peace in a chaotic city. Ace went to the gym to work out, and I leaned back, left the glass of wine on the deck table, and asked to talk with her. Sissy answered softly, as always.

"Sissy Jean, I have had an amazing day. I have spoken with people who have every reason to hate me as an American, and yet they have all been kind, respectful and welcoming. It has been an experience that has opened by heart more than ever before. These individuals and, perhaps a nation, have found a way to forgiveness and a view of the future that is underscored with hope and faith and kindness. What a glorious experience for a graduate student that walked in protest marches. I felt such anger when my friends were killed while a government that I loved and trusted was lying."

"Dear one, you are once again caught up in the alluring entertainment of illusions. Remember, they serve the purpose of teaching us to observe and learn, not to think that our experience is real. Your Vietnamese brother and sister experienced loss of family, land, government and safety. Their American counterpart lost faith, life, hope and trust. War left scars on the soul essence of all, as it always does. Without forgiveness, the survivors will live in hell."

"As in your own life, you hold on to hellish pain created by your reluctance to forgive what needs to be forgiven. Forgiving your ex-husband for the abandonment of his children does not mean that you accept his harmful behaviors, that his offending actions are acceptable, rather it says that you have released your anger and resentment, your judgment and angst. Your children were victimized, but they have forgiven their father. They are not pronouncing a pardon, but the fact is that they will not permit his obscene behavior to define their essence, their worthiness, their holiness. If the offended can forgive and fill their hearts with hope and trust, why do you hold on to the ugliness of non-forgiveness?"

"Sissy, I know you are right. I felt so much better when I was able to forgive the insensitive surgeon who coldly delivered my mother's death sentence and the school counselor whose competency did not include empathy or compassion, but who was limited, not mean. It took a little longer to forgive the two sexual assaults, but I got there... and was honest about it. Joe's lawsuits, calculated meanness with lies to me, the court and the children all entered into forgiveness slowly and over time. There is not a thing I can think of that I need to forgive of someone else except Joe's abandonment of his daughters. It is so inconceivable to me that my head wants to forgive, and my heart balks, admonishing me that I must be honest. Sissy, you know my heart, and it always tells me the truth. So I can't pretend I forgive Joe his heinous abandonment when I still know I harbor resentment and disbelief. The part of me that knows this is all an illusion to teach a lesson has not knocked me over the head yet. So until it's an honest forgiveness, I just keep working on it."

"Annie, you will get there, but do not forget that it is imperative that you DO get there soon."

"Sissy, I have forgiven myself for many offenses and granted myself so much more permission to speak my truth without fear of judgment. I hold beliefs that are foreign to some and, therefore, put myself forward to receive judgment. I think that does not bother me at all anymore. I am just grateful that I forgave myself for not telling my mother she was dying, for not helping Phil more when he was so lost and for not giving myself permission to divorce years earlier. And I'm pretty sure that I have made apologies, whenever possible, to those I have offended. I have this one sticky point with Joe and his behavior. It still feels like not forgiving him for leaving his children is some absurd way of still protecting them....still being a mother."

"Annalee Grace! You know that doesn't align with Spirit! But I am always here to nudge this issue along…and keep it at the forefront of your knowingness. When you feel that tickle at the back of your neck, it's me!"

I laughed out loud and said "thank you." I was so grateful to know that I had Sissy Jean always and forever. Knowing that everyone had a non-physical helper, I once again said my prayer that everyone's heart would open and connect with this precious beingness from the Other Side. I often felt I was cheating somehow because I had Sissy and KNEW it. What a profound blessing. I recalled, at that moment, a dear friend to whom I had told about Sissy after my retirement who said: "It's a good thing you didn't talk about her earlier or you would have been in the loony bin!" That would not happen. No harm has been done (or ever could be) by anything Sissy has ever said to me. It just doesn't get any better than getting messages and teachings from the Spirit Side that serve to help me and my world.

In Cambodia we rode elephants. Afterward, I asked for forgiveness for contributing to their daily mandated labor. They should be wild in the forests, but I had rationalized my ride by saying I wanted to be close to them. Ego Mind was rationalizing in full charge!

We were enchanted with Bangkok! And the river with boats that looked like they were straight out of THE KING AND I. The food was to die for. We skipped meals on the ship to be able to eat local fare. Wise tourists were we!

Singapore is an immaculate city with extensive orchid gardens. Its strict rules and subsidized housing for the greater percentage of citizens is a marvel. The airport was so scrubbed and polished that we teased we could eat off the floor. Traveling on Singapore Airlines to Tokyo and then L.A. was a treat. I am a walking advertisement for how they so kindly treat their passengers on such a long, long flight.

We were so satisfied that we had chosen the Asian cruise for our anniversary. Tired, but happy, we returned home to re-enter normal life. As usual, I picked up my phone messages and immediately felt profound sorrow. I packed my bags and knew that the next month was going to be anything but normal. My heart was breaking.

> Nothing in life is to be feared. It is only
> to be understood. Now is the time to
> understand more, so that we may fear less.
>
> Marie Curie

33

As I sat restless in the recliner provided by the hospice facility staring at him, I counted his respirations, watched for the chest to move ever so slightly and hated the gurgle in his throat that came intermittently. There was not a whisper of evidence that he was doing anything but sleeping. No machines, no tubing, no monitors, nothing but a comfortable looking bedroom with a bed holding a man barely alive. We, his wife and daughter and I, were sitting vigilant to bless him as he would exit. My brother, my twin, my partner in family survival, my polar sibling, was dying. The final step over was close.

My memories ran the gamut of his life, from infancy diapers to exit diapers. When he was little, I was his touchstone. He shadowed me everywhere, cried when he could not catch sight of me and screamed my name if he needed help. By age two, he crawled in bed with me because I was "warm." Mother and I were the only two trustworthy people in his world. He hid when Dad came home and he ventured out only when Dad kindly coaxed him. When Dad swooped him up and threw him in the air, he was terrified and ran to me once he was on the ground. I vividly recall my father exclaiming: "I sure as hell hope the whiney boy grows into a man sooner than later!"

Fippy was the town's Tom Sawyer. From second grade on, he had the clever skill of getting others to do his chores and pay him for the privilege. His collection of nickels from school friends was amazing. Describing chores as if they were rites of passage or worthy of regal recognition, he easily enticed his brethren to bicker and quarrel for the right to get one of "Phil's presents." Mother giggled about it, Dad didn't believe it, and I envied his talent. Once, when having to do a number of objectionable chores, I told on him. Immediately feeling guilty beyond description, I ran and told him that I had snitched on him and begged his forgiveness while crying. He hugged me and told me everything was all right…because no one would believe me. He was so right!

When I was in Mrs. Van Dyne's class in second grade, a really mean kid whispered to me as we came in from recess that he had "hanged" my brother behind the bus barn adjacent to the playground. I knew this little monster could and would do such a thing. So I ran out of the building, across the gravel parking lot, rounded the corner of the barn and found my brother with a rope around his neck. He was hanging from a low branch of a young tree with his toes barely kissing the ground. His hands had a pair of toy handcuffs that obviously worked, and his lips were slightly blue. I jumped in the air and caught the branch with both hands, ready to bend it down so Fippy's feet would be on the ground. My excited motion actually broke the tender branch, and I was able to slip the rope off. I removed the somewhat well-tied rope from his neck, and he coughed and vomited, after which he was ready to re-enter the school house. Pleading with me not to tell and afraid of the revenge of the meanest kid in school, he finally accepted that I had to tell because he was almost killed. He said he would trust me, telling me: "Annie, you always know what to do." Actually, I had no confidence in what I was about to do, but I was angry...and just seven years old!

One of my most courageous moments in memory was walking into the classroom of the principal, one of three teachers in the schoolhouse, and abruptly yelled that Tommy Deteridge had almost killed my brother. To his credit, the principal walked over to me, looked at Phil's neck and handcuffed hands and invited us into the hall. After several questions, he called my mother who came to get us at school. I, to this day, have no idea what was said to Tommy or his parents, but Fippy was safe at school from then on. And my brother told everyone how brave I was, and that I deserved a medal like our Daddy had. I thank Tommy Deteridge that he bragged about his "hanging" or my brother might not have had such a good outcome.

It was time for us to change places. Anita, Phil's wife, and his daughter, Kim, and I were rotating from the recliner to blow-up beds on the floor every two hours. Kim took my place, robotically moving into the recliner after softly touching her dad's hand. It was her turn to count inhalations, pray, reflect and pour love into this departing soul. His only child, his "forever-princess" and his anointed progeny now was on guard, promising to wake us at any turn in events. She nodded, unable to speak, desperate for this situation to be a bad dream. There are few children as loved as Kim was by her dad.

Luckily, we had not awakened Anita during the changing of the guard. She could get four hours of much-needed sleep before her rotation in the recliner. I felt gratitude for this small favor, knowing that if Fippy were conscious he would be protecting all of us, making us comfortable and sacrificing himself once again, as usual.

My memory of Fippy was actively reliving his life. He was always small, slight and far under the normal bar on the growth scale. His classmates were average or bigger than average, so Fippy was relegated to mascot or water boy status. His intelligence, ingenuity and personality filled the gaps that his physical body was unable to produce. Girls loved him! His guile began in the fourth grade, and he successfully perfected it through the years. His wit was so much more entertaining that the muscular pitcher on the baseball team or the captain of the basketball team. Remember, this was INDIANA where b-ball was everything! He was a testament to the fact that everyone likes entertainment, adventure, light-heartedness and well-intentioned teasing.

When we were nine and ten, respectively, we were wrestling on the living room hooked, wool rug that Mother had spent over a year making. All of a sudden, his face was ashen, and he stopped, stood up and backed off.

"Fippy, what's the matter?"

"Annie, I hurt you bad. Please don't die. I'm sorry," he whimpered.

"I'm not hurt. You didn't do anything bad. Why do you think you hurt me. I didn't scream or anything," I said matter-of-factly.

"Cause you are bleeding. It's all over your legs and on Mother's good rug," he breathlessly replied.

"What?" looking down at my legs under my cotton skirt and at the precious rug.

I knew immediately what was happening, and I was scared to death. I ran to the phone to call Mother. She had recently taken a job as a receptionist at a manufacturing company on the edge of town.

I told her I was bleeding from "you know where" and insisted she come home immediately with all the necessary personal hygiene items she had previously described in an embarrassing "life events" talk. She acquiesced and gave me the comfort and assurance a young girl, frightened of maturity and a life passage, needed. I also asked her not to explain things to Phil, and just tell him I was all right, and he didn't hurt me. Some years later, my brother and I laughed at the incident, with Phil expressing the traditional: "Better you than me" stupid-guy remark.

Almost two years ago he had called to say that his PSA was way out of range, but the doctor did tests and biopsies, and there were no abnormal results. His prostate was fine. Eventually, bladder cancer was discovered. After being told it was stage one, he sighed a breath of relief and proceeded with the prescribed protocol. It was difficult, but he improved. His vintage characteristic of dismissal of anything unpleasant kept most everyone in the dark. This was his purpose.

Then, the most horrific phone call came. Phil called Ace, not me, to say that Scott, Anita's only child, a married father of two sons, had been killed in a motorcycle accident. The news paralyzed the entire family, rendering most of us unable to think, believe or respond. Scott was more fun than monkeys at play, brighter than the dickens, talented beyond belief and always the tease that Phil had mentored. He was simply a fabulous nephew.

Phil rose to the occasion of comforting, caring for and loving his wife with the understanding of a true soul mate. As the father of an only child himself, he desperately tried to soften every emotion for her. He read her mind as much as he could to make everything she needed materialize and walk her through her grief. He did just that until he could no longer keep his secret of the ever-present pain in his groin. His cancer had returned.

Our sweet Anita was the wife who finally understood and loved my brother. Nonetheless, she desperately needed to have time for her grief and memories of her late son. At the same time, she was the manager of a law firm with massive, daily demands. Now she had to immediately take on the responsibility of getting Phil accepted for an evaluation at M.D. Anderson, the internationally-known, premier cancer research and treatment center.

The oncologic urologist spoke clearly and without hesitation. The cancer was now, actually, stage four, with zero percent survival rate. As was typical with Phil, he said he understood and would beat the odds. His wife and I were astounded. But we were aware of the defense mechanism of denial. We walked forward, knowing that Phil's enthusiasm for being the pioneer survivor of his diagnosis was absolutely integral in his personality. He was never, ever, going to be the loser our dad had defined.

After some unsuccessful experimental chemotherapies, he

returned to a Ft. Worth hospital for more treatments and care. I have to admit that I fought daily against the urge to push the oncologists up against the wall and scream that they had a duty to tell this patient the truth. Knowingness always whispered that Phil knew the truth, refused to believe it and was coddled by doctors trying to do their best. The day would come when he would know.

That day came when Anita had a private conversation with the head nurse, asking if there was any hope. God bless honesty. The nurse quietly told my sister-in-law that the most loving thing she could do was to take him to Community Hospice, a unique and reverent facility near-by. The nurse made the arrangements.

Anita returned to the room, told Phil that we were all going to hospice together and left to get the car. While she was gone, Fippy motioned me over to the bed. With another motion he summoned me closer so he could tell me something. In a very breathy and hoarse voice he said:

"You...can...have...my...dollar." I put my head on his chest and laughed and cried and laughed.

The first night at hospice, Anita's family came to the room. All of them were singers. Some of them were professionals and others were members of the church choir of which Phil was a member. They shut the door and proceeded to sing the most gorgeous old church hymns with exquisite harmony, all a capella. Soon the nurses knocked and asked to open the door because the families of other patients wanted to share in the blessing and beauty of their performance. Those kind singers transformed a house of death into an uplifting concert hall. I did not want the event to end because I knew what was to come. Despite my knowingness and faith, I did not want to lose him on this side. His goodness was such an additive to a chaotic world.

I saw Kim nudge Anita awake, change positions, and quietly, yet reverently, proceed with our mission of accompanying this soul on his exit journey. Burying my face in the pillow, I did not cry. I prayed. I prayed for an easy transition, a sweet awakening in the beauty of Truth, the reunion with Mother, a now-perfect Dad and beings of pure Love.

At that moment, one of the angel hospice nurses came to me and asked how I was. The thought crossed my mind that these nurses were attentive angels of death's journey. They were volunteers who knew the Truth and had returned from previous lifetimes and discoveries to help the souls who were so worthy, but needed assistance. I began to explain that my brother's wife had lost her only child one year ago on April 10th· and this was April 9th. I told her it really didn't matter in the scheme of things, but I thought it would be cruel to have them die on the same day. She nodded and told me she had a plan. Very quietly, she rolled his bed out of the room and took him to the room of "warm baths". Two nurses lowered him in a sling apparatus down into warm water, massaged him, touched his body with loving strokes while he languished in the warmth of the bath. When they toweled him dry, returned him to his bed and then to his room, he was calm, slightly breathing and ready to leave. We kept taking turns every two hours until Anita was in the recliner once again. All three of us fell asleep for a period of ten minutes or less, as if a mist had fallen over our bodies. Phil left during that time. It was like the last joke of his life. He knew that we were all there to support him, and he slipped to the Other Side in that rare moment of sleep with his three loved ones in attendance.

The angel nurse lovingly shook us awake with the quiet sentence: "I think he's gone." I was so glad that he had stepped over and so sad for his wife, his daughter, his friends, his church choir members, his relatives…and for me. I knew he was in the Light. His fear was gone. Phil had asked to be unconscious at the onset of death. I assumed because of fear. I so wanted him to be conscious and celebrate the reunion with total Love and Peace. We all do the passage in our own way. Phil had passed. I desperately wanted him back. I wanted one more hug, one more laugh, one more tease. I knew when I sat in the parking lot watching the body bag being loaded into the hearse that it was final. Good-bye, Fippy, my sweet, forever, brother…

Then, there was the funeral. I would prefer to not have a funeral. Rather I would embrace some sort of celebration, attended by friends, with wine, food, music and stories. Phil's funeral was traditional, with casket (closed because he didn't want to be stared at!), a church service with speakers who loved him and a minister who honored him openly. Telling one of the stories of his experience with Phil, he spilled the beans that the previous Christmas, when their chorale program, CHRISTMAS SPLENDOR, was going to be cancelled due to lack of funds, Phil had written a check to underwrite it saying: "This is Christmas Splendor, not Christmas Slender!!" Perfect example of Phil!! Anita has to be given so much credit because he did the service part, and she did the earning-the-nickel-to-make-it-happen part. What a team!

As the pallbearers lifted the casket to carry it up the aisle and out of the church to the waiting hearse, they all wore one of the musical hats from Phil's hilarious collection he had gathered over the years. Anita and her grandson had culled the unsuitable ones, and put the fun ones on display. Each pallbearer grabbed one as he passed the casket, plopped it on his head, pushed the start button for the accompanying jingle and returned to lift the box carrying the remains of this wonderful man.

Before I left my home in response to Anita's call for help, I had hurriedly packed a black suit, shoes and nylons. I guess I knew. Sissy always had my back when I was not into high awareness.

The day after his passing, I wrote to my friends: "The kindest soul I have ever known left the planet today."

My brother had died of a cancer usually caused by smoking or chemicals. He had never touched a cigarette, but he had worked with chemicals for years, cleaning out the inside of water tower tanks...one of his many business ventures in Texas. He was the third member of my family or origin to die of cancer before his time. Mother succumbed to ovarian cancer, Dad to Alzheimers while he had prostate cancer, and Phil to bladder cancer. I was the oldest living grandchild, cousin and sibling. Cancer was not my nemesis, at least not yet. My heavy yoke was the lung disorder that constantly had my attention. One day, in frustration, I asked Sissy: "So, why do I have this lung disease? I know we manifest the illnesses in our lives, but I really don't understand why it would be a lung issue!"

"Annie, you are an individual that needs to be aware...aware at all times. Nothing demands awareness like the breath of life. Your disease commands you to pay attention to each breath you take, thereby keeping you at high alert and in awareness at all times. You do not have the privilege or meandering through life unconscious of breath; you are in gratitude for every inhalation and exhalation. Now accustomed to the routine, the medications and the necessary, nightly machines, you go about your daily routine as though all these things were natural to anyone. Of course, they are not. They are specific to you to nudge you into higher awareness, higher vibrational frequencies and gratitude as you move through the illusions and their resolutions."

As I was sitting with Anita, Ace and our children at Phil's service, I remembered something and began to smile. When the singers at his hospice room were blessing Phil with heavenly song, I had looked up to the high ceiling corners of his room and had seen light. The light of beings standing watch over his exit, or maybe part of the welcoming committee that escorts one to the Other Side, back to the Collective, the pure energy of Love. I was mesmerized, but I had seen this before, standing next to patients making their transition. I was pretty sure every departing soul got the escort group, no matter the quality of their earthly experience. I liked to think that they sent the "A" team for my brother!

> For those who believe,
> no proof is necessary.
> For those who don't believe,
> no proof is possible.
>
> Stuart Chase

34

I was the only surviving member of my family of origin. It was time to do an inventory of my life, its meaning and its purpose. Sissy and I had the opportunity to spend much more time together, and I had very specific ideas about the subject matter to be discussed. Now in my late sixties, I waned philosophical as well as metaphysical and found myself yearning for more proximity to Truth. I desired more understanding about the path to peace, and most of all, an avid dedication to forgiveness in all its forms.

The inventory revealed contentment in my marriage and a true friendship with my husband. Sharing so many common beliefs, we were easily entertained with conversations about politics, planet conditions, family, friends and spiritual works. We found ourselves becoming naturally more charitable, more humorous and more understanding of difficult events or ideas. We found it was much more difficult than we first assumed to commit ourselves to a life plan of "no judgment." It was amazing how many times a day we found ourselves unintentionally thinking or commenting judgmentally on something. We were doing so, nonetheless. I, slowly, began to see that this dilemma circled right back to forgiveness. Finally, now or never, I fully owned that my refusal to approach the subject of full forgiveness was inextricably tied to judgment of my ex-husband and his abandonment of our daughters. My mind knew that forgiveness did not mean approval, accepted or excused behavior or that the event was forgotten. Without a doubt, I knew that forgiveness meant not allowing any issue to rob me of my internal peace. Indeed, I rarely thought of the issue, but I held onto the judgment of his behavior as some sort of misguided protection of my daughters.

During the course of my career as a therapist, I had helped hundreds of patients through their forgiveness issues and had witnessed the accompanying rewards of dissipated anger and hurt that no longer plagued their nightmares or daily relationships. Clearly, I knew the recipe for the peace of post-forgiveness work. Part of the walk to forgiveness always included an inventory of the patient's own regrets and shame. Sissy had insisted for decades that forgiveness was not possible without an unabashed examination of one's own ego. Therefore, I became a dedicated examiner of the shadow remnants still lurking, or maybe even cemented, in the recesses of my Ego Mind. If I had not had the knowledge and certainty of Spirit Mind, I could have easily gone bonkers with the meanderings which Ego Mind directed, choreographed and harshly judged. Knowing that I was being driven off course, I headed to one of the meditation benches on the ranch. It sat at the edge of a majestic stand of oaks, overlooking a pond which was the habitat for collections of ducks and blue herons. There was almost always a cool breeze that crossed the water and brought freshness and a sense of alertness as it passed by. Sissy and I often conversed on that bench as I imagined her curled up beside me, mimicking my behavior.

"Sissy, it is time. I no longer find any joy in avoiding the necessary forgiveness that I have withheld about issues concerning my ex-husband," I said softly.

"*My dear friend, I am happy to tell you that the forgiveness you have withheld all these years has nothing to do with the father of your children. You have not forgiven yourself. I invite you to find a way to truly forgive YOURSELF for decisions you made and have punished yourself for all these years. You have quietly hidden your guilt for having married him, for having stayed seventeen years hoping to find a workable solution, trying to protect your daughters and trying to avoid public judgment. The illusion of your first marriage and its ongoing disappointments, the divorce, the jury trials, the financial recovery, the introduction of a new husband into a family with two strong teen-age daughters, health issues and budding spiritual awareness all seemed real. Sit and embrace the lessons learned, the agony that turned to sweetness and the invitation to spiritual growth that pricked awareness and right-mindedness. Express the gratitude you feel. The manner needed to do so will become apparent, dear one.*"

As I walked back to the house, I affirmed once more that I would delight in being able to "see" Sissy in physical form and hug her with a bear hug like no other, introduce her to beloved friends who knew about her over the years and have her share openly in my life. Instead, my heart opened to pure, unadulterated gratitude for the good fortune of having her at my side and in my heart for decades.

During the exploratory process of taking a rigorous accounting of my self-forgiveness issues, I visited our older daughter, Eleanor. I enjoyed a weekend of soaking up the delight of being with our grandchildren and their multiple football and softball games. At one point, we found ourselves alone in her kitchen. That moment, serendipitously, offered an opportunity for a private conversation.

"Eleanor, I have already had this conversation with your sister because a good time presented itself. Now I want to tell you that I deeply apologize for parts of your childhood. I wish I had been home more, been able to salvage a marriage and not have put you through the pain of divorce."

"Mom, lots of kids go through divorce. We made it. We're all okay."

"I know lots of kids have to deal with what you went through, but every child deserves a wholesome family, and I am so sorry I could not provide that the way I wanted to. I have always believed that you and Emma felt my love and that you knew how precious you both were and are to me. There were many times that I know I over-protected or over-attended to you because I had some guilt about what you were missing. I will never understand your father's abandonment of his daughters. I think he was just too fragile to handle the situation. I still have not been able to forgive him."

"Oh, Mom, you HAVE to," Eleanor said forcefully and beseechingly. Her tone and facial expression instantly conveyed her concern for me and the ongoing theft of my peace. Her actions were pure, demonstrative love.

It was an instantaneous holy moment. Sitting frozen, I felt the soul of my daughter played out in the drama of a few sentences between us. My heart opened and swelled with the sweetness of abiding, forgiving love. The Mother had been freed by the Holy communication of the daughter. Peace pulsed through my body as it removed the Ego's chains of guilt and fear. This woman in front of me did not need the imagined protection that I thought was provided by my unforgiving attitude toward her father. She was an exquisite teacher.

How foolish of me to hold onto this Ego lie for years! Obviously, Ego Mind relished in feeding the fear that I had damaged the two most precious human beings in my world. Now I had to face the truth of the illusion. If his own daughters had long ago forgiven him, why did I insist, against all knowingness, to nurture a narrative that only furthered my angst? The answer had to be that I had not forgiven myself. Sissy's words echoed in my head as I confronted the only lesson, the only reason for being in this illusory world and waging battle with Ego Mind and the many very believable illusions of everyday life.

Upon arriving home, I made time that same afternoon to speak with Sissy. I had to tell her that I thought I now knew the purpose of my life...indeed, the purpose of every soul.

"Sissy, I am such a slow learner. Now I got it. It is so much more simple and satisfying that all the machinations of a life-time of illusions. I know that the ONLY purpose in life is ongoing, moment to moment forgiveness. If we don't judge the illusions, if we stay aware of the essence of The One in and around us at all times and forgive ourselves and others constantly, we create heaven and live with Spirit Mind. Holy Spirit, the purest communicator, is actually the highest part of our self, the perfect part, the eternal part. We can only separate from Oneness if we judge and forego forgiveness. The only dramas in our illusions are the ones fearfully created and exacerbated by Ego Mind. The roadmap to peace is so easy. The remembering of Truth with the nemesis of ego always nibbling away at our ideas is so hard. As I enter my last decade(s) of this earthly experience, I am overjoyed with my knowingness and the peace it brings. I can imagine Father Uribe smiling and slightly nodding his head affectionately."

As I walked the ranch trails meticulously kept by my husband, I let my mind wonder back over the dramas of my life that consumed me at the time and now were meaningless. I am so grateful that my mother was gracious and loving. I thought she was cheated out of a lifetime of family events. I now think she came for her own purpose, unknown to me, but intertwined with my growth. She added an immense amount to my life in her very limited time on Earth. The fragrance of her essence still remains.

My father was a dedicated, but harsh, teacher. He demanded excellence, self-sufficiency, resilience and tenacity. I learned those attributes early and they served me well. Also, I know he unintentionally and unwittingly led me to learn to forgive the absence of demonstrative love, affection and admiration. If I were to feel those human needs and have them fulfilled, I had to learn to give them to myself. Ultimately, I learned, via my dad, that one can absolutely learn to forage, adapt and choose a path compatible with oneself. One can leave the unworkable parts of the family of origin behind and find individualized happiness and tranquility. The numerous difficulties I had experienced with my father were due to his having little awareness of his own pain and forgiveness of himself, compounded by a life-long Ego Mind entrapment cycle fueled by unnamed fear. Knowing he would have other life cycles to find his answers, I smiled to myself as I felt the love I always carried for him. I wished he had a spiritual lens to the secret.

Children, whether born of self or another, are one's greatest gift in walking the daily illusion. I cannot image a full life without the experience of motherhood. It is the most fulfilling way I know to embrace charity, selflessness, exquisite love and courage. When the developing nature of a child is a mother's responsibility, it is ominous, honoring and satisfying to the core. I have known familial love, agape love, erotic love, messy love, broken love, lost love, imagined love and marital love. There is nothing that surpasses the love that happens at the moment one sees her newborn.

An ex-spouse is a demanding lesson in forgiveness and charity. The marriage started with so much hope and so many goals to be shared and enjoyed. My world went from my own ego oneness to a concept of co-mingled aspirations. My dreams became less selfish and more inclusive, with an awareness of the "other" and the necessity for the principle of sharing to achieve compatibility and fairness of spirit. I can unabashedly own that I did not feel or achieve that in my first marriage. Gratefully, I have achieved that glorious contentment in my present relationship. I suppose that as we traverse the illusions we choose, we simply need a practice run. Having taken years to accept that forgiveness was the only path, I think it made the lesson indescribably indelible...and never forgettable.

While on a brisk walk one day, I decided to turn the inventory upside down and smother myself with the best of memories...the ones that feel like never-forgotten gifts, aside from my husband and children. The videos of their faces and places played like a montage of movie clips.

Aunt Madge's motherly smile and ever-present warmth greeted me first, perhaps because I missed her so much. She passed several years after Phil. She had agreed to hernia surgery at age eighty-eight and entered the hospital with full confidence. Her doctor left town after her surgery, and she was not well attended. The illusion of her leaving was hard, but knowing that she was of Spirit was an easy consolation. What an incredible human being. Her legacy was that of a woman who gave and did not judge. She had a spiritual secret.

Every time I hear a French word, I instantly think of Jacqueline and our incredibly fun times in Paris. Her father and Reza spent four years hiring investigators to find her and her mother in Vietnam. They finally concluded that the two women had been victims of the war and whose bodies were never found or identified. When her father told me their conclusion, I wept. I still hold onto the hope that every loved one guards in his/her heart...that the MIA will miraculously reappear someday. My internal knowingness had long said she had stepped over. Her essence will certainly be additive to the Oneness. Jacqueline taught me to be able to laugh at myself. She, too, had a spiritual secret.

When I learned that Emma was moving to Indiana, I was surprised. Knowing that she loved four seasons and pioneer woman activities that many Indiana small towns embrace, I thought that she was on a quest to live a simpler life. Then, she shared that she had learned that her father, my ex-husband that had not connected with her for years, had dementia. Having alienated his brother and his family, her dad had no available caregivers, and a nursing home was his only option. Emma and her family decided to make their ministry that of caring for her dad. Although I knew the decision entailed a lot of hard work and responsibility, I was so grateful that her heart was charitable and forgiving. She had a developing spiritual secret.

Eleanor had given me the mandate to claim my freedom and peace through the ongoing forgiveness of everything. She is a woman who walks the walk, without judgment and with unbridled awareness. She knows she has a spiritual secret.

Fippy's humor was something I could always count on. Even though he often hid behind it, there were so many times he had us all doubled over in laughter. He could not abide the pain of anything ugly. He simply created something nice to counteract his unwanted feeling. I know he lived in a great deal of denial, but his brand of humor was entertaining and curative. I think he would have given anything to have a spiritual secret that would erase the fear.

I smiled and warmed myself with the memory of attending the wedding of my brother's widow, Anita. Alone for five years after the passing of Phil, she found another true love. We all adored him, believing that Phil had a hand in the selection. My niece, Kim, Fippy's daughter, and Lillie, his granddaughter, and I all did a "high five" as we witnessed the wedding ceremony that so generously included the blessing of my sibling. Spirituality was everywhere that day!

My patients have been my best teachers. I have learned something from each of them. Suffice to say, I learned plenty over the forty years of practicing psychotherapy. Witnessing the illusions of others always helped me maneuver around the ever-present reach of Ego Mind. As I closed the door to the office to go home each night, I said a "thank you" out loud to the bravest people I was privileged to meet. The souls that seek help exhibit a courage unknown to the ones whose overriding fear of self-judgment is so incapacitating that making the appointment with a therapist would be judged a weakness instead of an act of bravery. My patients learned to seek the spiritual discovery path in search of the secret. Many learned that forgiveness opened the way.

I ascribed early on to the belief that if I did not have a family of origin that fulfilled my needs, I would create a family from the friends I learned to love as sisters, brothers, mothers and fathers. As a recipient of great good fortune, I have lived over seven decades and am still enjoying my unique and distinguished collection of friends. They create a collage that answers the yearnings of my heart for closeness, safety and forgiving love. I have made sure that they all know my feelings because love deserves to be spotlighted, appreciated and cherished.

Sissy and I talk almost every day and have for the last year. I decided to indulge myself and ask every question that popped into my mind. One day I asked about the creation of the world I live in. She explained that, originally, the essence of souls separated from One (God) to live an experiment. At that moment they began the creation of illusions and Ego Mind as a counterforce to Spirit Mind. She explained that God did not create the world, our mind did. And of course, we began to create the dilemmas to experience duality, which is actually non-existent and a creation of the ego.

"My dear Annalee Grace, do you think God would create a world

of duality where there is darkness and bad opposed to light and goodness. Gracious, no. That would be impossible for the Essence of all Love. He could not be that cruel or vindictive or hurtful. He is always Loving Awareness, accessed through forgiveness, as you know. Now, dear one, spend your days living the Truth, forgiving yourself, loving others, speaking your knowingness and always assured that death does not exist, but that eventually taking one step over into the Light affirms all you have learned."

"Will we always be together as you promised?"

"My love, that promise was such an easy one because we are all one, indivisible and in the collective of Loving Awareness. So, yes, we are eternal with one another. Enjoy the peace of knowing that."

I often walk through the woods, knowing Sissy is with me, and I feel no fear. She enriched a life of many dramatic and informative illusions, and she loved me with every step and misstep. Best of all, she has been my best friend and the teacher that affirms all is well all the time. Anything else is a construct of illusion.

WITH SO MUCH GRATITUDE TO

The Ace-Man, my true love

The sister-friends: Dr. Nancy Glass, Dr. Jaine Fraser, Jean La Mont

The family lawyer extraordinaire: Steve Hulme

The two guys who were so accepting of Sissy: Tim Alderman and Baxter Lawrence

The retired dentist-turned editor: Dr. Steve Lowe

All the supportive friends that just wanted me to hurry up and finish the book: Rhonda Guard, Peggy Westerbeck, Dr. Sally Fryer, Melinda Rieken, Melissa Blackburn, Wendy and Jerry Meredith, Leslie Bowman, Mark Dietz, Maggie Alderman, Stacy Castillo, Rita Bennett, Stan Victor, Laurie Gatlin, Kathleen Harper, Janie Jones and Claude Menger.

And a special shout-out to Dan Millman, internationally renown author, who shared kind words and suggestions for a first-time author.

Printed in the United States
by Baker & Taylor Publisher Services